The Prayer That
Changes Everything®

To my friend dearest friend Karen — Get well soon you will — My prayers are with you + I know God wants you + will — Believe in him + you shall get better — God Bless you my dear and take care — + loving You are very special + caring! + how wonderful a person you are — don't forget you All my love + support!

Dee

5-19-08

The Prayer That
Changes Everything®

Stormie
Omartian

New York, New York

The Library of Congress has cataloged the Thorndike Press® edition as follows:

Omartian, Stormie
    The prayer that changes everything / by Stormie Omartian.
      p. cm.
    ISBN 0-7862-7888-9 (lg. print : hc : alk. paper)
    ISBN 1-59415-102-4 (lg. print : sc : alk. paper)
    1. Prayer.   I. Title.
BV210.3.O54 2005
248.3'2—dc22   2005013488

Special Introduction to the Guideposts Edition

Again and again in His Holy Word, God *tells* us how He wants us to pray!

In Philippians 4:6, He commands us to come to Him with "praise and thanksgiving" —before we turn the spotlight on ourselves and let our "requests be known."

So often we turn to God when we want something, without praising Him first for all He has given us. Or we go through tough times and get fearful or discouraged, instead of praising God in the midst of our trouble and seeing Him do great things.

When I fully embraced worship and praise as a way of life, it changed my life forever. God has brought me deeper into His presence. He has brought good out of situations I thought were hopeless, and He has shown me that there is no suffering without purpose and that joy always "comes in the morning."

He will do all this for you. You simply need to add this powerful way to pray to your life. You will see how God works in your life every day and you will find new peace of mind and a deeper faith.

—Stormie Omartian

This book is dedicated to You, Lord.

For without Your power and grace, I know I wouldn't be where I am today. You have spared my life so many times when otherwise I surely would have died. You still sustain me daily. I am increasingly aware of how I don't deserve the blessings You've given me. You've taught me to have Your love and compassion for others and Your heart for their greatest blessings, and yet into the midst of that I interject my selfishness. You've given me strong vision for the wonderful things You want to do, and even do through *me,* but into that vision I sometimes impose my fears, which threaten to derail it. You give me promises to cling to, and they sustain me, yet even then I let doubt sway me. Why You put up with me so much I'll never understand. That's because I cannot comprehend the depth of Your love. How You could come to earth to suffer and die for me the way You did is incomprehensible, especially when I'm not certain that I could bring myself to do the same thing for You. I'd like to think I could, but when I frequently pray for my precious brothers and sisters in Christ throughout the world, who are being tortured and even martyred because of their service to You, I don't know if I could go through what they do.

It amazes me that even though I don't always do or say the right thing, You have still allowed me to live and to serve You. That You have given me the privilege of writing this book is most humbling to me. While I am no expert on anything, let alone praise and worship, one thing I do know is that You are worthy of all praise, both now and forever. My credibility lies in my experience and all that You have taught me. The fact that You would allow the praises of Your people to be to their own greatest blessing is something only an amazing God of love would do. I pray that You will give me the ability to communicate the greatness of who You are and the reasons You are deserving of praise, and also help people to remember to praise You in all situations and at all times. Help me to reveal the full extent of the blessings You have for us when we focus on You in worship and praise.

Because You first loved me, I am now free to love You. And I do.

Your devoted servant,
Stormie

Acknowledgments

With special thanks:

- To Christopher, Amanda, John, Rebecca, Stephanie, Derek, Matt, Suzy, and Louie. Thank you for living. Your mere existence gives me joy and strength. I praise God for you every day of my life.
- To Michael. Thank you for being a faithful husband and never giving me any reason to doubt that. I couldn't do this without your support.
- To Susan Martinez. Thank you for your prayers and love, your diligence and organization, your ability to rise beyond the call of duty, your kindness and graciousness to answer calls, letters, e-mails, faxes, and doorbells, the volume of which could have driven a lesser person crazy long ago.
- To Roz Thompson. Thank you for being my faithful friend and prayer partner all these years. You have been a strength and an inspiration to me far more than I can ever tell you.

- To Erik Sundin. Thank you for all your meticulous help on this project. You are the best.
- To Patti and Tom Brussat, Michael and Terry Harriton, Bob and Sally Anderson, Donna and Bruce Sudano. Thank you for your prayers. I don't see you often enough, but I feel your prayers every day.
- To my pastors: Jack and Anna Hayford, Rice and Jody Broocks, Tim and Le'Chelle Johnson, Stephen Mansfield, Dale and Joan Evrist, Jim and Cathy Laffoon, John and Maretta Rohr, Ray and Elizabeth McCollum. Your richness in the things of God has made me rich in my spirit too. I don't know where I would be without all the great things of the Lord you have taught me and the countless times you have prayed for me.
- To my wonderful sisters in Christ and great women of God: Joyce Meyer, Beth Moore, Lisa Bevere, Kay Arthur, and Florence Littauer. Thank you for your love and kindness to me, your wealth of knowledge of God's Word, and your work for the kingdom. It is with great humility, along with love and respect for you and all that you do, that

I count it a great privilege to know you. You have each taught me so much and have been such an inspiration and a strength to me. You have given me encouragement beyond what you can ever imagine.

- To my amazing family at Harvest House: especially to Bob Hawkins Jr., Carolyn McCready, Julie McKinney, Teresa Evenson, Terry Glaspey, John Constance, Mary Cooper, LaRae Wiekert, Peggy Wright, Betty Fletcher, and Kim Moore. Thank you for your love, patience, kindness, graciousness, untiring work habits, and professionalism. You make it all happen.

Contents

What Is the Prayer That Changes Everything?

Proclaim the praises of Him who called you out of darkness into His marvelous light.

1 Peter 2:9

If you're like me, you don't want to live a lukewarm, mediocre, "barely making it," sad, lonely, hopeless, miserable, frightened, frustrated, unfulfilled, meaningless, ineffective, or fruitless existence. You don't want to be imprisoned by your circumstances or chained to your limitations. You want to live an *extraordinary* life. A life of peace, joy, fulfillment, hope, and purpose. A life where all things are possible.

The kind of life I just described can only happen when we enter into a close relationship with God.

I mean *really* close.

There are many people who *believe* in God. Some of them live their lives with a sense of God in the back of their mind. Others do religious things for God. Still others love God and serve Him to the best of their ability, but they long for more in their relationship with Him. Yet not many are *really* close to Him.

You may be thinking, *How close* is *really close exactly?*

It's close enough to know Him intimately. Close enough to communicate your whole heart to Him on an ongoing basis. Close enough to be able to direct your attention away from yourself *completely* and place it on Him *entirely*. Close enough to understand who *He* really is and then allow that knowledge of Him to define who *you* really are. It's loving Him with all your heart and letting Him love you with all of His.

You know how it is when you fall in love. That special person occupies your every thought, and it's hard to focus on other things. You experience a constant wellspring of joy bubbling up from within you that seems as if it could never run dry. You long for that person when you're not with them, and you can't wait to be in their presence again. Being near them takes your breath away. You love them so much it sometimes makes your heart hurt. You delight in all you see in them, and you seek to know everything there is to know about them. You want to wrap your arms around them as tightly as you can and never let go. You want your souls to intertwine until you can no longer tell where that person ends and you begin. And every time you embrace, new strength and fulfillment flow into your being. You feel as though you have finally connected to someone at a depth you always dreamed about. You complete each other. Your heart has found a home. The world is wonderful. And all is good.

It's a *glorious* way to feel.

This is also the way God wants us to feel about *Him*.

All the time.

When you are in love you wish you could feel that way forever. But if you did, then your heart would hurt every day and you would never get anything done. So as the *extreme intensity* of your love fades — which it must do or we would never live through it — the *depth* of it must grow. It must be watered and fed and nurtured and become like a beautiful oak tree that cannot be shaken because the roots have gone down so deep.

That's what God wants to happen in your relationship with *Him*.

I'm not saying that your first love for God needs to fade. I'm saying that it needs to grow. After that beginning rush — that initial spiritual high — your relationship with God needs to be nurtured and deepened.

But how does all this happen? How do you develop that kind of love for God? What should you do to make your relationship grow deeper? How do you get *really* close to Him?

One way is to read His story. The Bible. It reveals who He is. It shows how He works. It tells us of His desires and plans for our lives. It speaks of His great love for us.

Another way is to receive His Son, Jesus. And then spend every day for the rest of your life trying to fathom love so great that He would willingly lay down His life in brutal torture and crucifixion on a cross, just so you could always be close to God.

Another way is to pray.

My definition of prayer is simply *communicating with God.* It's a love relationship first and foremost. Prayer is baring your soul to the One who loved you before you even knew of Him and letting Him speak to your heart.

Far too often prayer becomes a complicated issue for people. In fact, there can seem to be so many aspects to it that many people become intimidated. They fear that they can't pray well enough, or right enough, or long enough, or eloquently enough. They are afraid that their prayers won't be heard because they themselves are not good enough or holy enough or knowledgeable enough. In all the books I have written, I have sought to dispel that kind of fear and intimidation and make prayer accessible to everyone.

In this book I want to focus on one very important form of prayer — or *communicating with God* — and that is worship and praise. (I know that worship and praise can be considered as two separate ways we honor God, but they are so interconnected that I'm going to refer to them as one expression.) Worship and praise is the *purest* form of prayer because it focuses our minds and souls entirely away from ourselves and on to Him. What it communicates is pure love, devotion, reverence, appreciation, and thankfulness to God. It's exalting God for who He is. It's communicating our longing for Him. It's drawing close to Him for the sake of being close. When we worship God, we are the closest to Him we will ever be. That's because praise welcomes His presence in our midst.

One of the most wonderful things about God is that He lives in our praise. He inhabits the praises of His people. "But You are holy, enthroned in the praises of Israel," the Bible says (Psalm 22:3). When we worship Him, it's not like worshiping some cold and distant deity. He's a loving God who *wants* to be with us. And when we worship Him, He is.

Isn't that amazing?

What an awesome gift! *When we praise and worship God, His presence comes to dwell with us.* And the most amazing thing about that is when it does, things change. Always! You can count on it. Hearts change. Situations change. Lives change. Minds change. Attitudes change.

Every time you praise God, something changes within you, or your circumstances, or in the people or situations around you. We can't see all that is being affected, but we can trust that it is, because it is impossible to touch the presence of God and there not be change. The reason for that is you are coming in contact with all that *God* is, and that will affect all that *you* are.

Praise is the prayer that changes everything.

Enough About You, Let's Talk About Me

When I first came to the Lord, I didn't understand the power of praising God. I thought praise was something you did on a

Sunday morning in church while waiting for all the people to get there who were coming in late. It was a prelude to the main event — the sermon. That's what we were there for, wasn't it? It seemed a little like when the appetizers are served at a dinner party, during which time all the guests arrive. And once everyone is present, the dinner is served.

After I received Jesus into my life, however, I started going to a new kind of church. One where worship and praise was a priority. I had never seen anything like it.

Growing up as a child, I didn't go to church much. Just Christmas, Easter, funerals, and one extended visit to a relative's house, when my mother left my dad, where that family went to church every week! Of course they *had* to, since the father in that home was the pastor. It was the family business, after all. But even with going to church every week, I never found much life in it. I don't remember any real worship time, except for a hymn or two. The choir performed what music there was. It was nice, but I was always with the adults and didn't understand much of what was going on or being said. Plus, I was with my mother, and she had a completely distorted view of God, church, and the Bible. It made me never want to go any further into it.

My mother was mentally ill. Only no one understood it back then or knew what to do about it. And there was a social stigma attached to it, so that if anyone found out you had a mentally ill relative — especially a parent — you were suspect from then on and socially ostracized. Not that we were all that socially accepted in the first place. We lived isolated lives. But the few people who had anything to do with us would have been reduced to zero at first knowledge of something like that. So my mother's problem was swept under the rug.

My dad always loved my mother in spite of how mean she was to him. He wouldn't have her committed, even at the urging of her own family, because he always hoped she would "someday snap out of it." He said he first realized something was wrong on their honeymoon when she thought people were following them and trying to kill her. Because of that, they couldn't go to the hotel they were supposed to stay in. They had to travel to three different hotels before my father finally put his foot down and said, "This is it. We are staying here!"

Untreated, my mother's mental illness grew worse throughout the years. The way she coped with me as a child was with violence and abuse and keeping me locked in a

24

closet for many hours at a time. I never knew *exactly* why I was put there, but I thought I must have done something really bad. And then at other times, she seemed so far away in her own world that she wasn't aware I existed. So the pendulum would swing, with no predictability, from physical abuse to abandonment.

As a result, I grew up with serious feelings of rejection, fear, depression, anxiety, hopelessness, painful loneliness, and a sadness that planted a perpetual lump in my throat. It was the kind of lump you get when you have a constant ache in your heart and you must continually choke back a lifetime of uncried tears. You have kept them back for so long that you know they have become a torrential flood building up behind a dam. You learn to keep that dam from breaking at all costs because, if it ever did, it might destroy everything in its path. The kind of tears I'm talking about can only be released in the presence of unconditional love and acceptance. And where on earth can you go to find that?

My dad never went to church that I recall except the day of his funeral. My family and I had a simple service for him and buried him the way he had requested. He always said his dad *never* went to church, but his mother made him go twice on Sunday and once in the middle of the week to sit for four hours at a time on hard benches while the preacher screamed about going to hell. He said he knew there was a God and he believed in Jesus, but he was never going to enter a church again as long as he lived. As far as I know, he kept his promise.

After I grew up and was out of the house, I tried everything I could get my hands on to be rid of the emotional pain I had inside. It was unbearable. I apologize to anyone reading this book who knew me during those years, because there must have been times when you wondered what was wrong with me. I could *appear* normal for a while, but I just couldn't keep it up. And then I would break down, suddenly withdraw, clam up, or be distant. It was all about hiding who I really was. It was all about holding back the tears.

One of the ways I coped was to drink way too much alcohol. I drank until I was giddy, but I wouldn't stop there. I had to keep going until I was drunk and passed out on someone's couch. I took drugs until I nearly killed myself many times. I went into the occult determined to make contact with some kind of spiritual being who could help me because I knew no human could. I did make contact with a spiritual being, all right, and whatever it was frightened me to death. My fear and depression continued to increase. I explored Eastern religions, but their gods were cruel, distant, and cold. If I wanted cruel, distant, and cold, I could go back and live with my mother. At least she was familiar, and by this time I understood where she was coming from.

In my twenties I had a number of relationships with men. But that old spirit of rejection was always in control. As a result I made sure I rejected *them* before they could reject *me*. There were several young men who were quite wonderful, but they didn't know the *real* me. The broken, hurting, sad, anxious, desperate, suicidal me. And I could never risk letting them see that side. If I were to tell them the truth about my life and my emotional state, rejection was a sure thing. So I ended the relationships while everything was still good. The young men were baffled about why I left with no explanation. It was because my situation was beyond explanation. At least *I* couldn't explain it.

Out of all those relationships I ended up getting two abortions. One in the back room of an old rundown house in Tijuana where the doctor who performed it told me if I died during the operation, he would have to dump my body in the desert. He apologized in advance just in case that happened. The other abortion happened in a hotel room in Las Vegas with no anesthetic. I was blindfolded and gagged, and another man, the doctor's "assistant," laid across my body with his full weight and put his hand over my mouth so I could not move or scream. It was worse than a nightmare because there was no hope of waking up from it. During both of those times, killing a child never entered my mind. Staying alive another week was always my only goal.

Finally, when I was 28, I couldn't keep up the front anymore. Everything in my life failed. I had a career as a singer, dancer, and actress on television, but all the shows I had been doing were canceled. There was a major industry transition away from musical variety and comedy shows. That was okay with me because I no longer felt like singing and nothing was funny to me anymore.

I had a short first marriage which I expected to fail. And it did. My health, mind, and emotions failed right along with it. I couldn't keep up the front anymore. All of my attempts to find a way out of the pain had come to nothing, and I could no longer fight the suicidal thoughts I had battled every day for as long as I could remember.

I planned my suicide. I began collecting enough sleeping pills and various drugs from friends to do the job right. I did not want to wake up in a hospital somewhere after having my stomach pumped. I didn't want to wake up at all. I wanted to be rid of the pain forever. I knew I had become what my mother had often predicted — a worthless failure who would never amount to anything. All the degrading profanity she used to describe me summed up how I felt about myself and my life. And I couldn't bear it anymore.

At this crucial time my friend Terry came to me and told me about Jesus. She had talked about Him before in a gentle way, but I wasn't listening then. She was more insistent this time because she could see I was in bad shape. We were singing together on a record session, and she took me aside on a break and gave it to me as straight as anyone could. She said she had been praying for me for the past four years we had been working together in television. She extended the love of God to me like a lifeline and begged me to come with her to meet her pastor. It wasn't as much *what* she was telling me as it was the love and concern with which she said it that convinced me to say yes.

We met Pastor Jack Hayford at a popular restaurant close by, and he spent two hours talking to me in a way I could understand about who Jesus really was. His words were compelling. And if what he said was true, I wanted the life Jesus promised. He gave me books to read, one of which was the Gospel of John, and asked us to meet him again the following week. While reading the books during that week, my eyes were opened to the truth and reality of the Lord. When we met with Pastor Jack again, he asked me if I wanted to receive Jesus and find the life God had for me. I said yes, canceled my suicide plans, and he and Terry prayed for me. I wasn't sure what I was getting into, but I could sense the love and peace of God in these two people, and I wanted what they had.

Immediately my life began to change. I started going to Pastor Jack's church, and the minute I walked in, the love of God was so strong it brought me to tears. The dam was starting to break. And I wasn't the only one. Everyone else felt the same way. The saying that went around at the time was that you shouldn't go to this church without Kleenex and waterproof mascara.

The first thing I learned in church was the importance and power of worship and praise. Pastor Jack led worship, but he didn't just lead the music. He also taught us *how* to worship God and *why* God was deserving of all the praise we were giving Him. He taught us about how much God loved us, and how we could love Him back through our praise and worship.

In every service I attended, the worship was life-transforming. Even though we were all there to praise God, *we* were the ones being blessed, empowered, enriched, fulfilled, and changed. Each time I was in a worship service, *I* was changed. I came to worship *God,* but in the process God changed *me.* That happened years ago, but I remember it as though it were yesterday. That's because it changed my life completely.

I attended that church for 23 years before my family and I moved to a different state. From then on, every time I have gone into a church the first thing I look for is that kind of life-changing worship. The kind that changes everything every time you do it. The kind that changes you. Changes your perspective. Changes your mind, your life, and your circumstances.

Whether we admit it or not, or even recognize it in ourselves, we all pursue, seek after, idolize, or worship something or someone. And whatever we worship will become the main motivation in our lives. Some people worship celebrities. Others worship money and material possessions. Others worship their job or position. Still others worship such things as nature, beauty, food, hobbies, sex, music, friends, or entertainment. Whatever we worship will influence our lives.

The truth is, we become like what or who we worship (Psalm 115:4-8).

When we worship something, it affects who we become as a person. This doesn't mean if you worship a rock star you are going to develop a raspy voice. It means you are worshiping something that doesn't have the power to save you from anything. When we idolize and seek after other gods, they can't change us, transform us, or help us find our destiny. But when we worship God, He can do all those things and more.

The more we worship God, the more we become like Him.

Who or what you worship affects what emanates from your life. When we seek after the Lord and worship *Him,* then we become all we were created to be.

I have found that *we* — most people — don't praise God as much as we should. Or could. And the reason for that is we don't really know enough about who God is. We don't understand the many reasons why we should worship Him. Plus, we can't comprehend the powerful impact that praising Him has on our own lives. We don't recognize the *gift* that praise is to us, and therefore we don't fully understand the *power* to be found in it.

It's like receiving Jesus. If people understood who He really is and all that He did for them, only the hardest of hearts would hesitate to receive Him into their lives. But so many lies are told about Him, and there are so many misconceptions about what He did and what He is doing today, that people have a distorted view of Him.

If we truly understood who God is, our praise would be unending. It could not be contained.

We don't really know how to *worship* God until we come to *know* Him. We may appreciate His creation, but that is not the same as appreciating *Him.* In fact, when we appreciate His creation more than we do Him, it shows that we don't know Him. Every time we praise and worship God, we receive new revelation of God's character. We understand more about who He is. And the more we know who He is, the more we want to show our love and adoration to Him.

Just as God created man and woman in His image, the gods we choose to worship manifest their attributes in the worshiper. So in deciding what or whom to worship, you are making life decisions regarding your values, your priorities, and how you are to live.

— Jack Hayford

We were born to worship God. But God did not create us to be robotic beings who tell Him how great He is. He created us to be in communion and partnership with Him. Every time we praise God for who He is and all that He has done, it unleashes His life-changing power in our lives. His presence comes to soften our hearts so they can be molded into whatever shape He wants. *Praise is the means by which God transforms our lives and enables us to do His will and glorify Him.*

That is the most amazing thing about

praising God. There is a gift found hidden within that seems to make praise and worship of Him to be as much for *us* as it is for *Him*. I doubt that God needs to be reminded of who He is, but He knows *we* certainly need to be. God is secure in the knowledge of His greatness, perfection, and power. *We* are the ones who forget. And *we* are the ones who need to show Him that we know who *He* is. And when we are praising God, we demonstrate all that to Him.

Worshiping God is the way He can pry us loose from ourselves and make us stop holding on to the world and start holding on to *Him*. God intends worship to restore us, fill us, motivate us, bless us, and fulfill us in ways we never dreamed possible. There are certain blessings that He wants to give us that will only come into our lives as we worship Him.

I never knew the meaning of joy until I found it in worship. I remember a specific day when many people were worshiping together and we could sense the power of the Holy Spirit filling the room. Suddenly God broke through the hardness of my heart. I didn't think it was hard until the hardness was gone. And then I sensed the amazing love of God and the joy of the Lord. I had never known that before. It fully existed without depending on circumstances, material possessions, or acceptance of man. It was there because of the presence of God alone. That was my day of freedom. My personal independence day. Joy did not depend on anything other than being in the presence of God and allowing His presence to overflow me with His love. I received all that while praising God.

Our greatest blessing comes when we take the focus off of ourselves and put it entirely on God in worship and praise. Isn't it just like our wonderful Lord to make something that is all about Him be the thing that blesses us the most when we do it?

Praise becomes the very means by which God pours Himself into our lives. It's not something we can manipulate God into doing. It's a gift He gives to those who have a true heart of love and reverence for Him. Only those who put God first will uncover the hidden power of praise.

Making Praise a Priority

Just recently I went through two months of the most empty, paralyzing, depressing time. On the outside it looked as if I had nothing to be concerned about. But on the inside I felt paralyzed to the point of not being able to do much of anything. And I had so much I needed to be doing. Good things. Things I have always wanted to do. Yet I couldn't bring myself to do any of them. I had not been like this since I became a believer.

I prayed time and again about this problem, but I just could not get through it. I had lost my vision for the future and couldn't seem to regain it no matter how I tried. I felt useless, aimless, and alone. Even despairing at times. I couldn't see beyond the day, and the day was a struggle to get through. I had trouble concentrating. It was impossible to focus. It seemed as though I were being squeezed in a vise and then wrung out like a rag to dry in the heat of the day. I felt trapped by my own blessings — by the answers to my own prayers. I wanted to be anywhere but where I was, if that meant I could escape the misery. And this was a hard place to be, because I had so many responsibilities and deadlines that going anyplace except to my laptop would have been criminal. Possibly even prosecutable under certain standards. The harder I tried, the less I was able to get done. Of course I prayed about this with my prayer partners and a few friends and family members, but to no avail. Nothing changed.

One night I became so desperate to break through this painful malaise that I reached out to God yet again from the depth of my being and cried, "Lord, what is the matter with me? What is this about? Am I doing something wrong? Tell me what I should be doing differently. I can't seem to make myself do anything at all. Am I just burned out? Have I worked too hard for too long? I thought You had instructed me to do the things I'm doing, yet I feel incapable of working on any of them right now. Did I misunderstand Your leading? If so, what am I supposed to do? Please speak to me, Lord. Help me to understand. Take away this heaviness so I can breathe freely and think clearly again."

Finally I felt a distinct impression upon my heart that I knew was the Lord. It was like the sun breaking through clouds after a tornado. Everything was calm and peaceful in direct contrast to the intensity of the moments before.

He said, "Simply worship Me."

I understood this was not to be a prelude to anything else, but an end *entirely* in itself. It was not to be for just that moment or until the next morning. I was to worship Him until He told me otherwise.

That was very hard for someone who likes

to pray about everything, covering all the bases and possible scenarios. Yet God wasn't saying I couldn't pray for other people and situations. Just that I was not to ask for anything for myself right then. My stance in the midst of my miserable condition was to be one of worship and praise before God. That's all.

"Simply worship Me," He said.

It's not as if I didn't know how to praise God in the midst of difficult situations or had never done that. I had learned this powerful principle many years before and had made praise and worship of God a priority in my life. I knew *what* to do. I knew *how* to do it. I knew *why* I was doing it. But this time, I was to do it as the *ultimate* end in itself. As if nothing else would ever follow.

"God, are You preparing me for eternity?" I asked.

"That is always true," He spoke to my spirit again. "But this is not your time to die. I am preparing your heart to do the work I have for you to do, and I need your full attention. Don't come to Me with your lists right now, even though the things you need are important to Me and I desire that you look to Me for all your needs. There will be a time for that kind of prayer again soon, but right now you must trust that I know what you need. In this season, I want you to simply worship Me. Exalt My name and praise Me for all that I am. Let Me fill your heart with *My* thoughts and not your own."

So that's what I did. I simply worshiped Him.

It wasn't easy. It felt as though I were standing in the middle of a raging storm and the winds of temptation, depression, hurt, and torment would tear me apart. It seemed at times that I wouldn't survive it. I feared I might cave and look somewhere other than God for relief. It wasn't as though I couldn't have gone to someone for pastoral counseling or prayer support. I am richly surrounded by all of that, and I have made use of it far more often than I'm sure most of these kind people had time for in their busy schedules. But I knew this was between me and God. He was doing something that I couldn't understand or explain to anyone else right then. And I had to go through it with *Him alone.*

I cried every single day. Many times throughout the day. Actually, crying is not a strong enough word. Gut-wrenching sobs is more like it. I was continually blinded by rivers of unending tears. Even when the tears weren't visible on the outside, they flowed silently inside. Without any warning they would overtake me in an instant and spill over into the visible so profusely that I would have to excuse myself from where I was or pull over to the side of the road. Sometimes my insides would be so strongly constricted by sobs that it was hard to breathe. It was not merely emotional; it was deeply spiritual. And I felt as though I were in a battle. A battle for my soul. A battle for my life. For my existence. A battle for my future. Not a battle with God, but with the enemy of my soul. The enemy who wanted to destroy me and had tried so often and hard to do so in my past.

I kept all this hidden. I couldn't explain it, and I didn't even want to try. Once again I had to lay down every dream I ever had. I'd done that in the past. Numerous times, actually. I surrendered my dreams to God and let them die. Then He took away the ones that were not from Him and resurrected the ones that were. The difference now was that these were the dreams I thought God had resurrected. They were the ones He had given me, and I thought they were mine to keep. These had been my joy to think about. And now it hurt unbearably to let them go. It tore at the fabric of my being. But I had to surrender *everything* to the One who would ultimately determine whether I ever saw those dreams realized or not.

It was pointless to resist.

Through it all I remained with my heart bowed at my heavenly Father's feet, humbled before His throne, and clinging to the hem of His garment. I cried every time I thought of Him. Actually, I cried just about every time I thought of *anything,* but *especially* Him. And particularly when I thought of all He had done for me. How He had sent Jesus to earth for *me.* And countless other people too, of course, but that wasn't the point right then. The point was that God wanted me to take our relationship personally. I thought I had been doing that, but He wanted more. What He had done in my life up until that point would pale in comparison to what He wanted to do in my heart now.

God wanted to have such free reign in my heart that I would allow Him to break it, pummel it, grind it into sand, and then make something new. That's because He wanted to *do* something new. Ultimately not just for me and my benefit, but for others as well.

And I was willing.

Boy, was I willing! When God has a hold

of you, it's best to not resist. It's better to go with the program and see it through. Life will never be the same if you do. It will be always missing something great if you don't.

Through it all I came to see in deeper measure how awesome and wonderful our Lord is. How great is the depth of His love. How worthy of our praise and worship He is. We see so little of His greatness with our finite minds. We are practically clueless in our approach to Him. He desires so much more *from* us because He has so much more *for* us. And when we let Him, He will reveal more of Himself to us. As much as we are able to contain.

It took months of every kind of test and temptation that you can imagine until one day the storm ceased. The vise parted. The hold on my life finally broke. I got my vision back. I could think ahead again. And I knew He was preparing me for something. To write this book perhaps. That remains to be seen. But God definitely wanted me to make worship and praise a greater priority in my life than it had ever been before.

During that time I learned a lot more about the power of worship and praise. I see that sometimes it is *all* God wants. Sometimes worship is to be our *only* weapon, along with the Word of God, of course, because it allows Him to fight the battle for us.

God sees into the heart of every worshiper. He knows whether they are sincere, truthful, honest, and pure in their motivation. You know how you can always tell when someone comes to you acting nice, but they have ulterior motives? Maybe they haven't called you in months, but now they want something from you and try to convince you of their affection so they can get it. Many parents have seen that in their children.

"Mom, you look so beautiful. Can I have a new video game?"

"Dad, you're the greatest. Can I borrow the car?"

Maybe that's how God feels. Like a holy sugar daddy or lucky slot machine. Surely He longs to have His children sometimes just express their affection for Him and that's all. I am not saying we shouldn't pray for things. That's not scriptural, and it's certainly not what I believe. I am saying that in our praying we can't forget to make praise and worship a priority. It should be a part of every prayer.

We were created to worship God. It's a state in which our soul finds true peace, rest, and purpose. But it must become a condition of the heart, a way of life, a pattern that is woven into the fabric of our being. Worship must become so ongoing that it is no longer even a decision that has to be made because the decision has *already* been made. Worship must become a lifestyle.

When you make worship a lifestyle, it will determine in whose image you will be formed and what you will become.

Sometimes praise and worship will be the only thing you do in a situation. You will stand and praise God while the tornados of life swirl around you, and you will see God move on your behalf. And then you will understand the hidden power of praise. When you understand that concept, it will change your life.

It's not your saying, "I'll give it everything I've got, and the Lord will bless it," but rather it's the Lord saying to you, "You just bless My name, and *I'll* give it everything *I* have." That's the hidden power in praise!

— Jack Hayford

Worship is a choice we make. Whether we

worship God or not is always an act of our own will. Our will determines whether we make it our first reaction to things that happen to us — or *don't* happen to us — or a last resort. If we *don't* make it our first reaction, then we cannot possibly make it a way of life. And if we don't make praise a way of life, we will never experience all God has for us.

Taking It Personally

One of the most important things you can do in your life is to worship together with other believers. I can't emphasize that enough. This kind of *corporate* praise can pull you in and take you someplace you couldn't get to without it. There is something that happens when we worship God together with other believers that doesn't happen to the same degree when we don't. It becomes a force that ignites change in the world around you. There's a renewing, reviving, and refreshing of our own souls. It's amazingly life-transforming, and when you let yourself be swept up into it, it will melt and change your heart. But if you have to always rely on a group to draw you in, you are missing an important element in your personal walk with God. Your own spirit and soul need to connect with God in a way that can only happen through frequent and on-going praise and worship.

It's not enough that you should read about worship, hear worship songs, or listen to other people worship, you must actually worship God yourself. It's in your own per-sonal worship times that you will develop an intimate relationship with Him. If you are ever worshiping God by yourself and you don't sense His intimate presence, continue to praise and worship Him until you do. It's not that you have to try hard to get God to be close to you. He has chosen to dwell in your praise. But you do have to give Him time to break down the barriers in your soul and penetrate the walls of your heart so that He can pour Himself into you.

God must always be the complete focus of your worship. But when you worship Him, there will be gifts and blessings that He will pour out on you.

In worship you will sense why you were created. You will hear God speak to your heart because He has softened it and made it less resistant. In worship you will experi-ence God's love. He will change your emo-tions, attitudes, and patterns of thought. He will pour out His Spirit upon you and make your heart open to receive all He has for you. He will make your mind clear so you can better understand His Word. He will refresh, renew, enrich, enlighten, heal, free, and fulfill you. He will breathe life into the dead areas of your existence. He will infuse you with His power and His joy. He will redeem and transform you and your situation. He will fill your empty places, liberate you from bondage, take away your fear and doubt, grow your faith, and give you peace. He will break the chains that imprison you and restore you to wholeness. He will lift you above your circumstances and limitations, and motivate you to help others find life in Him.

Need I go on?

No religion has ever been greater than its idea of God. Worship is pure or base as the worship entertains high or low thoughts of God . . . We tend by a secret law of the soul to move toward our mental image of God.

— Jim May

Worship is really a gift God gives us. It's the means by which we find our purpose in life and then see it realized according to His will. In worship we not only acknowledge God and who He is, but we begin to understand who we are in relation to Him. It's a way of expressing our utter dependence upon Him and our submission to Him. But in order to see all this realized, praise must become a way of life. Like the air we breathe. King David spoke of praising God constantly. He said, "I will bless the LORD at all times; His praise shall continually be in my mouth" (Psalm 34:1).

The way we keep praise continually in our mouths is by letting praise continually live in our hearts through an ongoing attitude of worship.

God looks for true worshipers because through them He can accomplish His purposes here on earth. "The hour is coming, and now is, when the true worshipers will worship the Father in spirit and truth; for the Father is seeking such to worship Him" (John 4:23). He wants to reveal Himself, His glory, and His power to those who look to Him. "From there you will seek the LORD your God, and you will find Him if you seek Him with all your heart and with all your soul" (Deuteronomy 4:29). Only when we seek God in worship will we find our true purpose in life and begin to understand why we are here. And only then can we actually begin to see that purpose realized.

When I learned to make praise and worship a priority, it transformed me and my circumstances. I want this to happen to you too. I want you to truly understand the hidden power of praise because when you do, it will become the prayer that changes everything in your life.

The Rest of the Book

The rest of the book is divided into two main sections:

Part I gives you Fifteen Reasons to Praise God Now. These are the things that are always true about God. They remind us of who He is, no matter what is happening in our lives. Of course, there are far more reasons than that to praise God, but these are the important ones we tend to forget.

Part II gives you Fifteen Times When Praise Is Crucial. These are the situations in our lives during which we often forget to praise God. Again, there are far more than 15, and I am sure you will think of some of them as you read. When these examples find a place of full understanding in your heart, they will change the way you relate to God on a daily basis for the rest of your life.

Part 1

Fifteen Reasons to Praise God Now

Why We Need to Know God Better

One of the most powerful experiences I've ever had helped me gain a greater understanding about who God really is. It happened in a church service where Pastor Jack Hayford was teaching about the awesome attributes of God. In the middle of his teaching he asked the people in the congregation to spontaneously speak out a name or an attribute of God that had meant the most to them.

One at a time people spoke out loud enough for all to hear.

"Savior," said one.

"Redeemer," said another.

"Healer," said someone else.

"Deliverer," said yet another.

"Lord."

"Peace."

"The Word."

"All-Knowing," "All-Powerful," "Light of

the World," "Creator," "Heavenly Father," "All-Sufficient," "God with Us."

Names poured forth in succession from every part of the large sanctuary. And with each name came a surge of joy from deep within the souls of those listening. With each name the light of hope glowed more brightly in our hearts.

It was not only hearing God's name spoken, but we could tell that the person speaking the names either *knew* God as that name from personal experience, or they were *hoping* in faith to know Him in that way. I was the one who called out "Deliverer" because God had delivered me from the hands of death and brokenness so many times that I knew I was alive because of His deliverance. He had set me free from the loneliness, sadness, fear, and depression of my childhood and restored me to wholeness. When I said, "Deliverer," I *knew* Him as my deliverer.

With each name spoken, everyone increasingly sensed the awesome greatness of God. It was as if each name brought a rising of faith regarding that particular attribute of God. It touched all of us so powerfully that many of us openly wept. When it was finished, the entire place erupted into spontaneous praise. No one was reluctant, no one had to be coaxed or invited. No one hesitated to raise their voice or their hands to God. In fact, we couldn't stop ourselves. The praise went on and on. Hearing God's names had filled us with new hope and increased our love for Him.

This happened more than 30 years ago, and I have never forgotten the full impact of it. It proved to me that the better we know God, and the more we understand all of who He is, the less we will be able to contain our praise for Him.

ATTENTION ALL READERS! What I am saying here is that we are to worship *God.* I am *not* saying we are to worship His attributes. I *am* saying that God is multifaceted, and we don't understand all that He is. We could spend a lifetime alone just trying to fathom that He is God the *Father,* God the *Son,* and God the *Holy Spirit.* But He is also many other things.

In the Bible God has numerous names. If we were able to grasp all of who God is on our own, He would not have needed to inspire the writers of the Bible to speak of Him using His many names. It's obvious that there is no way our finite minds can understand even a fraction of who He is without knowing these things about Him. The Bible wasn't written so that God would have a record of who He is and what He has done in case He forgot. It is written for *us* in case *we* forget. The Bible was written to help us know Him better. To help us understand things about Him that we otherwise could not.

God doesn't hide who He is and what He has done. We can clearly see Him if we will open our eyes with humility. We see Him in His Word. We see Him in His creation. "Since the creation of the world His invisible attributes are clearly seen, being understood by the things that are made, even His eternal power and Godhead, so that they are without excuse, because, although they knew God, they did not glorify Him as God, nor were thankful, but became futile in their thoughts, and their foolish hearts were darkened" (Romans 1:20-21).

In other words, when we know God and do not thank Him as we should, we become fools bathed in futility and darkness. It seems to me that we need to spend more time appreciating who God is.

Our image of God influences our life more than we realize. That's why the more we know of Him and His nature, the more we will love Him and want to worship Him. Worship is responding to the greatness of God by openly loving and honoring Him.

But if we don't understand all of who He really is, we may not worship Him with the passion we need to have. When we understand His greatness, we will be like children in a candy store, wanting everything we see. "Out of the mouth of babes and nursing infants You have perfected praise" (Matthew 21:16). Innocent, childlike appreciation, and the unrestrained joy of showing it, is what God wants from us.

God must always have first place in our hearts. He says, "You shall have no other gods before Me" (Exodus 20:3). We must be very careful that we not allow anything or anyone to usurp His position. The better we know Him, the easier that will be. Below is a list of the names of our Lord that are good to read over frequently. Speak them out loud and declare that aspect of God as a reality in your life. They will remind you of *His greatness* and inspire *your gratefulness.*

Names and Attributes of God

He is Good (1 Chronicles 16:34)
He is Powerful (1 Corinthians 1:24)
He is Great (Psalm 86:10)
He is Excellent (Psalm 8:1)
He is Love (1 John 4:16)

He is Wisdom (1 Corinthians 1:24)
He is Holy (Psalm 22:3-4)
He is Patient (Romans 15:5)
He is Changeless (Malachi 3:6)
He is Merciful (Psalm 116:5)
He is Almighty (2 Corinthians 6:18)
He is Glorious (Exodus 15:11)
He is Righteous (Deuteronomy 32:4)
He is Just (Isaiah 45:21)
He is Grace (John 1:14)
He is Majestic (Isaiah 33:21)
He is All-Knowing (John 16:30)
He is All-Wise (Proverbs 3:19-20)
He is True (Jeremiah 10:10)
He is Pure (1 John 3:3)
He is Sinless (1 Peter 2:21-22)
He is Radiant (Hebrews 1:3 NIV)
He is Faithful (Deuteronomy 7:9)
He is Magnificent (Isaiah 28:29 NIV)
He is Worthy (Psalm 18:3)
He is my Creator (Psalm 139:13 TEV)
He is my Redeemer (Isaiah 59:20)
He is my Strength (Isaiah 12:2)
He is my Truth (John 14:6)
He is the Lifter of my Head (Psalm 3:3)
He is the All-Sufficient One
   (2 Corinthians 12:9)
He is my Savior (Luke 1:47)
He is my Hope (Psalm 71:5)
He is the Son of God (Luke 1:35)

He is my Resurrection (John 11:25)
He is the Holy Spirit (Genesis 1:1-3)
He is the Light of the World (John 8:12)
He is the Lord of Lords (Deuteronomy 10:17)
He is the King of Kings (Revelation 17:14)
He is my Authority (Matthew 28:18)
He is my Consuming Fire (Deuteronomy 4:24)
He is my Restorer (Psalm 23:3)
He is my Comforter (John 14:15 TLB)
He is my Stronghold in the Day of Trouble (Nahum 1:7)
He is my Resting Place (Jeremiah 50:6)
He is my Refiner (Malachi 3:2-3)
He is my Deliverer (Psalm 70:5)
He is my Refuge from the Storm (2 Samuel 22:3)
He is my Overcomer (John 16:33)
He is my Peace (Ephesians 2:14)
He is the Bread of Life (John 6:35)
He is my Fortress (Psalm 18:2)
He is my Everlasting Father (Isaiah 9:6)
He is my Shade from the Heat (Isaiah 25:4)
He is my Healer (Malachi 4:2)
He is my Counselor (Psalm 16:7)
He is the Author of my Faith (Hebrews 12:2)
He is my Rewarder (Hebrews 11:6)
He is my Hiding Place (Psalm 32:7)
He is my Shield (Psalm 33:20)

He is my Purifier (Malachi 3:3)
He is my Sustainer (Psalm 55:22)
He is the Sovereign Lord
   (2 Samuel 7:28 NIV)

The "Fifteen Reasons to Praise God Now" in the following 15 chapters are only a few out of many, but they are important ones we often forget, especially when we go through difficult times. No matter what is going on in your life, they will always be cause for praise.

Remember, we value God's attributes. We worship *God.*

1

Because He
Is My Creator

Let's start at the beginning, shall we?

I mean the *very* beginning. Back when God created heaven and earth. On page 1 of Genesis.

God started the creation process without any preexisting things. He began with nothing. With the presence of His Holy Spirit and the entrance of His Word, creation happened. He brought order, light, life, and beauty out of chaos and darkness. Every time He said, "Let there be . . ." it happened.

God doesn't need anything in order to create something great. Aren't you glad about that? I know I am. Even in our lives, God doesn't need much to work with. He can create something from nothing. He has certainly done that in my life.

Everything God Created Is Good

Not only can God create something from nothing, but everything He creates is good. Seven times in the story of creation, God said that what He had made was good (Genesis 1:4,10,12,17,21,25,31). If everything God makes is good, doesn't that mean you are too? Of course, sin came in and perverted things, but God created you for good, and He is redeeming your life to that end. He is all about redemption. And He never makes an error. Even if something happens to ruin or pervert what He has made, He provides us a way back to complete restoration.

Let me tell you some words God *never* utters.

Ten Things God Never Says

1. "Oops!"
2. "What have I done?"
3. "How did I let that happen?"
4. "I made a mistake."
5. "It was an accident."
6. "I don't know what to do."
7. "I'm afraid of what will happen now."
8. "I can do better than this."

9. "What do *you* think I should do?"
10. "Why didn't *I* think of that?"

The reason it is important to know these things that God never says is because it means He never says them about *you* either. Everything God created is good. He says so Himself. That includes you and me.

If all God created is good, then anything that has been spoiled must be *our* doing. Whenever we see anything of God's creation that doesn't seem to be good, we can be sure that man has done something to ruin it. Sin spoils everything. We spoil the good things in our lives when we transgress our relationship with Him by not living His way. And when we don't give God the reverence that is due Him through our own worship and praise, we are not living His way. We are not fulfilling the original intention of all God created us to be and do.

God Created You in His Image

Having a close resemblance to your heavenly Father is an amazing thought. "God created man in His own image; in the image of God He created him; male and female

He created them" (Genesis 1:27). That means you have your Father's eyes. And you have your Father's heart. You also are a brother or sister to His Son, Jesus, and you are destined to become like Him. That means you are part of a *really big* family. "For whom He foreknew, He also predestined to be conformed to the image of His Son, that He might be the firstborn among many brethren" (Romans 8:29).

What are some of the characteristics of God you would like to inherit? What about His strength? His goodness? His wisdom? His patience? His faithfulness? His peace? God wants to impart all of those things and more to us as we are ready to receive them. God wants to share Himself with us. He wants to train us up to be like Him. That doesn't mean we are actually going to be God someday. It means that He wants to show us how to run the family business down here, and we need to have His qualities and abilities to do it.

God wants us to remember Who it is Who gave us life and Who it is we are supposed to resemble. "Is he not your Father, your Creator, who made you and formed you?" (Deuteronomy 32:6 NIV). God wants you to be thankful for the way He made you. I'm not saying don't get your teeth fixed or try to improve yourself in any way. Fix what you can, but also be grateful for who He made you to be.

God Loves All He Created

God loves His creation just as a mother loves the child that is growing in her womb — sight unseen. She is already completely in love with that tiny person before he or she is ever born.

Your Creator loved you before you were born too. You were wanted. You were not an accident. You didn't evolve from a monkey. You weren't *accidentally* born to someone who could not raise you, and so you were later adopted. God gave you life, and you are a part of His plan. He created you and you are valued, precious, and priceless to Him. He loves you because He made you and He knows who He made you to be.

You are unique. There is no one like *you*. There never was and never will be. And God has a purpose for you that is unique as well. He has big plans for your life. Remember, God never makes mistakes. Therefore you are not one.

We Were Made for His Glory

The ultimate reason God created you is to be with Him. To glorify Him. He says, "Everyone who is called by My name, whom I have created for My glory; I have formed him, yes, I have made him" (Isaiah 43:7). And we were made to worship Him. "This people I have formed for Myself; they shall declare My praise" (Isaiah 43:21). Praising God is the main purpose for which we were created. We were created for worship. We just have to get it straight in our heart exactly where our worship is to be directed.

> At the root of God's revelation to His creation, worship is shown as the prerequisite for man's ability to receive and live within the high possibilities and rich benediction of God's plan.
>
> — Jack Hayford

God Loves His Creation and So Should We

All too often we don't take time to step back from the world to appreciate God's creation. To thank Him for it. To praise Him as our Creator. When we do, it gives us a whole new perspective. It takes away darkness, futility, and foolishness from our minds. It helps us see the world through different eyes.

His!

That means we need to praise God for other people. But that's not always our first thought, is it? It's so much easier to praise God for His sunset, His ocean beaches, His trees and flowers. But His people? Waking up every day and thanking Him for other people? They may not be *our* first thought, but they are *His*.

All that God created is beyond our full comprehension, but this is especially true when it comes to *people*. Every person in the world is entirely unique, down to their fingerprints and DNA, and we need to respond to God's greatness as our *Creator* by praising Him for all those *whom* He has created. This is not worshiping the creature rather than the Creator (Romans 1:24-25). This is *worshiping* the Creator and *appreciating* His creatures.

When we praise God for other people, it helps us to gain His heart for them. He *loves* them. *All* of them. We definitely don't do that in the natural. Our love for other people has to be ignited in the Spirit. God has to impart that ability to us. And He does it when we praise Him for the people He has created.

Think of that the next time you are at an amusement park, standing in line for an hour with a thousand other people, trying to get your children on a ride. Or when you are at a sporting event, concert, or meeting, and it's wall-to-wall bodies and some of them don't smell as fragrant as others. Or you are at the grocery store just before a snowstorm or after an earthquake and all the batteries, bottles of water, bread, and milk are gone. Think of it when you are hopelessly stuck in a traffic jam that shows no sign of moving because of the number of cars and trucks in front of you. These are the times to especially thank God for all the people He created, and that they each have a unique calling and purpose that is important to Him.

We also need to appreciate everything else in God's creation. We can sometimes become so wrapped up in praising *man's* creations that we ignore *God's* completely. If there were no other reason for our praise, the fact that God is the Creator of all would be enough. "The heavens declare the glory of God; and the firmament shows His handiwork" (Psalm 19:1). All of God's creation is an expression of His love for us.

Every time I look at an ocean sunset with explosive shades of red, pink, yellow, lavender, and orange dancing in lavish combinations on the water as far as the eye can see, I feel God's love and find that praising Him comes automatically. But God wants us to see the beauty of His creation at *all* times and in *all* places. No matter where we look. Even in the depravity of the world around us, His creation can still be seen and appreciated. His love can still be found there.

When you are going through a difficult time, don't let yourself become so overwhelmed by your concerns and blinded by your situation that you can't see anything else but that. Praise God as your Creator and thank Him for His creation. It's important to our well-being to acknowledge that everything under heaven is God's (Job 41:11) and to praise Him for it. "Then at last they will think of God their Creator" and have respect for Him (Isaiah 17:7 TLB). When we *don't* think of God as our Creator and don't give Him the proper respect, there are ramifications for that. "For this is a people without understanding; so their Maker has no compassion on them, and their Creator shows them no favor" (Isaiah 27:11 NIV).

This is serious. It's not a good idea to lose God's compassion and favor. God loves His creation. He surely doesn't love all that has happened to it, but He knows the way He created it to be. He sees its potential, He knows its purpose. He wants you to see that too.

The same is true for you. You are His creation and He loves you. He may not love all that has happened to you or all that you have done, but He loves you and He knows the way He created you to be. He sees your potential, and He knows your purpose. And what He can create in your life now is without limits.

The hidden power of praising God as your Creator releases Him to create new life in you.

WORSHIP IS

... celebrating Him as our Creator and thanking Him for all that He has created.

I Give God My Praise

Lord, I worship You as the Creator of

heaven and earth. All things were made by You and everything You created is good. I praise You for all of Your beautiful creation. You placed the earth on its foundation so that it can never be moved (Psalm 104:5). Your right hand stretched out the heavens (Isaiah 48:13). Thank You that You have blessed us with light and dark, sun and rain, food and water, land and sea, trees and flowers, days and seasons. "The heavens are Yours, the earth also is Yours; the world and all its fullness, You have founded them" (Psalm 89:11).

"When I consider your heavens, the work of your fingers, the moon and the stars, which you have set in place, what is man that you are mindful of him, the son of man that you care for him? You made him a little lower than the heavenly beings and crowned him with glory and honor. You made him ruler over the works of your hands; you put everything under his feet" (Psalm 8:3-6 NIV). I know that "both men and women come from God their Creator" (1 Corinthians 11:12 TLB). "How many are your works, O LORD! In wisdom you have made them all; the earth is full of your creatures" (Psalm 104:24 NIV).

O Lord, thank You that You created me and gave me life. "You formed my inward parts; You covered me in my mother's womb" (Psalm 139:13). I praise You, "for I am fearfully and wonderfully made; marvelous are Your works, and that my soul knows very well" (Psalm 139:14). I praise You for every breath I take and thank You that I was created for good things. Help me to be renewed in the image of You, my Creator (Colossians 3:10 NIV). I know You made me to be so much more than I am now and that You will help me become all You created me to be.

I praise You for the people You have created, each one unique and valuable and carrying in their spiritual DNA a purpose that is distinctive and priceless as well. I am grateful for the potential for good that You have placed within each one. Help me to value others as Your creation and see them the way You do. Thank You, Jesus, that You are "the image of the invisible God, the firstborn over all creation" (Colossians 1:15). "You are worthy, O Lord, to receive glory and honor and power; for You created all things, and by Your will they exist and were created" (Revelation 4:11). I worship You as my Creator and I praise You for all that You have created.

God Gave Me His Word

Christ himself is the Creator who made everything in heaven and earth, the things we can see and the things we can't; the spirit world with its kings and kingdoms, its rulers and authorities; all were made by Christ for his own use and glory.

Colossians 1:16 TLB

By You I have been upheld from birth; You are He who took me out of my mother's womb. My praise shall be continually of You. I have become as a wonder to many, but You are my strong refuge. Let my mouth be filled with Your praise and with Your glory all the day.

PSALM 71:6-8

Therefore let those who suffer according to the will of God commit their souls to Him in doing good, as to a faithful Creator.

1 Peter 4:19

Woe to the man who fights with his Creator. Does the pot argue with its maker? Does the clay dispute with him who

73

forms it, saying, "Stop, you're doing it wrong!" or the pot exclaim, "How clumsy can you be?"

Isaiah 45:9 TLB

Since they show no regard for the works of the LORD and what his hands have done, he will tear them down and never build them up again.

Psalm 28:5 NIV

Giving It Some Further Thought

1. Write out a prayer of praise to God, worshiping Him as your Creator and thanking Him for His creation. Take a moment to experience God's creation right where you are. What do you recognize in the world around you of God's creation for which you are especially grateful? What of God's creation reveals His love for you? Write out praise to God for those specific things.

2. Read Psalm 104:1-24 in your Bible. Write out a prayer of praise for the things listed there that God created.

3. Read Psalm 28:5 in your Bible. What happens to people who do not show any regard for what God has done?

4. Read Romans 1:24-25 in your Bible. Why did God give these people over to their own lusts? What should you remember to do?

5. Read Genesis 1:27-31 in your Bible. Who did God create and what did He tell them to do? How did He feel about His creation?

2

Because He Is My Heavenly Father

I'm always amazed at how many people have a hard time relating to God as their *heavenly* Father. And it's often because they didn't have a good relationship with their *earthly* father. If their father was too busy and pre-occupied, they feel God might be too. If their father was emotionally detached, they may view their heavenly Father as being distant. If their father was gone a lot and never there for them when they needed him, they may doubt that their Father God will actually be there for them either. Or if they had a father who was abusive and cruel, they may regard their heavenly Father as unloving and uncaring.

I know of someone who had a drug addicted mother and a father who deserted her and never spoke to her or saw her again. She ended up in different foster homes, one in which she was sexually abused. As a result, once she became a believer, she had a very difficult time relating to God as a loving Father. After a time of Christian counseling, she finally broke through that barrier and was able to forgive her father for abandoning her. It was crucial to her healing and to establishing her relationship with God as her heavenly Father. When she was finally able to receive His love and go to Him as a child would to a loving dad, she began a healing process that brought her into the wholeness God had for her.

Each of us needs the love of a father. Some of us never had one — at least not one we knew. Maybe you had a father, but you did not feel loved and accepted by him. Or even worse, you felt disliked, disrespected, uncared for, or even hated by him. The truth is, you can't develop to your fullest potential without a father's love. There will always be something missing. There will always be something in the back of your mind that only trusts His love so far. (Do you dads see how important you are, and how much your love means to your children?) That's why God wants you to know that He is your heavenly Father, and He unfailingly loves you as a father should — with strength, care, guidance, consistency, and rules for your own good.

So often we forfeit the wholeness God has for us because we can't relate to Him as our heavenly Father.

Forgiving Your Earthly Father

The day I began to truly trust God as my heavenly Father was the day I recognized my own unforgiveness toward my dad. I was in a counselor's office talking with her about the anxiety and unrest I had in my soul. She was the person who had taught me how to forgive my mother. But this time she felt I had unforgiveness toward my dad. I told her that was impossible and I was sure she was totally wrong about that. Even though my dad wasn't openly affectionate, I knew he loved me. And, besides, he wasn't abusive. But she insisted, saying, "Just ask God about it and see what *He* says."

Driving home from her office I did ask God about it, knowing He would surely say that a good and faithful servant like me would never harbor such terrible feelings about my dad. But quite the opposite happened. I felt as though I had been struck through the heart with a sword. I had to pull to the side of the freeway because I was doubled over with sudden sobs. As I sat there, with tears blinding my eyes so that I could not see to drive, God revealed how I had felt abandoned by my dad for not coming through for me. He never protected me from my mother's abuse. He never unlocked the closet door or came to my rescue when she became violent. I had not realized how much I held against him. And down deep inside I felt that God probably wouldn't come through for me either.

Forgiving my father freed me to cry a lifetime of uncried tears and to be able to love him more. It also freed me to love my heavenly Father and fully receive *His* love for *me*. It was a major time of healing, and I came to a new place of peace and rest in my life. Soon after that my ministry in writing broke forth, and I believe there was a significant connection between the two.

In order to have the healing, wholeness, and restoration you want for your life, you must be able to forgive your earthly father for all he did or did not do and receive your heavenly Father's love. If you are unable to fully view the Lord as your heavenly Father, it will affect every part of your life, from your relationships to your view of yourself.

In order to have a long, fruitful life and

move into all God has for us, we must honor our father and mother. Some of us had parents who were around and provided food and a place to live — and for that we certainly need to be grateful — but they never put anything of themselves into our lives. We could never expect Dad or Mom to support, encourage, or to teach us anything. But we still need to honor them. If for no other reason than that they gave us life. Without them, we wouldn't be here.

But you can't fully honor your father and mother if you haven't forgiven them. No parent is perfect. No parent always does everything right. And even if your parents *were* perfect, forgive them for giving you an impossible standard to live up to. Ask God to show you if there is anything you need to forgive. Even if they are no longer living, forgiving them will clear the way for you to fully see God as your heavenly Father and to feel His love for you. He will heal and restore whatever you suffered or lost in your relationship with them. "When my father and my mother forsake me, then the LORD will take care of me" (Psalm 27:10).

If you have ever felt alone in your life because one or both of your parents were not there, know that your Father God *will* be. Your heavenly Father is not like an earthly

81

parent. He will never abandon you, mistreat you, ignore you, or be too preoccupied to have time for you. He is *always* there for you, He *always* loves you, and He *always* has your best interests at heart.

Know to Whom You Belong

You will never really understand your true identity unless you can forever settle in your heart that you are a true son or daughter of God. The Bible says of Jesus that "as many as received Him, to them He gave the right to become children of God, to those who believe in His name" (John 1:12). Once you settle this issue and come to know God as your heavenly Father, your life will change. You'll begin to take on a family resemblance. You will have your Father's eyes, heart, and mind.

Have you ever heard someone talk about God in a way that made Him so stern and demanding that He seemed untouchable? He became someone to avoid, because to be around Him meant being reminded of what a failure you are. If so, this is another good reason for you to learn to see God as your heavenly Father. He is only frightening when you don't know Him, don't love Him, and don't reverence Him as one who loves you. He wants to have a close relationship with you.

> The reason God desires our worship is because He desires a personal relationship with each of His children.
> — Patrick Kavanaugh

When Jesus taught us how to pray, He told us to first establish our relationship with God as our heavenly Father, and then praise and exalt His name. He said to pray, "Our Father in heaven, hallowed be Your name. Your kingdom come. Your will be done on earth as it is in heaven" (Luke 11:2). And He said, "When you pray, go into your room, and when you have shut your door, pray to your Father who is in the secret place; and your Father who sees in secret will reward you openly" (Matthew 6:6).

As a child of God, we have privileges that other people don't have. We have become part of a large family. We have a special place to live for eternity. We are provided for. We receive many wonderful blessings and gifts. We have security. We have an important position in the "family business."

And we have an amazing inheritance. God says that the thoughts He thinks toward us are "of peace and not of evil" to give us "a future and a hope" (Jeremiah 29:11).

One of the ways a parent loves a child is by having rules for their protection and benefit. God's rules are a sign of His love for us. Because we are His son or daughter, there are things that are expected of us. One of the ways we love and acknowledge Him as our Father is living by His rules. One of His rules is that we honor Him with worship and praise. That is also the way we come to know Him better.

When you worship God as your heavenly Father, you gain a greater understanding of what it means to be His child, and it will be the very means by which your Father-and-child relationship will deepen. This is the hidden power of praising God.

The unconditional love of an earthly father is something you may have missed. But the unconditional love of your heavenly Father is something you need *never* live without. Your heavenly Father is waiting to hear from you, so call home.

> . . . the way we honor our heavenly Father and thank Him that we are one of His beloved children.

I Give God My Praise

Heavenly Father, I worship You this day. I am so grateful that You are not a distant or remote Father, but a close and loving one. You are closer to me than an earthly father ever could be. Your love for me is unconditional and everlasting. I know that no father on earth is perfect, but *You* are. Thank You that as my Father, You care about what happens to me. You provide for me, teach me, plan for my future, supply all my needs, and because You love me You will never let me get away with disobedience to Your rules. Thank You that "You have given me the heritage of those who fear Your name," and I have inherited great and eternal riches from You (Psalm 61:5). "LORD, you alone are my inheritance, my cup of blessing. You guard all that is mine. The land You have given me is a pleasant land. What a wonderful inheritance!" (Psalm 16:5-6 NLT).

Lord, help me to forgive my earthly father for anything he did or did not do. Show me if there is anything I have not forgiven that I am not seeing. I don't want my lack of forgiveness to stand in the way of my intimate relationship with You. As Your child, I long to make You proud. Help me to always do what is pleasing in Your sight. I want to be separate from all that would keep me separated from You (2 Corinthians 6:17-18). Thank You that I have been predestined to be adopted as Your child through Jesus because it gives You pleasure and it is Your will for my life (Ephesians 1:5). I praise and honor You as my Father God and give thanks always for all things, especially Your Father's love (Ephesians 5:20).

God Gave Me His Word

Therefore do not be like them. For your Father knows the things you have need of before you ask Him. In this manner, therefore, pray: Our Father in heaven, hallowed be Your name.

Matthew 6:8-9

If you then, being evil, know how to give

good gifts to your children, how much more will your heavenly Father give the Holy Spirit to those who ask Him!

Luke 11:13

Seek the kingdom of God, and all these things shall be added to you. Do not fear, little flock, for it is your Father's good pleasure to give you the kingdom.

Luke 12:31-32

Your heavenly Father knows that you need all these things.

Matthew 6:32

Whatever you do in word or deed, do all in the name of the Lord Jesus, giving thanks to God the Father through Him.

Colossians 3:17

Giving It Some Further Thought

1. How would you describe your relationship with your earthly father? For example, was it close or distant or somewhere in between? Was it loving or abusive or somewhere in the middle? How does the relationship you had with your dad make you feel today?

2. What do you feel was most lacking in your relationship with your earthly father? Describe it in a prayer to the Lord and ask Him to fill in what has been missing in your life because of it. If there was nothing lacking in your relationship with your earthly father, write out a prayer of praise and thanksgiving to God for the fact that your earthly father was everything you needed him to be.

3. List the greatest attributes of your earthly father. If you never knew him, or barely knew him, list the attributes you would have most desired in a father. What names and attributes of God most correspond to those you have listed? Do you believe that your Father God can be all that to you now?

4. Write out a prayer of praise thanking God that He is your heavenly Father. Ask the Lord to show you any place where you have put something on Him that was really due to a failing on the part of your earthly father.

5. Read 2 Corinthians 6:17-18 in your Bible. While God's love for you as His child is unconditional, He still has rules and requirements as any good parent would for their children. What are the requirements stated in these verses?

3

Because He Loves Me

When my son was about three years old, I often told him that I loved him more than any other little boy on earth. In return he would say, "I love you too, Mom." Then he would spread his hands as wide apart as he could and say, "I love you *this* much."

Every time he did that he would spread his hands farther and farther apart until one day they finally touched together in back of him. Then he started saying, "I love you two hands behind the back."

That became our private saying to each other for several years. This to us was an expression of loving someone with your whole being. It meant "I love you with everything I've got in me. As far as I can go." It was full circle. It was complete.

That's exactly the way God wants us to love *Him*. With everything we have. As much as we can. With all of our being. Unconditional. Full circle. Completely.

And that is the way God loves *us*.

But what if you've never been loved unconditionally? Or at least never felt as though you have been. Can you really give a return of love if love has never been invested in you? Can something be poured out if it hasn't first been poured in? In other words, how do you know the way to love completely if you've never been loved that way before?

I used to wonder about that. I felt unloved and unlovable for most of my life, and I was always seeking someone to love me. I wearied myself, and probably everyone else around me, in pathetic and futile ways trying to find unfailing love. I think I may actually have found it more than once, but because I was so needy I couldn't love that person the same way in return. I felt that when you love someone, you need to offer them a whole person. And I knew I wasn't.

When I first came to the Lord, I could sense the love of God. I sensed it in the church when I walked in. I sensed it in the people around me who trusted in Him. It was easy for me to believe God loved *them* because I sensed His love *in* them. But I didn't think God would ever love me as much as He loved them. Convinced as I was that I was unlovable by human standards, I certainly didn't feel worthy of *God's* love.

But when I came to know God better, and learned who He really is, I began to understand more and more the depth of His love for each one of us. Even me. He doesn't love us because we deserve it. He loves us because He is a God of love. That's who He *is*. He cannot be something He isn't. And He loves *you* because you are His creation and He is your heavenly Father. There is no way He cannot love *you*.

Parents love their child sight unseen. I loved each of my children even as they were growing in me. Your Father God loved you in that same way. He loved you unconditionally *before* you were born, while you were still being formed. Long before you ever knew Him. "We love Him because He first loved us" (1 John 4:19). That's why we can love Him now.

God says there is nothing that can separate us from His love. Nothing in life, and nothing in death (Romans 8:38). The love of man will always be shallow and limited, but God's love is deep and unending. Sometimes we can find ourselves in the lowest valley and question God's love for us there. But His love is not minimized in valley times. No matter how difficult tough times are, they don't reflect God's love for us in the way *we* think of it. We think, *If God really loved me, He wouldn't allow me to suffer this way.* But the truth is, even in the lowest valley and most difficult time, we cannot be separated from His love. He will love us *through* it. And we have to let Him.

Too often, though, we don't let Him.

We don't let God love us every time we *doubt* His love for us. We don't allow Him to fully love us when we don't let ourselves love *Him*. We don't let Him love us when we don't *worship* Him. For worship is the most significant time when we show our love for Him and He pours His love into us. Worship is the way we love God in return.

Of course, there are other ways we need to show God that we love Him, such as by obeying Him. "Whoever keeps His word, truly the love of God is perfected in him. By this we know that we are in Him" (1 John 2:5). Obedience is not trying to get God to love us by being good. That's not the way it works. He loved us first, remember? At our *worst.* The way we *are.* It's that when you love someone, you want to do whatever makes them happy. Obedience makes God happy. Living God's way makes Him happy.

And one of the steps of obedience He wants us to take is to make worship and praise a priority and lifestyle.

Facing the Love Issue

The love issue is a big one. There is no one who doesn't want or need love, especially if it was completely missing during some period of their development as a human being. But we don't have to live without it, because God loves us completely and continually. There is nothing you can do that would make Him love you any more or any less than He does right now. And God's love is the same for everyone.

When you think of the worst person on earth, whom do you think of? An evil dictator? A serial killer? A child molester? A wife abuser? Well, God loves each one of them. He hates their sins, just the way He hates yours and mine. But He loves the person. It's hard to imagine, but it's true.

When a child does things his parents don't like, they still love him. It's the same with your heavenly Father. His love is always there for you no matter what you have done. *People's* love for us may change, depending

94

on what we do or don't do to please them. But *God's* does not. He loves you with an eternal, undying, everlasting, unconditional love. The love we feel from people too often depends on how valuable we are to them at the moment. God says we are valuable to Him at all times.

The times when I most sense God's love for me is when I worship in a group of people gathered together for that purpose. An extremely powerful dynamic happens when people worship together. I'm not talking about just getting together to sing nice songs *about* God. I'm talking about worshiping God for who He is with all we have in us. There is nothing more healing, restoring, or life changing. Once you sense God's love through those times of corporate praise and worship, you won't want to ever live without it.

God doesn't want us to praise Him just with our mouths; He wants us to praise Him with our whole hearts. He doesn't want us to praise Him just because someone said to; He wants us to praise Him because we love Him. "These people draw near with their mouths and honor Me with their lips, but have removed their hearts far from Me, and their fear toward Me is taught by the commandment of men" (Isaiah 29:13). When you understand how much God loves you, you can't help but praise Him for it.

> To be a worshiper is to fall in love with God, the Author of love, and accept the love He has for you. He adores you. God gave you His Word as a living love letter that contains everything you will ever need to get through this life and beyond.
> — Darlene Zschech

One of the wonderful things that happens when we worship the God of love is that He fills us with His love and then we become a conduit of His love to others. His love *for* us causes love to grow *in* us for other people, many of whom we would probably never even think to love. "He who does not love does not know God, for God is love" (1 John 4:8).

The hidden power of praise is that the more we praise the God of love, the more His love is released into our hearts and through our lives.

One thing about falling in love with someone who loves you back is that no matter how much you see each other, it is never enough. You always want more. Once you feel God's love *for* you, *in* you, and *around* you, you will want to be in His presence all the time.

Jesus said, "You shall love the LORD your God with all your heart, with all your soul, and with all your mind" (Matthew 22:37). *That's a lot of love.*

That's with everything we have in us.

With our whole being.

Unconditional. Full circle. Complete.

It's "two hands behind the back."

WORSHIP IS

> . . . opening up the channel through which we communicate our love to God and God transmits His love to us.

I Give Him My Praise

Lord, I worship You and thank You that You are the God of love. Thank You for loving me before I even knew You. I praise You especially for sacrificing Your only Son for me. There is no greater love than that. Your love brings healing to me for all the times and ways I have felt unloved in my life. I know that no matter what is happening in my life or what *will* happen in my life, Your love for me will never end. Because of Your love, "I will praise You, O LORD, with my whole heart; I will tell of all Your marvelous works. I will be glad and rejoice in You; I will sing praise to Your name, O Most High" (Psalm 9:1-2).

Thank You, Lord, that "You number my wanderings" and "put my tears in Your bottle" (Psalm 56:8). They are in Your book. Thank You that "when I cry out to You, then my enemies will turn back" (verse 9). I know that You are for me. Jesus, I know that whatever I ask in Your name You will do, so that God the Father may be glorified. I ask that You would pour out Your love upon me in a way that I can feel today. I pray that I will be so filled with Your love that it overflows from me to others and can be seen by everyone around me. May Your love be greatly evident in all that I do and say. May Your grace, Your love, and Your Holy Spirit be with me always (2 Corinthians 13:14).

It is amazing that You love me so, even though I have done nothing to deserve it. "What is man, that You should exalt him, that You should set Your heart on him?" (Job 7:17). Thank You that You "see my ways and count all my steps" (Job 31:4). Thank You that Your "favor is for life"

(Psalm 30:5). O Lord, "because Your lovingkindness is better than life, my lips shall praise You. Thus I will bless You while I live; I will lift up my hands in Your name" (Psalm 63:3-4). Lord, I love You with all my heart, mind, and soul, and I worship You as my God of love.

God Gave Me His Word

> For I am persuaded that neither death nor life, nor angels nor principalities nor powers, nor things present nor things to come, nor height nor depth, nor any other created thing, shall be able to separate us from the love of God which is in Christ Jesus our Lord.
>
> Romans 8:38-39

> In this is love, not that we loved God, but that He loved us and sent His Son to be the propitiation for our sins.
>
> 1 John 4:10

> We have known and believed the love that God has for us. God is love, and he who abides in love abides in God, and God in him.
>
> 1 John 4:16

Can a woman forget her nursing child, and not have compassion on the son of her womb? Surely they may forget, yet I will not forget you. See, I have inscribed you on the palms of My hands.

Isaiah 49:15-16

Beloved, if God so loved us, we also ought to love one another. No one has seen God at any time. If we love one another, God abides in us, and His love has been perfected in us. By this we know that we abide in Him, and He in us, because He has given us of His Spirit.

1 John 4:11-13

Giving It Some Further Thought

1. Are you convinced that God is a God of love? Do you feel God loves you as much as anyone else in the world? Why or why not?

2. Read 1 Corinthians 13:1-3 in your Bible. What happens to us when we

don't have the love of God in us and
flowing through us?

3. Read Jeremiah 31:3 in your Bible. In
   light of this Scripture, how long will
   God love us? How has God drawn us
   to Himself? Write out your answer as a
   praise to God. (For example, "Lord, I
   praise You for Your love and that it
   is . . .")

4. Read Ephesians 2:4 in your Bible. Why
   does God show us mercy?

5. Read Romans 5:5 in your Bible. Why should we never lose hope? How do we receive God's love in our hearts?

4

Because He Laid Down His Life for Me

Do you know anyone who would love you enough to lay down their life for you? Someone who would die in your place? Someone who would pay the penalty in their body and person for your mistakes and sins? Someone who would take the fall for you? Suffer what you deserve? And do it willingly? All the while knowing that at anytime he could stand up and say, "Forget this. Send in the angels. I'm out of here."

I know of only one who would do that for me. And He already did it. That really takes the pressure off my family and close friends.

If you can't think of anyone who would die to save you, think again. God sent His only Son, Jesus, "the image of the invisible God" (Colossians 1:15), the manifestation of Himself in the flesh. He came. He taught. He displayed His power in the miracles He worked. He laid down His life in unimaginable suffering and torture and an agonizing death by crucifixion on a cross in order to bear all the consequences for our errors, failures, and mistakes. And then He rose from the dead and forever broke the power of death and hell in our lives.

He did all this for you and me.

He paid the price for you. He took the fall for you. He suffered the consequences for you. All because He loves you. One of the greatest demonstrations of God's love for us is that while we were sinners Jesus died for us (Romans 5:8). Could anyone love you more?

The greatest thing about Mel Gibson's film *The Passion of the Christ* was that it drove home the magnitude of the sacrifice Jesus *willingly* made for all of us. He paid an enormous price so we would not have to pay it ourselves. I had *read* the account of Jesus' life countless times and gave full value to what He accomplished in His suffering and death. But in seeing it on the screen, it became so real that I felt as though I had been there to witness it.

The deepest emotion I felt each time I saw the film — and I felt many — was that I painfully regretted every time I ever took lightly what Jesus did for me. I felt deep remorse for the moments I took God's laws lightly and walked in disobedience or carelessness. I thought about the time as a teenager when I tried to kill myself because I didn't want to wake up to another day with the pain I felt inside. What was my pain compared to *His?* And if I had succeeded in killing myself, I would never have come to know Him and the wonderful life He had for me. I would have spent eternity separated from God. And yet before I ever knew Him, He had already rescued me.

There is a realm that God operates in, and we are unable to be a part of it until we acknowledge Jesus in our life. He said, "I am the door. If anyone enters by Me, he will be saved, and will go in and out and find pasture" (John 10:9). We cannot begin to understand the reality of the kingdom of God until we walk through that door and are born again in our spirit. Because Jesus paid the price for us, we have a free ticket into the kingdom by receiving His life into ours. It's not God saying, "I see your sin but I'm going to forget about it." It's Him wiping it so completely off the record it is as if it never even happened.

Jesus saved us from an eternity separated

from God. He said, "He who believes in me will have everlasting life" (John 6:47). We can go to be with God when we die because Jesus took in His own self the penalty for our sin. He also saved us from a pointless existence here on earth. Once we receive Jesus, we now have the Holy Spirit of God living *in* us, and we can enter into a fruitful, purposeful, and meaningful life. With Him we have more life in *this* life, as well as in eternity.

Every day we need to fall in love with Jesus all over again.

Seven Good Reasons to Praise Jesus as Lord

1. **Because of Jesus, I am forgiven.** "Whom God set forth as a propitiation by His blood, through faith, to demonstrate His righteousness, because in His forbearance God had passed over the sins that were previously committed, to demonstrate at the present time His righteousness, that He might be just and the justifier of the one who has faith in Jesus" (Romans 3:25-26).

2. **Because of Jesus, I have peace with God.** "Therefore, having been justi-

fied by faith, we have peace with God through our Lord Jesus Christ" (Romans 5:1).

3. **Because of Jesus, I don't have to live with guilt or condemnation.** "There is therefore now no condemnation to those who are in Christ Jesus, who do not walk according to the flesh, but according to the Spirit" (Romans 8:1).

4. **Because of Jesus, I have a great inheritance.** "If children, then heirs — heirs of God and joint heirs with Christ, if indeed we suffer with Him, that we may also be glorified together" (Romans 8:17).

5. **Because of Jesus, I always have someone interceding for me.** "It is Christ who died, and furthermore is also risen, who is even at the right hand of God, who also makes intercession for us" (Romans 8:34).

6. **Because of Jesus, I have eternal life with Him.** "If Christ is in you, the body is dead because of sin, but the Spirit is life because of righteousness. But if the Spirit of Him who raised Jesus from the dead dwells in you, He who raised Christ from the dead will also give life to your mortal bodies

through His Spirit who dwells in you" (Romans 8:10-11).

7. **Because of Jesus, I can have more life in this life.** "The thief does not come except to steal, and to kill, and to destroy. I have come that they may have life, and that they may have it more abundantly" (John 10:10).

Remember What Jesus Did on the Cross

Jesus showed us who God is and what God's rule means. He demonstrated His authority over death, sickness, hopelessness, brokenness, poverty, and the enemy of our souls. He bore in His body the penalty of our sin so that we don't have to bear it ourselves. When He said, "It is finished" on the cross (John 19:30), it not only meant His life on earth was finished, but the things He accomplished on the cross were finished too. Done. Nothing can change that. The power of death and hell was conquered on the cross and defeated for all time. When we let our hearts fill up on that reality, praise and worship can't be contained. It becomes like a sunrise in the heart that will flow out of us in one way or another. When that happens, then we can shed our idea of worship as only a formal prescribed liturgy or a predictable order, and we will then know the newness of the living Christ in us.

> What people need is Jesus Christ, not the Christian religion. Religion is just another futile attempt to reach God by trying to be good. Jesus Christ is the life of God in us, and no human can ever achieve it without Him. This is how ordinary men live extraordinary lives.
>
> — Jim May

Jesus does not want us to ever forget what He did. He wants us to remember it daily. He instructed His disciples in the way the sacrifice of His body and blood should be remembered in the drinking of wine and eating of bread. And we must do that often as well. But when we worship Him and praise Him for His suffering, death, and resurrection, we give Him the reverence and worth He deserves. We remind ourselves of all that He sacrificed and accomplished.

There is an intimacy in sharing a meal with someone. There is a deepening or a connecting that happens in the relationship.

Jesus waits for us to invite Him into our lives so we can do the same with Him. He says, "Behold, I stand at the door and knock. If anyone hears My voice and opens the door, I will come in to him and dine with him, and he with Me" (Revelation 3:20). That He will come and dine with us is a precious promise of intimacy. Every time we praise Him, we are opening that door and further deepening our relationship with Him.

The hidden power of praising Jesus is that by our very praise, He increases our knowledge of Him and all that He accomplished on the cross. It makes an indelible impact on our souls, enabling us to move into all the freedom He gained for us.

I've often heard people say, "Isn't heaven going to be boring — wearing the same white robes and singing worship songs all day?" Actually, that sounds good to me. No pain, no sickness, no fear, no one hurting you, no more worry about where your next meal is coming from or how you're going to pay the bills. And, besides, I love white! As far as praise being boring — there's no way. We are going to be so impressed with the awesome wonder of God that we are not going to be able to contain it. Worship will pour out of us and be a continual thrill.

We owe Jesus so much. Our payment is to

love Him and praise Him forever. Let's start now, shall we?

WORSHIP IS

. . . honoring, adoring, glorifying, and thanking Jesus for all He did for us on the cross.

I Give God My Praise

Lord, thank You for sending Your Son Jesus to be my Savior and Redeemer. Praise You, Jesus, for the price You paid, the sacrifice You made, and the unthinkable suffering and death You willingly endured on the cross for me. Because of You, I am forgiven and now have made peace with my Creator.

I worship You, Lord, and thank You that even before the creation of the world You chose me to be holy and blameless in Your sight. Thank You that because of Your great love, You predestined me to be adopted as Your child through Jesus in accordance with Your will. Thank You, Jesus, that because of You I have been redeemed through the shedding of Your blood. Lord, I know that I have sinned and fall far short of Your glory (Romans 3:23). Thank You for forgiving me. Thank You that even though I was dead in sin, You have made me alive in Christ (Ephesians 2:4-5). Thank You for the richness of Your mercy and grace which You have lavished on me.

I praise You, Jesus, as the rock upon which I stand. Thank You for giving me new birth into a life of hope because of Your resurrection. Now I have an eternal inheritance that can never be defiled or diminished (1 Peter 1:3-4). "You have also given me the shield of Your salvation; Your gentleness has made me great. You enlarged my path under me; so my feet did not slip" (2 Samuel 22:36-37). Lord, I thank You that I have been saved and reconciled to You because of Your Son, Jesus (Romans 5:10-11).

Pray This Prayer if You Would Like to Receive Jesus

Dear God, thank You for sending Your Son, Jesus, to die for me. Thank You, Jesus, that because You suffered and died in my place, I can be completely forgiven of all my sins and have eternal life with You forever. Forgive me for everything I have done that is not Your will and Your way for my life. Cleanse me with Your forgiveness so that I can be free of all guilt, shame, and any sense of failure. I believe that after You were crucified, You rose from the dead and now live in the hearts of all who receive You. I believe "there is no other name under heaven given among men by which we must be saved" (Acts 4:12). I receive Your love and Your life and invite You to live in me today by the power of Your Holy Spirit. Help me to live in a way that is always pleasing in Your sight so that I can become all You created me to be. All glory be to Your name and "let the God of my salvation be exalted" (Psalm 18:46).

God Gave Me His Word

Blessed be the God and Father of our Lord Jesus Christ, who according to His abundant mercy has begotten us again to a living hope through the resurrection of Jesus Christ from the dead, to an inheritance incorruptible and undefiled and that does not fade away, reserved in heaven for you.

1 Peter 1:3-4

Nor is there salvation in any other, for

113

there is no other name under heaven given among men by which we must be saved.

Acts 4:12

And you, being dead in your trespasses and the uncircumcision of your flesh, He has made alive together with Him, having forgiven you all trespasses, having wiped out the handwriting of requirements that was against us, which was contrary to us. And He has taken it out of the way, having nailed it to the cross. Having disarmed principalities and powers, He made a public spectacle of them, triumphing over them in it.

Colossians 2:13-15

For God so loved the world that He gave His only begotten Son, that whoever believes in Him should not perish but have everlasting life.

John 3:16

God demonstrates His own love toward us, in that while we were still sinners, Christ died for us. Much more then, having now been justified by His blood, we shall be saved from wrath through Him.

Romans 5:8-9

Giving It Some Further Thought

1. Read Ephesians 1:3-6 in your Bible. Write these verses out in your own words as a praise to God for all the things contained in them for which we should be thankful.

2. Read Ephesians 2:4-5 in your Bible. How did God prove His love for you?

3. Read Ephesians 5:2 in your Bible. What are we supposed to do and why?

4. Read 1 Peter 3:18 in your Bible. Why did Jesus suffer? Write out a prayer of praise thanking Jesus for all He has done for you. Ask Him to reveal as-

pects of what He accomplished on the cross you are not even fully aware of yet.

5. Read Romans 5:1-2 in your Bible. What have we been given through Jesus? What are the reasons for praising Him listed here? Write out your answer as a prayer of praise to God.

5

Because He Has
Forgiven Me

One of the reasons we can go through life not feeling good about ourselves, and not experiencing the intimacy with God that we want, is because we never get free of the guilt of our own failings.

We *think* we do.

We were, after all, forgiven of our past sins when we received Jesus, right? Then why do we sometimes still feel condemnation in the presence of God? Why is it that there can be times we suspect He is not overjoyed to see us when we go to Him in prayer? Is that coming from Him or from us?

I believe it happens because we are carrying around guilt like an overloaded backpack.

Sometimes we don't know it's guilt that we're carrying because we don't feel bad about anything specific that we've done. But we don't feel entirely good before God either. We find ourselves crawling into His throne room to talk with Him, but we are so afraid He might step on us like a bug that we crawl back out without having made real contact. What is *that* all about?

For my entire life before I met the Lord, I always felt as though I were a failure. As though I had to apologize every day for my existence. I never had peace about who I was and the life I was living. I knew I had done many things I wasn't proud of, but it didn't seem that what I had done was worse than what everyone else around me was doing. The only difference between them and me was that I felt bad about it all the time and they didn't.

When I received Jesus, I also received forgiveness for all my sins. It was part of the whole package. The gift of God's grace to us. A "get out of jail free" card. An undeserved reward for making a good decision. And I felt a huge burden lift off my shoulders at the time. But even though I didn't feel nearly as bad about my life as I had before, I still didn't feel completely great either. I looked at others who seemed to be entirely free and wondered how they did it.

Of course, guilt was my MO. My *modus*

operandi. My mode of operating. The way I lived. I had been raised with it. My mother had always told me that I never did anything right, never mind that I wasn't taught how. She punished me for things I *didn't* do and ignored the things I *did* do that I knew were wrong. In later years, even after I understood that she had far less than a sound mind, there was still a lot of confusion about the sin issue. And so guilt became a way of life for me.

One day, however, while reading God's Word, I knew I had to decide if I was forever going to hold my mother responsible for my peace, my happiness, and my future. Was I going to accept *her* words as gospel, or was I going to believe *God's?* I easily remembered her words because they played over and over in my head daily. I had to get God's words to do the same.

That day I read: "There is therefore now no condemnation to those who are in Christ Jesus, who do not walk according to the flesh, but according to the Spirit. For the law of the Spirit of life in Christ Jesus has made me free from the law of sin and death" (Romans 8:1-2). I had often read these verses before, but this time they were engraved on my soul.

I said to myself, "If there is no condemnation for those who are in Christ Jesus, and I am in Christ Jesus, then why do I feel condemnation? And if the Holy Spirit is in me, I must be walking in the Spirit, so why do I give place to the flesh? Why do I say and do things I regret? And how often can I keep going before God to confess the same things and expect Him to keep forgiving me? If I repent and do them again, does that mean I didn't really repent in the first place? But this verse says I don't have to live in guilt. Not for the things I did in the past. Not for the things I did last night or this morning or just a few minutes ago. And not for the things I will do in the future. I can go to God as often as I need to and ask for forgiveness as long as I do it with a repentant heart. And He will set me free from all failure and guilt."

What a life-changing revelation! We *never* have to live in guilt.

I knew this was not a license to drive through life doing what I wanted as long as I was willing to pay a repentance fee when I was caught and pulled over. Rather, it was God saying, "I have given My Spirit to live in you. If you will travel through life with *Me,* I will teach you what to do and help you when you are about to get off the path. I will even set you in the right direction when you take a wrong turn."

I'm not saying I never felt guilt over anything again after that, but I didn't live there anymore. I didn't let guilt come between me and God. I now understand that if there is something that makes me feel distant from Him, it is from *my* end of things and not His. I have to do what is necessary to move into the forgiveness that Jesus — after paying such a huge price — had secured for me.

Okay, I know that this may sound like "Sunday School 101" to you, but it was a great revelation to me. And it set me free. I have known way too many people who have taken "Sunday School 101" and are still living today with a less than satisfying relationship with God because they are carrying around so much guilt. And I am talking about committed believers. That's not what God has for us.

Forgiveness as a Way of Life

God wants His forgiveness to be something we breathe in like air. A way of life. Not just a one-time thing. Not just a pay-as-you-sin issue. Not a you-be-good-and-maybe-I'll-love-you arrangement. God is a *forgiving* God just as He is a *loving* God. Forgiving us is something He chose to do a long time ago, and Jesus did what was necessary to make it happen. We hurt Him all over again when we don't receive it.

The point is, we don't have to live in guilt. And too often we do. Take it from an expert on guilt, God doesn't want us to live there. He wants us to be free so we can move on.

A Christian is not a man who never goes wrong, but a man who is enabled to repent and pick himself up and begin over again after each stumble — because the Christ-life is inside him, repairing him all the time, enabling him to repeat (in some degree) the kind of voluntary death which Christ Himself carried out.

— C. S. Lewis

Let's face it. As hard as we try, we all make mistakes. We don't live God's way in everything we think and do. The Bible says, "There is not a just man on earth who does good and does not sin" (Ecclesiastes 7:20). There now. Doesn't that make you feel better? You are in good company.

Every one of us deals with guilt over something at some point. It's part of life. Parents, for example, know that children are an ongoing guilt trip. Who among us is the perfect parent and has never made a mistake? Anything that goes wrong with one of your children makes you feel like a failure. And if you are *divorced* with children, guilt can become a way of life. But it doesn't have to be.

Reasons for guilt and condemnation can be found everywhere, and the enemy of your soul is determined to see you weighed down with them. When he succeeds, guilt controls your life. It colors the decisions you make and the things you do. It gets in between you and God and undermines your relationship.

God doesn't want that for you. He wants you to live free of condemnation. The forgiveness He has for you is a gift that cost Him dearly. A great sacrifice. If you don't receive His gift, it's as if His sacrifice were for nothing. I'm not trying to make you feel guilty for that too. All I'm saying is, *RECEIVE THE GIFT!*

Yet Another Sign of His Love

How many of *us* could tell everyone we know that no matter what they do *to* us or *against* us, we forgive them? God does that for *you*. Forgiving you is one of the many ways God demonstrates His love for you. When you don't let Him do that, you can't receive all of His love. Guilt will always hinder the way you sense God's love for you.

God's love for you is so great that His forgiveness not only releases you from your past, but it also *will* release you from the mistakes you make in the future. God forgives again and again as you come before Him with a humble heart and confess. Now that's love!

Just as one of the best ways to receive God's love is to enter into worship, likewise, one of the most effective ways to receive the forgiveness God has for you is also to enter into worship. And specifically to praise Him that He is the God of forgiveness.

When we worship God, we are enabled to receive God's love and forgiveness in a deeper way.

King David did some terribly wrong things — far worse than anything I hope you or I will ever do — but when he was confronted with his sin, he did three things right. He repented. He prayed. And he worshiped God. As a result, God forgave him and the situation was eventually redeemed.

He will do the same for us.

Time after time the Israelites were disobedient and unfaithful to God — and they had seen far greater miracles than you or I have ever seen — yet He was always willing to receive them back to Himself when their hearts turned toward Him in repentance and worship.

He will do that for us too.

God is not sitting up in heaven waiting to strike us with lightning if we don't obey Him. When we humble ourselves before Him in repentance, He is quick to forgive. He wants to save us, not condemn us. "God did not send His Son into the world to condemn the world, but that the world through Him might be saved" (John 3:17). When we confess, repent, and worship Him, He is quick to restore. It doesn't matter how badly we have strayed from His ways or how far we have gone from Him, He will receive us back.

The problem is, we forget that His forgiveness is always there for us. We run with the guilt instead. We think we have to *do* something to make up for what we've done. But we can't. He already *did* it.

If there is always doubt in your heart about whether you are forgiven, it will close off your relationship with the Lord because you will feel as though you can't come to Him.

If you've done something wrong, confess

it and ask Him to help you to not do it again. If you haven't done anything wrong and you are just suffering from "habitual guilt syndrome," then lift up praise to God, the Forgiver of your soul, and let Him pour the wonderful freedom of forgiveness into your being.

The hidden power of praising God is that as we worship Him for who He is and praise Him as the God of forgiveness, we open up the channels through which we are better able to understand and receive His forgiveness in our minds, hearts, and lives.

WORSHIP IS

. . . not just a song, it's a way of life. It's not just for musicians and good singers, it's for everyone. It's not just 20 minutes once a week. It's an ongoing daily attitude that reminds us of His greatness and our dependency upon Him.

I Give God My Praise

Lord, I worship You as the awesome God of my life. You are the keeper of my heart and the forgiver of my soul. I praise You for sending Your Son to die for me so that I could be forgiven. Thank You that You forgive my wickedness and will remember my sins no more (Hebrews 8:12 NIV). I know that I was dead in sins, but You, O God, have made me alive in Christ and have forgiven me of everything (Colossians 2:13). I am grateful that there is no condemnation for those of us who walk with Jesus (Romans 8:1).

Thank You that the law of the Spirit of life has set me free from the law of sin and death (Romans 8:2). I praise You as my Lord and wonderful God of forgiveness. Thank You that You are continually willing to forgive me and mold me into a whole person. Thank You for convicting me of my sins so that I can come humbly before You and confess them. Thank You that no matter how far I stray from Your ways, You will always receive me back when I repent and cry out to You for forgiveness. Forgive me for my sins today. Remind me whenever I stray from Your laws so that I can confess and repent and receive Your forgiveness. I don't want any sin of mine to come between us. I don't ever want to live apart from You in any way. Cleanse me of all that is not of You. I worship You, O Lord, my Forgiver and Redeemer.

If we confess our sins, He is faithful and just to forgive us our sins and to cleanse us from all unrighteousness.

1 John 1:9

In him we have redemption through his blood, the forgiveness of sins, in accordance with the riches of God's grace that he lavished on us with all wisdom and understanding.

Ephesians 1:7-8 NIV

To whom little is forgiven, the same loves little.

Luke 7:47

According to the law almost all things are purified with blood, and without shedding of blood there is no remission.

Hebrews 9:22

Whenever you stand praying, if you have anything against anyone, forgive him, that your Father in heaven may also forgive you your trespasses. But if you do not forgive, neither will your Father in heaven forgive your trespasses.

Mark 11:25-26

Giving It Some Further Thought

1. Read Psalm 103:12 in your Bible. How much does God forgive us? Do you believe you are completely forgiven or do you struggle with guilt over something? Explain your answer.

2. Are there any areas in your life where you feel you specifically need to be forgiven by God? If so, write it out as a confession to Him and praise Him for His forgiveness.

3. Read Acts 2:38-39 in your Bible. What do these verses tell us to do? What will happen when we do it? Who is included in this?

4. Write out a prayer of praise and worship to God for forgiving you. Tell Him what His forgiveness means to you specifically. What have you been forgiven of that makes you most grateful?

5. Read Ephesians 1:7-8 in your Bible. Why do we have the privilege of being forgiven? Who deserves our praise and why?

6

Because He Has Given Me His Holy Spirit

About 15 years ago I had a terrible dream. I woke up gasping for breath. My heart was pounding. And a desperately sick, hopeless feeling had overtaken my entire being. What occurred in that dream was so real that it changed my life forever.

In the dream I had fallen into temptation to immorality. I had not acted upon it, but I knew I had already succumbed. In other words, even though I had not actually done anything wrong at that point, I had made the decision in my heart to do it. In the moment it took to make that split-second decision, the Holy Spirit lifted off of my life and I could feel the devastating loss. The most horrible and excruciating sense of dread and remorse settled on me like an inescapable death. I had given myself over to something that grieved the Holy Spirit.

The Bible clearly instructs us: *"Do not grieve the Holy Spirit of God, by whom you were sealed for the day of redemption"* (*Ephesians 4:30*).

I had seriously disobeyed God and lost the anointing of the Holy Spirit that was on my life. It was not that I had committed the "unpardonable sin" and would never be forgiven. And it was not that I wouldn't be able to be reconciled to God. But I knew my life would never be the same again. I could never become all that God had intended for me to be.

The whole incident was so real and vivid and carried with it such a profound impact that I knew it wasn't merely a dream. It was a sign. A warning to be careful. To be watchful. What it meant to me was that there would be things coming to me in the future which would present themselves as a great temptation to get off the path God had for me. And I had to be extremely diligent to see that I not only did not *do* something wrong, but that I did not even give the *appearance* of doing something wrong.

I'd had a strong sense for quite a while that God had a calling on my life and He was preparing me for it. I didn't know exactly what it was, but I knew there would come a time when I would be given the opportunity to speak into the lives of people with a message of hope. And I knew that any compromise on my part would weaken that message.

When I realized that I had awakened from a dream and it wasn't reality, I praised God over and over. The prayer of David came to my mind and I prayed it repeatedly. "Do not cast me away from Your presence, and do not take your Holy Spirit from me" (Psalm 51:11).

Would David have prayed that prayer if it were not possible? I thought.

My desperate plea was that I would never lose the most valuable thing in my life. I can't imagine anything more terrible than to live life again without the Holy Spirit.

No wonder blaspheming the Holy Spirit is the unpardonable sin — the only sin that can never be forgiven (Luke 12:10). Even if someone speaks against Jesus, they will still be forgiven. But if they speak against the Holy Spirit, they will not. I believe the reason for that is there is no way someone can know the Holy Spirit of God and reject Him unless that person is hopelessly evil.

Once you have known the Holy Spirit's touch on your life, there is nothing in the world more precious. *"For it is impossible for those who were once enlightened, and have tasted the heavenly gift, and have become partakers of the Holy Spirit, and have tasted the good word of God and the powers of the age to come, if they fall away, to renew them again to repentance, since they crucify again for themselves the Son of God, and put Him to an open shame"* (*Hebrews 6:4-6*).

The Holy Spirit is the most wonderful of all the gifts the Lord gives us. And in turn, the Holy Spirit gives us gifts which are more valuable than any other we can ever receive. To treat *this* gift and *His* gifts lightly would be a travesty. To reject the Holy Spirit, to blaspheme Him, or to speak against Him would be unthinkable for anyone who knew Him. To grieve Him by our actions is something to avoid at all costs. Once you have sensed the presence of the Holy Spirit dwelling within you and guiding your life, you could never tolerate life without Him.

The Holy Spirit — symbolized as many things in Scripture, including a dove (Matthew 3:16) and water (John 7:38) — is given to anyone who asks of God (Luke 11:13). There are countless reasons to ask and to praise God for His Holy Spirit. The following are just a few.

Twenty Good Reasons to Praise God for His Holy Spirit

1. **The Holy Spirit comforts us.** Jesus called Him the Comforter (John 14:26 TLB). How wonderful that God loves us enough to send His Spirit to comfort us. "Walking in the fear of the Lord and in the comfort of the Holy Spirit, they were multiplied" (Acts 9:31).

2. **The Holy Spirit convicts us of wrongdoing.** He convicts us of wrongdoing, but He doesn't condemn us for it. There is a great difference. One leads to restoration, and the other leads to defeat. "When He has come, He will convict the world of sin, and of righteousness, and of judgment" (John 16:8).

3. **The Holy Spirit enables us to obey God.** It is impossible to obey God in all things without the enablement of the Holy Spirit. "We have been delivered from the law, having died to what we were held by, so that we should serve in the newness of the Spirit and not in the oldness of the letter" (Romans 7:6).

4. **The Holy Spirit guides us.** We can't get to where we need to go without the

guidance of the Holy Spirit. "When He, the Spirit of truth, has come, He will guide you into all truth; for He will not speak on His own authority, but whatever He hears He will speak; and He will tell you things to come" (John 16:13).

5. **The Holy Spirit teaches us.** What the Holy Spirit teaches us is far beyond what we can learn from man. "The Helper, the Holy Spirit, whom the Father will send in My name, He will teach you all things, and bring to your remembrance all things that I said to you" (John 14:26).

6. **The Holy Spirit gives us power.** We are completely powerless in our lives without the Holy Spirit. "May the God of hope fill you with all joy and peace in believing, that you may abound in hope by the power of the Holy Spirit" (Romans 15:13).

7. **The Holy Spirit gives us spiritual gifts.** The gifts of the Spirit help us to live successfully and bear fruit for God's kingdom. "God also bearing witness both with signs and wonders, with various miracles, and gifts of the Holy Spirit, according to His own will" (Hebrews 2:4).

8. **The Holy Spirit sanctifies us.** He clears the slate for us so we can always make a fresh start. "That I might be a minister of Jesus Christ to the Gentiles, ministering the gospel of God, that the offering of the Gentiles might be acceptable, sanctified by the Holy Spirit" (Romans 15:16).

9. **The Holy Spirit helps us to pray.** We cannot pray effectively without the enablement of the Holy Spirit. "For we do not know what we should pray for as we ought, but the Spirit Himself makes intercession for us with groanings which cannot be uttered" (Romans 8:26).

10. **The Holy Spirit brings us to Jesus.** If we have made Jesus Lord over our lives, the Holy Spirit has brought us to this point and filled us with Himself. "Therefore I make known to you that no one speaking by the Spirit of God calls Jesus accursed, and no one can say that Jesus is Lord except by the Holy Spirit" (1 Corinthians 12:3).

11. **The Holy Spirit makes us strong.** He will give us added strength when we need it most. "That He would grant you, according to the riches of His glory, to be strengthened with might

through His Spirit in the inner man"
(Ephesians 3:16).

12. **The Holy Spirit raises us from the dead.** That same Spirit who raised Jesus from the dead will also raise us up to spend eternity with the Lord. "For Christ also suffered once for sins, the just for the unjust, that He might bring us to God, being put to death in the flesh but made alive by the Spirit" (1 Peter 3:18).

13. **The Holy Spirit works miracles.** Because of the work of the Holy Spirit in our lives, we can experience the miraculous. "In mighty signs and wonders, by the power of the Spirit of God . . . I have fully preached the gospel of Christ" (Romans 15:19).

14. **The Holy Spirit gives us words to say.** We can be led by the Spirit whenever we speak to anyone. "The Holy Spirit will teach you in that very hour what you ought to say" (Luke 12:12).

15. **The Holy Spirit renews us.** The ability to be renewed and revived comes entirely from the work of the Spirit in our lives. "Not by works of righteousness which we have done, but according to His mercy He saved us, through the washing of regeneration

and renewing of the Holy Spirit" (Titus 3:5).

16. **The Holy Spirit helps us when we are weak.** He enables us to do what we could not do on our own. "Likewise the Spirit also helps in our weaknesses" (Romans 8:26).

17. **The Holy Spirit gives us knowledge and understanding.** There are things that can only be known and understood by the power of the Holy Spirit. "The Spirit of the LORD shall rest upon Him, the Spirit of wisdom and understanding, the Spirit of counsel and might, the Spirit of knowledge and of the fear of the Lord" (Isaiah 11:2).

18. **The Holy Spirit gives us revelation and wisdom.** The Holy Spirit reveals things to us and gives us wisdom without which we can't survive. "That the God of our Lord Jesus Christ, the Father of glory, may give to you the spirit of wisdom and revelation in the knowledge of Him" (Ephesians 1:17).

19. **The Holy Spirit reveals the things of God.** The only way we can understand the things of God is by the power of the Holy Spirit. "God has revealed them to us through His Spirit. For the Spirit searches all things, yes,

the deep things of God" (1 Corinthians 2:10).

20. **The Holy Spirit assures us that we are God's children.** We need to know for certain that we are a beloved child of God because this will affect everything we do in life, and the Holy Spirit helps us to recognize that. "The Spirit Himself bears witness with our spirit that we are children of God" (Romans 8:16).

Value the Holy Spirit in You

In the years following my dream, every time there was about to be a major breakthrough in my work for the Lord, the enemy would bring some temptation into my life to get me off the path God had for me. But I would remember vividly the way I felt in that dream and knew that nothing or no one on earth was worth that. The presence and anointing of the Holy Spirit is way too precious to risk anything that would jeopardize His full impact in my life.

The Bible says that our gifts and callings are irrevocable (Romans 11:29). But the full anointing of the Holy Spirit isn't. A good example was when "the Spirit of the LORD departed from Saul" because he violated God's commands (1 Samuel 16:14). What a sad end to a promising career. I've also seen a number of people who had a powerful anointing of the Holy Spirit on their lives, but when they fell into temptation and gave themselves to adultery, the full power of that anointing lifted. I'm not saying they weren't restored or forgiven. I'm not saying they didn't still have their gifts. But the extent of the anointing that they had was never there in that same power again.

I'm also not saying that they lost the Holy Spirit, for where can we go from His Spirit's presence? (Psalm 139:7). And I'm not saying that there isn't a way to get back what has been lost. God can restore anything. It's just that I have never seen anyone regain the same powerful anointing once it was lifted.

Was it worth it for them? I've never asked. It wouldn't be for me.

I'm not criticizing people who experience that kind of temptation. In fact, my heart goes out to them. Everyone has needs. And the need to be loved and appreciated is one of the strongest of all. In a weak moment, when you desperately need someone to love you, attractions between people can happen. The attraction is not the sin. It just means you are human. It's what you do with it that counts.

If you fall into immorality, there is a steep price to pay. God will forgive you when you repent and stop doing it. But if the Holy Spirit is grieved to the point of withdrawing the anointing and special grace that is on your life, it is not worth it. Resist it with everything that is in you. Cling to God with every fiber of your being. Worship God and thank Him that He has given you His Holy Spirit to dwell in you. Say, "It's Your love I want more than anything, Lord. Renew a right spirit in me" (Psalm 51:10).

If we can't say Jesus is Lord without Him, how can we worship in spirit without the power of the Holy Spirit? There must be an impartation of the Holy Spirit into our spirit enabling us to worship in spirit, God, who is Spirit.

— Sam Hinn

The hidden power of praising God is that the very act of worshiping the Father, the Son, and the Holy Spirit opens the channel through which the Holy Spirit pours more of Himself into you. More of His power, strength, enablement, revelation, and ability to resist temptation.

There is so much to be grateful for with regard to the Holy Spirit, and praise to God for *giving* us His Spirit is the place to begin. Praise God every day for the Holy Spirit's presence in your life. Thank Him that "you are the temple of God and that the Spirit of God dwells in you" (1 Corinthians 3:16). Do whatever you have to in order to keep your temple pure and not cause the Holy Spirit grief.

Ask yourself, "What would my life be like without the Holy Spirit?"

WORSHIP IS

... the key to unlocking our lives. It helps us find the life that God planned for us to have, the way it was meant to be.

I Give God My Praise

Lord, I worship You and praise You and thank You for Your Holy Spirit in my life. Thank You, Jesus, for sending me the Comforter and Helper to teach and guide me every day. Thank You, Holy Spirit, that You enable me to do what I could never do on my own. I praise You for the wisdom, revelation, and knowledge that You impart to me. I love You and the joy You bring into my life (1 Thessalonians 1:6).

Lord, fill me afresh with Your Spirit this day. I let go of all else and open to all of You. Holy Spirit, may I never grieve You (Ephesians 4:30). Enable me to always resist the temptations of the flesh that would cause me to stray from the path You have for me. I don't ever want to minimize all that You want to do in my life. Help me to be ever mindful of Your presence in me, and may I always hear Your clear leading.

Thank You that I have been "sealed with the Holy Spirit of promise" (Ephesians 1:13). I know that I cannot understand the things of God in my flesh, but I can discern them in my spirit because of You dwelling in me. Thank You, Lord, for the gift of Your Holy Spirit in me. Thank You, Holy Spirit, for Your gifts manifesting in my life. I want to show my love for You by embracing You with my worship and touching You with my praise. Teach me all I need to know about how to worship You in ways that are pleasing in Your sight.

I will pray the Father, and He will give you another Helper, that He may abide with you forever.

John 14:16

Now hope does not disappoint, because the love of God has been poured out in our hearts by the Holy Spirit who was given to us.

Romans 5:5

And we are His witnesses to these things, and so also is the Holy Spirit whom God has given to those who obey Him.

Acts 5:32

But you shall receive power when the Holy Spirit has come upon you; and you shall be witnesses to Me in Jerusalem, and in all Judea and Samaria, and to the end of the earth.

Acts 1:8

Unless one is born of water and the Spirit, he cannot enter the kingdom of God.

John 3:5

Giving It Some Further Thought

1. What do you feel are the most important elements that the Holy Spirit brings into your life? What aspects of the Holy Spirit's work do you most need and appreciate?

2. Read 1 Corinthians 3:16 and 1 Corinthians 6:19 in your Bible. Knowing that the Holy Spirit of God resides in you, and considering the things the Holy Spirit does listed in this chapter, what gifts would you most like to receive from Him right now? (For example, "I need the Holy Spirit's guidance," or "I need to see more of the power of the Holy Spirit working in my life" . . .).

3. Read Romans 8:14 in your Bible. What is an important indication that you are

a child of God? In what ways have you felt led by the Spirit of God?

4. Read 1 Corinthians 2:12-14 in your Bible. Why have we received the Holy Spirit? Why do we need spiritual discernment in our lives?

5. Read Isaiah 63:8-10 in your Bible. How did God show His love toward His people? What happened to make Him turn against them?

7

Because He Gave
Me His Word

Back in the '60s, before I knew the Lord, I tried everything I could to make my way in the world. But I didn't do well at it. I lived in tremendous sadness, depression, misery, and confusion. I made countless bad choices. That's because there were no absolutes. There were different levels of morality — or lack thereof — depending on which people I associated with at the time. It was totally confusing. We did things in the name of freedom — for instance, drinking to the point of drunkenness or getting stoned on drugs to nearly heart-stopping dimensions. Those fleeting moments of a chemical high would temporarily relieve some of the gut-wrenching pain in my soul, but then the experience became like a rapid fall into hell. And I fell deeper each time.

How free is that?

Someone once said, "If you remember the '60s, you weren't really part of them." I guess I wasn't really part of them because I remember more of that time than I would like. For example, I clearly remember being with my boyfriend one night at his house after just getting off the road on a concert tour together. He was the lead singer in a well-known band at the time and another girl and I sang backup for them. It was at the peak of the group's career, and the intense schedule we had been on for months had left us beyond exhausted.

He and I made a batch of brownies from a mix and into it we added a large amount of marijuana he had bought from a neighbor down the street. I don't know exactly how great a quantity it was because he poured it in loose from a plastic bag. We baked the brownies and then ate them warm from the pan. It was one of the popular things to do back then.

The problem was, I was a chocoholic. Once I started eating chocolate, I couldn't stop until it was all gone. Whenever someone gave me a box of chocolate candy, I never could just eat one or two pieces like a normal person. I had to eat the entire box. There were always consequences for that, and far too often I was willing to pay them.

While we were eating the brownies, my boyfriend put on the new Beatles album. The long-awaited *Sergeant Pepper's Lonely Hearts Club Band* had just been released that day, and his record company had secured a copy for him. Most of my generation could tell you where we were when John Kennedy was shot, the first time we heard Barbra Streisand sing, and when we experienced *Sergeant Pepper's Lonely Hearts Club Band.*

As we sat there listening to the album, my boyfriend ate about three brownies and I devoured nearly the rest of the pan. The brownies tasted wonderful, but about halfway through the album I started feeling so dizzy I thought I was going to pass out. I stumbled to the couch and laid face down, wrapping my arms around a seat cushion and holding on as tightly as I could. I felt as though I would go flying into space if I let go. By the time the album ended, I was so dizzy, sick, and wasted that I couldn't even respond when my boyfriend called my name. He left me on the couch and went into the bedroom and fell asleep on his bed fully clothed.

I never slept at all. I just kept clinging to that couch.

In the middle of the night I lifted up my

head and could see him sleeping on his bed. I called his name several times to come help me, but I couldn't wake him. Silently I pleaded with a god somewhere in the universe that if I could just live through this night, I wouldn't do drugs ever again. We'd eaten the brownies about eight that evening, and I laid awake in that one position, clinging to the couch, until five the next morning. Finally, when I was able to stand up, I knew I had once again cheated death.

All my life I grabbed for anything and anyone who could make me feel better about myself for one night or even one hour. The problem was, each one of the things I tried destroyed part of me. This time I was nearly destroyed completely. I knew I had almost killed myself doing something that promised merely a temporary relief from the pain I felt.

All because I had no absolutes.

God's Word Makes Life Work

For years I seriously involved myself in different occult practices that taught there was no evil, only good. The only evil that existed was in your mind, they told me. So if you could control your mind, or convince yourself that every evil thing you did was actually good, then you could feel good about yourself and your life. The problem was that I was never able to make that work. No matter how I tried to justify my actions, I didn't have peace about any of the things I did. I only did them because everyone else around me was doing them. And if there was no evil, then everything I did was okay as long as it wasn't hurting anyone else but me.

See how messed up a life without boundaries can be?

It wasn't until after I received the Lord and started reading the Bible with newly opened eyes that I began to see what was really right and wrong. I could never comprehend the truth before because my spiritual eyes were blinded to it. It's that way for all of us. We may be able to sense that something is wrong in our lives, but we can't identify what it is.

Without God's Word we will always be more influenced by the relativism that pervades the world than we are by the revelation of the Holy Spirit.

God gave us His Word so that we would know the right way to live. That's why I love it so much. It spells everything out. It tells us this is right and that is wrong. When you live *this* way, life works. When you live that way, life *doesn't* work. God's Word builds you up, it feeds your soul, and gives you strength, direction, guidance, hope, encouragement, and faith.

God's laws are for *our* benefit. He doesn't come up with rules so that He will have a reason to strike us with lightning when we don't obey all of them perfectly. He wants to show us how to avoid the things that will hurt us or ruin our lives. That's why He has provided this wonderfully reliable tool. So we can always know the truth. And in it we will always find comfort and strength. Wisdom and knowledge. Love and faith. Peace and joy. Deliverance and liberty. Clarity and direction. Wholeness and restoration. Fruitfulness and purpose.

There are consequences for continued and willful disobedience to God's ways. And those of us who have tested those waters and paid the consequences know the pain of that testing. Those of us who have tried God's ways and have seen that they are good, understand how wonderful it is to have God's Word guiding us every day. When we refuse to look to the world for our counsel and instead find all we need in God's Word, then we become planted solidly where the river of God's life constantly flows into ours (Psalm 1:1-3). And that kind of life will bear fruit that lasts.

> God speaks to us through the reading
> and preaching of His word in Scripture.
> It is important for our worship to recog-
> nize that when we hear or read the Word
> of God, we encounter God Himself.
>
> — John M. Frame

Believing in the promises of God enables us to escape the corruption that the lust of our eyes and flesh brings into our lives. God's Word has "given to us exceedingly great and precious promises," that through them we "may be partakers of the divine nature, having escaped the corruption that is in the world through lust" (2 Peter 1:4). His Word lifts us above ourselves and helps us to attain a holy nature like His. It takes us out of a dead-end life like the one I used to live.

God's Word Protects Us

God's Word is a weapon of spiritual warfare we can use to protect ourselves. "Take the helmet of salvation, and the sword of the Spirit, which is the word of God" (Ephesians 6:17). But in order to use it as a weapon, we must *read* His Word, *think* about His Word, *speak* His Word, and *praise* God for His Word every day.

God's Word tells us how much He loves us and shows us to what extent He has gone to prove His love to us. That's why it touches a place deep in our hearts. Nothing penetrates our souls or changes our lives more profoundly than true love. And His is the truest of all. When we read God's love letter, we can better understand His heart of love for us.

When I first read God's Word after I became a believer, I knew I had finally found something that made sense. Something I could rely on that would not fail me. There were now boundaries for my life that would help me live rightly. Something I could go to anytime I needed to correct my thoughts or fill the emptiness of my soul.

I recently talked to a friend from my past who I suspected was searching for God. He already knew where I stood on the subject because he had read a number of my books. He was frustrated that things never worked out for him in his relationships with women. His marriage had failed, and he had not found another woman with whom he could be in a committed relationship. I told him that if he would surrender his life to the

Lord, God could bring the right person into his life.

"If I surrender my life to God, doesn't that mean that sex outside of marriage will be wrong?" he asked point-blank.

"Yes," I said. "Sex outside of marriage is not God's plan for our lives. But when you find the right person and marry her, you won't want to have sex outside of marriage."

Unfortunately, he was not willing to give that up. He could not see that whatever we give up of our fleshly desires in order to live God's way, the Lord will replace with something so much better. That kind of vision is ignited only in the spirit. And only in the spirit can we recognize His Word as reliable truth.

We need to praise God every day for His Word. Without God's Word we do things that destroy our lives. Without God's Word we attempt to find fulfillment in things that don't last. Without God's Word we try to live life on our own terms and wonder why we are not happy. Without God's Word we end up clinging to a couch for nine hours in the middle of the night.

When you praise God that His Word is dependable and unfailing, that it gives us life, fulfillment, and absolute direction, that it feeds our empty spirits and enriches our lives to the fullest, then the hidden power of praise will cause God's Word to penetrate deeper into your soul than it ever has before.

WORSHIP IS

... coming to God and praising Him for His Word, His great love letter to us. In its pages we find out everything about why and how we are to worship Him.

I Give God My Praise

Lord, I worship You and praise Your name. I praise and thank You for Your Word. How I love that it gives me the guidance I need for my life. My delight is in Your law. Help me to meditate on it day and night (Psalm 1:2). "Your testimonies also are my delight and my counselors" (Psalm 119:24).

Help me to fully understand all that I read in Your Word. Reveal everything I need to know. "Open my eyes, that I may see wondrous things from Your law" (Psalm 119:18). Thank You that every time I read Your Word, I know You better.

Lord, Your law is perfect. It changes my heart, enriches my soul, and makes me wise.

All Your commandments are true, right, pure, dependable, edifying, and life-giving, and that makes me glad. They instruct me, and I find great peace when I obey them (Psalm 19:7-11). Help me to hold "fast the word of life, so that I may rejoice in the day of Christ that I have not run in vain or labored in vain" (Philippians 2:16). "I will worship toward Your holy temple, and praise Your name for Your lovingkindness and Your truth; for You have magnified Your word above all Your name" (Psalm 138:2). Thank You that Your Word will stand forever because You, Lord, are the Living Word who always was and forever will be.

I love that I can forever trust Your Word. It never lets me down or leads me astray. It always brings comfort and guidance. It always edifies my soul. Your Word is a love letter to me, showing me how much You love me. And every time I read it, I love You more.

God Gave Me His Word

Blessed is the man who walks not in the counsel of the ungodly, nor stands in the path of sinners, nor sits in the seat of the scornful; but his delight is in the law of the LORD, and in His law he meditates day and night. He shall be like a tree planted by the rivers of water, that brings forth its fruit in its season, whose leaf also shall not wither; and whatever he does shall prosper.

Psalm 1:1-3

For the word of God is living and powerful, and sharper than any two-edged sword, piercing even to the division of soul and spirit, and of joints and marrow, and is a discerner of the thoughts and intents of the heart.

Hebrews 4:12

I will bless the LORD who has given me counsel; my heart also instructs me in the night seasons. I have set the LORD always before me; because He is at my right hand I shall not be moved.

Psalm 16:7-8

Be diligent to present yourself approved to God, a worker who does not need to be ashamed, rightly dividing the word of truth.

2 Timothy 2:15

The law of the LORD is perfect, con-

verting the soul; the testimony of the
LORD is sure, making wise the simple.

$\qquad$ Psalm 19:7

Giving It Some Further Thought

1. Read James 1:21-25 in your Bible.
   How are we supposed to respond to
   God's Word? What happens when we
   don't respond that way? What happens
   when we don't just *hear* the Word but
   we *do* it? Why is this a reason to praise
   God?

2. Read Romans 4:20-22 in your Bible.
   What did Abraham choose to believe?
   How did God respond to his faith?

3. Read Psalm 19:7-11 and Matthew
   24:35 in your Bible. Write out a praise
   to God for all that is good about His

Word as described in these verses. Include what you are most grateful for with regard to your life right now.

4. Read Joshua 1:8 in your Bible. What are we supposed to do in response to God's Word? What will happen when we do that?

5. Read 2 Timothy 3:16-17 in your Bible. How was Scripture given to us? How does it profit us? What does it accomplish in us?

8

Because He Is
a Good God

I lived in a place that looked like a slum when I was growing up. Actually, it *was* a slum. Everything there was ugly, run down, dirty, rotten, and unloved. It was a plot of dirt with a shack on it. It just wasn't declared a slum until after we moved and everything there was torn down. Living in that kind of environment hurts your spirit. That's because God did not create that kind of environment for us to live in. Man does that on his own.

Everything God creates is beautiful and good.

The place I live in now is beautiful and good. Not only the house, but the area around it. There are countless trees, bushes, and flowers, and grass that is so vibrantly green it feeds your soul. The air is always clear and the sky blue. Every season is stunning. Even wintertime, when most of the trees are bare sticks, has its own stark gray beauty. You can tell that the houses are loved because they are well kept. This place is the exact opposite of where I grew up.

The amazing thing is that I never forget the ugliness of that terrible place where I spent my childhood. But I quickly forget how beautiful the place is where I live now. I don't forget that it's beautiful. I just forget *how* beautiful.

The thing about true beauty is that it always surprises you. It is always more beautiful than you remember it. Have you ever known someone who is so beautiful or handsome that you forget how attractive they are until you see them again? That's true beauty. For some reason our minds can't retain the fullness of it.

There is a place in Big Sur, California, like that. Where you can stand on a high cliff overlooking the majestic and vast blue ocean bordered by enormous lush green pine trees. It's like being in the best of the mountains and the best of the beach at the same time. I could never retain how completely awesome the beauty of that place was, and so each time I went there it took my breath away.

What are some of the most beautiful

things you have ever seen? A field of vibrantly colored flowers? A waterfall? A loved one's smile? A crystal clear lake? A painting? A baby's face? A sparkling jewel? An act of love toward someone? Take everything that has ever touched you deeply with its beauty, put them all together, and you have only a fraction of the beauty of the Lord. It's hard to imagine.

Everything God *is,* is beautiful and good.

When you think of the *goodness* of the Lord, what do you think of? Perfection? Purity? Grandness? Holiness? Love? Grace? Mercy? Our minds can't comprehend it. Just like His beauty, God's goodness is *so* great that we have a hard time fully grasping it. We know God is good, but we forget *how* good. When something happens to us that hurts, we often fail to remember what a good God He is. We start having doubts and wonder, *If God is good, why did He let this happen?* We forget that God is good even when things are bad.

Remembering God's Goodness in Bad Times

I once heard Pastor Jack's mother speak a simple but profound message. She said, "God is a good God." By the time she finished talking, I was convinced. I never forgot it. And it's a good thing, because there were many times when I had to hold on to that truth with everything I had in me in order to get through some extremely difficult times, including one particular life-and-death situation.

Several years ago I was in and out of different hospitals for about six months with terrible pain and nausea in my stomach. I saw various doctors and specialists, but no one could find anything wrong with me. They didn't know what to do.

One night I was unable to sleep due to extreme pain and nausea. At about 3:00 a.m. I felt something explode in my body. My husband rushed me to the emergency room because I knew I didn't have time to wait for an ambulance. Once again no one could figure out what was wrong with me. I laid in the ER for eight hours in agonizing pain, barely able to breathe, let alone speak. I knew I was going to die if someone didn't do something. "Help me, Lord" was my one audible prayer.

God, is it my time to die? I asked silently. *I really don't want to. I want to see my children get married and have children of their own. But if this is my time to go, please give me peace about it.*

I grew weaker and weaker. I turned yellow from the poison in my body. The unbearable pain was so unrelenting that I felt my heart might stop from that alone if nothing was done soon. The situation didn't look promising. But I kept reminding myself, *God is a good God. God is a good God. He wouldn't let anything bad happen to me unless something good was going to come of it.*

"Praise You, Lord. Thank You that You are a good God," I whispered.

Finally a surgeon came in who was courageous enough to say that even though all the tests proved inconclusive, he was going to take me into surgery and see if my appendix had ruptured as he and I both suspected. If that wasn't the problem, then he would find out what it was and correct it.

As it turned out, my appendix not only *had* ruptured, but, as the surgeon later told me, the poison had spread so far throughout my system that in one more hour he would not have been able to save my life. He said that even after the surgery I was still in danger. He had to leave the 12-inch vertical incision open and not stitch it closed because a large tube had to be left in my body which was attached to a machine that suctioned the poison out. And I had to be completely opened up every day so that a special team of medical people could clean it out.

The pain of the recovery was excruciating. Even with morphine and Demerol, I still was in agony every time they took off the bandages, removed the tube, and inserted the sponges and instruments to clean out my incision. It was so horrendous, in fact, that I cried every time they did it. Throughout the entire process, especially on the worst days, I continually reminded myself that God is a good God. And the suffering He allows in our lives will be used for good. His glory will be revealed in it. And I praised Him for that.

It took five months for the wound to close, and when it finally did I was left with an ugly, long, wide, uneven, jagged scar. As much as I hate the way it looks, I have come to see the scar as a sign of God's goodness. If it weren't for that scar I wouldn't be here. The whole ordeal greatly changed my perspective on what was important and what was a waste of time in my life. I thought I had already learned that, but apparently not well enough. God also wanted me to better understand His goodness to me, of which His mercy and grace are the biggest part. Because of His grace and mercy — His goodness — I am alive today.

Learning to Trust His Goodness

You may be thinking, *Everybody knows God is good. You're not telling me anything I haven't heard before.* But the truth is, many of us know in our *heads* that God is good, but we don't know it completely in our *hearts* when bad things happen. That's when belief in the goodness of God really gets tested. If you ever *doubt* that God is good, then you don't really believe it.

In other words, if you really believe that God is good, then you will never doubt it, no matter what is happening.

One of the ways we can learn to completely trust that God is a good God is to praise Him for His goodness. Every time we do, it opens up the channels through which that particular aspect of His nature is poured into our heart. The more you praise God for His goodness, the more you will see it manifested in your life. That's the hidden power of praise.

You will be amazed when you pray this way how God will open your eyes to see things you haven't seen before. The Lord has done or is doing so many good things we don't even think to give Him credit for. We either don't see them, or we take them for granted.

> Praise is not complete until it has been expressed. The goodness of God gives us ample opportunities to be thankful.
>
> — Tony Evans

Only *God* is good.

Even Jesus said, "Why do you call Me good? No one is good but One, that is, God" (Matthew 19:17). David said, "You are my Lord, my goodness is nothing apart from You" (Psalm 16:2). The Bible says to "taste and see that the LORD is good; blessed is the man who trusts in Him!" (Psalm 34:8).

In tough times we can doubt that God is really good. We may know it in our heads, but we forget it in our hearts. That's because, just like His beauty, His goodness is greater than we can imagine. Our minds cannot even comprehend the breadth and the depth of it.

That's why, when we go through bad times, we have to *remind* ourselves of God's goodness. Otherwise we too easily forget. The way we keep ourselves reminded of God's goodness is to read His Word, worship Him as our wonderful Lord, and praise Him for His goodness. It will help us remember that no matter what happens, He is a God of mercy and grace. "For You, Lord, are good, and ready to forgive, and abundant in mercy to all those who call upon You" (Psalm 86:5).

God's mercy and grace are what I received in the hospital the day I didn't die. His mercy means He has compassion on us. His grace means He gives us what we don't deserve. His mercy and grace are a sign of His goodness. His goodness is a sign of His amazing love. And I love that about Him.

David said, "One thing I have desired of the LORD, that will I seek: that I may dwell in the house of the LORD all the days of my life, to behold the beauty of the LORD, and to inquire in His temple" (Psalm 27:4). Above all else, David wanted to look on the splendor, radiance, holiness, goodness, and glory of God, and be close to Him forever.

Isn't that what *we* want too?

And because of Jesus, we can experience God's goodness whenever we come to Him and worship Him. Our praise magnifies His goodness in our lives.

And that's a beautiful thing!

WORSHIP IS

. . . exalting who God is and affirming our unending love and loyalty to Him.

I Give God My Praise

Lord, I worship You as the God of heaven and earth. I praise You for Your greatness and Your goodness. Thank You that You are a good God and Your mercy and grace toward me will endure forever (Psalm 118:1). May I never forget all the good You have done for me and how You have filled my life with good things.

Lord, I desire, as David did, that I may dwell in Your house all the days of my life, to behold Your beauty and to be in Your temple (Psalm 27:4). This day I will enter Your gates with thanksgiving and Your courts with praise. I bless Your name, for You are good. Your mercy is everlasting, and Your truth endures to all generations (Psalm 100:4-5). You are my God and Lord, You are loving and patient, and You abound in goodness and truth (Exodus 34:6).

Help me to trust that You are a good God no matter what is going on in my life. Help me to believe without any doubting that even if bad things are happening, Your goodness will reign in the midst of them all. Thank You that Your plans for me are for good. Thank You that the future You have for me is good. Thank You that You bring good things into my life. Reveal Your goodness to me more and more so that I may praise You for it. How great is Your goodness to those who trust and fear You (Psalm 31:19).

O Lord, how excellent is Your name in all the earth (Psalm 8:1). I am so grateful that the earth is full of Your goodness, and that Your goodness endures continually (Psalm 52:1). You are good, and all You do is good. Teach me Your ways, for I know that they are good too (Psalm 119:68). Surely Your goodness and mercy will follow me all the days of my life; and I will dwell with You forever (Psalm 23:6).

God Gave Me His Word

Oh, that men would give thanks to the LORD for His goodness, and for His wonderful works to the children of men!
                                    Psalm 107:8

He loves righteousness and justice; the earth is full of the goodness of the LORD.
                                    Psalm 33:5

The LORD is good to those who wait for Him, to the soul who seeks Him.
                                    Lamentations 3:25

172

Oh, give thanks to the LORD, for He is good! For His mercy endures forever.

Psalm 107:1

I would have lost heart, unless I had believed that I would see the goodness of the LORD in the land of the living.

Psalm 27:13

Giving It Some Further Thought

1. Read Psalm 118:1 in your Bible. Write out a prayer of praise to God for all the good things you see from Him in your life.

2. Read Psalm 65:4 in your Bible. God chose you, and now you can come before Him in prayer and praise anytime you want. As a result, where can you expect to live your life? What will always satisfy your soul?

3. Read Psalm 145:8-9 in your Bible. Write out a prayer of praise and thanksgiving to God for all the good things listed in these verses.

4. Read Psalm 31:19 in your Bible. For whom has God laid up His goodness? Does that include you? Give the reason for your answer.

5. Read Psalm 23:6 in your Bible. How long is the mercy and goodness of the Lord extended to us? Write out a prayer of praise and thanksgiving to God for His goodness that will be manifested in your future. Thank Him that no matter what happens you can trust that He is a good God and His goodness will always be extended toward you.

9

Because He Is Holy

Did you ever wake up one day and realize that the life you've been living is all off? Your eyes are suddenly opened, and you see that you're miles away from the place and purpose God has for you. You've been covering up the broken pieces of your life and sweeping them under the rug for so long that now, just in the normal course of walking through each day, the accumulation has become a stumbling block. And you trip over it every time you try to move. Your own lack of wholeness has become blatantly apparent to you, especially in the presence of the wholeness of other people. You now understand the worth of God's holiness and are saddened by your own lack of it.

I experienced a time exactly like that. A time when the life I had been living was laid stark naked next to the life I was *supposed* to have. It was a sad awakening in one respect, but a hopeful one as well. I was a new believer and had not yet learned about God's restoration. It's hard to describe the depth of regret I felt every time I came into contact with someone who knew the Lord and had never done any of the things I used to do before I received Him. I sensed their purity, and the rightness of it, and I was painfully sorry I had never known to value that. I felt sick with regret that I had lived so far from God. It actually broke my heart. It grieved me. I can't imagine how it must have grieved God.

Yet on the other hand, I learned that God's holiness is something He wants to *share* with us. That He desires to impart who He is to *us* is one of the greatest signs of His love.

Holiness is the core attribute of who God is. All the other attributes of God are seen in the light of His holiness. It's the attribute that affects all the others. That means every part of God is holy. Holiness is attributed to each Person of the Godhead: the Father (John 17:11), the Son (Acts 4:30), and the Holy Spirit, who imparts God's holiness to us. Only God is morally excellent and entirely free from anything that would limit this aspect of His nature. "No one is holy like the LORD" (1 Samuel 2:2). *Holiness is what radiates out of Him.*

When I was in the presence of those who lived holy lives, it made me repentant for the manner in which I lived so far removed from God's ways. It made me feel unclean, and I desired more than ever to be cleansed of all failure and be able to live in the holy manner God wanted me to. *When we come in contact with something pure, after being filled with the Holy Spirit, we become acutely aware of anything in us that is not pure.*

When Isaiah, one of God's greatest prophets, had a vision of God with the angels worshiping Him around His throne, he realized his own unworthiness and sin. He said, "My destruction is sealed, for I am a sinful man and a member of a sinful race. Yet I have seen the King, the LORD Almighty!" (Isaiah 6:5 NLT). When Isaiah confessed his sin, God touched him and purified him. God's holiness made him aware of his own lack of it. It also made him whole.

Sin chips away pieces of our soul. With enough sin, we become a pile of broken pieces. But God's holiness is what purifies us and helps us to separate ourselves from all that is *unholy.* There is a correlation between God's holiness and our wholeness.

That's why when we are in His presence, we become more whole. *God's holiness makes us whole.*

Whenever the great men of faith in the Bible, such as Job, Abraham, and Moses, had a close encounter with God, they saw their own failings.

That's what happens to us too.

You may be thinking, *Why do I need to become more aware of my own failings? I am already well aware of them. Thinking about them is just going to make me feel worse about myself than I already do.*

But understanding God's holiness doesn't make you feel bad about yourself in a way that leads to depression. It makes you feel drawn toward His holiness in a way that leads to restoration. It convicts you rather than condemns you. It's actually liberating.

How in the World Can I Be Holy?

God calls us to reflect His holiness. "As He who called you is holy, you also be holy in all your conduct, because it is written, 'Be holy, for I am holy' " (1 Peter 1:15-16).

God is not saying, "You be holy!" as a parent would say, "You be quiet!" to a child. He is saying, "I am inviting you to share My

178

holiness. Let My holiness live in you. Come apart and be separate from all that is unholy and allow My holiness to grow in you. Let it become a well in your soul from which you draw your own holiness of character."

It's the difference between telling someone "Go with me!" and making it a stern command and saying the same words — "Go with me" — and making it a gentle invitation. With God, it is always a gentle invitation. He doesn't *command* something that we can't begin to do. How can we make ourselves holy like God on our own? We can't do it without *Him*.

To worship is to quicken the conscience by the holiness of God, to purge the imagination by the beauty of God, to open the heart to the love of God, and to devote the will to the purpose of God.
— William Temple

Jesus is the greatest example on earth of a holy life and character. He was wholly devoted to God and to God's will in His life. What Jesus did by dying on the cross for us and sending us the Holy Spirit was to ensure that we are guaranteed a way to be released from our unholiness and be holy like God. Because of Him, our sin does not keep us from approaching God's throne. If it did, who could ever come before Him? Instead, our sin is the *reason* to come before Him in confession and repentance, and to praise Him for His holiness.

The more we worship God, the more we see His holiness, wholeness, purity, and goodness making us holy, whole, pure, and good. Coming before God in worship reveals sin in our lives we might not have even been able to acknowledge. What better way to wash it out of us than being in His presence?

When we encounter the holiness of God and recognize it for what it is, it exposes who we are at that moment and reveals what we are supposed to become.

Becoming holy should be the goal of our lives because it makes us distinctive. This doesn't mean we gain a holier-than-thou attitude and *lord* it over others. It means we aspire to a holy-as-the-Lord lifestyle so we can be a *blessing* to others.

But we don't just get up one day and say, "I'm going to be holy," and suddenly we are. A deep recognition of the holiness of God and a desire to do whatever it takes to become like Him is absolutely necessary. We can't *make* ourselves holy, but we can *seek* to be holy as God is holy.

How do we seek that when holiness seems so elusive? So unattainable? We do it by worshiping God. And specifically praising Him *for* His holiness. That's what the angels in heaven are doing around the throne all the time. Isaiah heard them saying, "Holy, holy, holy is the LORD of hosts; the whole earth is full of His glory!" (Isaiah 6:3). When we praise God for His holiness, we have a closer understanding of what it means to be holy. It is as if His holiness rubs off on us by means of the close proximity we have with God. We become like that which we worship, remember?

The hidden power of praise is that the more we worship God and praise Him for His holiness, the more of His holiness will be worked into our lives. He imparts His holiness to us as we praise Him.

Of course there are other steps we need to take too.

How to Be Holy in Seven Not-So-Easy Steps

1. **Go after it.** "Pursue peace with all people, and holiness, without which no one will see the Lord" (Hebrews

12:14). We have to *want* it. And we must want it badly enough to do whatever it takes to have it.

2. **Claim what God gave you.** "Put on the new man which was created according to God, in true righteousness and holiness" (Ephesians 4:24). God has provided everything we need in order to be holy as He is holy. Don't let the enemy of your soul tell you that because you are not perfect and you've made mistakes that you can't ever be holy.

3. **Don't defile your body.** "If anyone defiles the temple of God, God will destroy him. For the temple of God is holy, which temple you are" (1 Corinthians 3:17). We have choices, and we have to make right ones so that we don't pollute our lives. Value your body, because the Holy Spirit lives there. Value your life because it is God's instrument to see His purposes fulfilled on earth.

4. **Copy God.** "Therefore be imitators of God as dear children" (Ephesians 5:1). Study Him. Be in His presence as much as possible in prayer, praise, and worship. Be fully aware of all His names and attributes so you can better understand all of who He is.

182

5. **Be loving and merciful.** "Therefore, as the elect of God, holy and beloved, put on tender mercies, kindness, humility, meekness, longsuffering" (Colossians 3:12). If there are any two qualities that would make you more like Christ, they would be to show love and mercy toward others. In every situation ask yourself what is the merciful, kind, humble, gentle, and patient thing to do.

6. **Stay on the path of obedience.** "A highway shall be there, and a road, and it shall be called the Highway of Holiness. The unclean shall not pass over it, but it shall be for others. Whoever walks the road, although a fool, shall not go astray" (Isaiah 35:8). The road is narrow, and we have to be watchful that we don't stumble off it. Read God's Word and ask Him to help you follow it. Communicate with God frequently each day in prayer and praise.

7. **Be like Jesus.** "He who says he abides in Him ought himself also to walk just as He walked" (1 John 2:6). In Jesus we have the perfect role model. Study Him in the Scriptures. Examine every word He said. Walk with Him. Talk

with Him. Let Him live in you and rub off on you.

Praise Him in the Beauty of His Holiness

When Jehoshaphat stood before people who were facing the biggest challenge of their lives, he instructed the worshipers to go out before the army, singing to the Lord and praising Him for the *beauty of His holiness*. When they did, they won the battle, defeated their enemy, and were blessed with more than they could handle (2 Chronicles 20:1-27).

That kind of praise is powerful. The Bible instructs us to "give unto the LORD the glory due to His name; worship the LORD in the beauty of holiness" (Psalm 29:2). When we do that, great things happen in our lives.

God's holiness is beautiful. God's beauty is a reflection of His holiness. When you worship Him, the beauty of *His* holiness makes you beautiful. I have seen it time and again in both men and women. The more they are in the presence of God and praise Him for His holiness, the more attractive they become. That's why Moses' face glowed with such radiance when he came down from the mountain with the Ten

Commandments. He had been in the presence of God and had witnessed firsthand His holiness and glory.

When you spend time in the Lord's presence in worship and praise, when you worship the Lord in the beauty of holiness, your countenance will be changed too. The change that happens in your soul will be seen in your face. When you bask in the beauty of His holiness, it will exude a compelling radiance through you more profoundly than anything else can. And it will be magnetically attractive to a world that longs for what you have, even though they can't identify what it is.

WORSHIP IS

. . . coming in contact with the holiness of God by the power of the Holy Spirit, and letting the beauty of His holiness rub off on you and make you beautifully holy and wonderfully whole.

I Give God My Praise

Holy, holy, holy are You, Lord, and worthy to be praised. I worship You and thank You that You are perfect and lovely and pure and wonderful. The beauty of Your holiness is awesome beyond words. Thank You for wanting to impart Your holiness to me.

Lord, I need Your holiness to penetrate my life and wash away anything that is unholy in me. Take away any attitude, any hidden sin of the mind, any activity or action that I do which is not what You would have for me. I know You did not call me to uncleanness, but to holiness (1 Thessalonians 4:7). Show me the way to holiness in my own life. Make me into a holy person who is separate from anything that separates me from You. Enable me to reject whatever is not Your best for my life so that I can be a partaker of Your holiness (Hebrews 12:10). I don't want to limit what You desire to do in me because of any sin or impurity of character. Help me to be holy as You are holy. Establish my heart "holy and blameless" before You (Colossians 1:22). Give me clean hands and a pure and humble heart.

You who are mighty have done great things for me; holy is Your name (Luke 1:49). I exalt Your holy name above all names and will give praise and thanks to You every time I think of it (Psalm 30:4). Who does not reverence You, Lord, and glorify Your name? For only You are holy (Revelation 15:4). I give You the glory due Your name, and I worship You in the beauty of Your holiness (Psalm 29:2). "Oh LORD, You are my God. I will exalt You, and I will praise Your name, for You have done wonderful things" (Isaiah 25:1).

God Gave Me His Word

Who may ascend into the hill of the LORD? Or who may stand in His holy place? He who has clean hands and a pure heart, who has not lifted up his soul to an idol, nor sworn deceitfully.

Psalm 24:3-4

For thus says the High and Lofty One who inhabits eternity, whose name is Holy: "I dwell in the high and holy place, with him who has a contrite and humble spirit, to revive the spirit of the humble, and to revive the heart of the contrite ones."

Isaiah 57:15

Who is like You, O LORD, among the gods? Who is like You, glorious in holiness, fearful in praises, doing wonders?

Exodus 15:11

Let them praise Your great and awesome name — He is holy . . . Exalt the LORD our God, and worship at His footstool — He is holy.

Psalm 99:3,5

Glory in His holy name; let the hearts of those rejoice who seek the LORD!

1 Chronicles 16:10

Giving It Some Further Thought

1. Read Romans 6:6, 13, and 19 in your Bible. What are we *not* to do? What are we *supposed* to do?

2. Read Revelation 4:8 in your Bible. How much is God praised in heaven? What do you think we will be doing a lot of in eternity? Write or speak these same words of worship as a praise to God.

3. Read Ephesians 1:4 in your Bible. Whom has God chosen? When did He make that decision?

4. Read 2 Corinthians 7:1 in your Bible. What are we to cleanse ourselves from? What are we to aspire to?

5. Read Luke 1:74-75 in your Bible. How are we to serve God? How long are we to serve Him?

10

Because He Is All-Powerful

I experienced my first airplane ride when I was in my early twenties. It was the most amazing thing to me. Because I didn't understand the aerodynamic construction of the aircraft, I felt that by tightly squeezing the armrests of my seat, I could somehow effect the success of that plane getting off and on the ground safely. Because I couldn't comprehend where the power was coming from and how it operated, I mistakenly believed I could somehow assist in making it happen. Eventually I realized that clutching the armrests until my knuckles turned white didn't help the plane fly at all. Actually, deep down inside I knew that all along. It was just that this was all I could do to appear to have some control over what was happening.

How often do we do that with God?

God is trying to take us somewhere in our lives, and just as He is about to lift us out of our situation and help us soar over the obstacles and mountains and rough terrain that stand between us and our destination — our destiny — we try to take control and help out. We white-knuckle it by hanging on to what we know instead of trusting the very thing that can get us to where we need to go. That's because we don't understand His power and how it works.

How much better would it have been for me on the plane if I could have just sat back and relaxed. Or even better yet, if I had prayed, released myself into God's hands, let go of the armrests, and turned my hands toward heaven and praised God for His protection, love, and sustaining power. How much better if I could have trusted that God not only knew the way I was supposed to go, but He also had the power to get me to my destination.

I didn't have to understand *how* the power worked in that airplane. I just had to *trust* it to work. I would certainly have enjoyed the ride far better if I could have released my grip and let the plane carry me in peace. How hard it is sometimes for us to let go of the material, physical, and earthly things we cling to and let God handle everything.

191

There have been so many times in my life when I've worn myself out trying to help God get me to where I thought I should be. I've worried about how it was going to happen, or if it really *could* happen, or if God's power was strong enough to carry someone with as much baggage as I had. But the more I learned to praise the all-powerful God of the universe, the more I could sense His power working in my life. I was relieved of my burden. And I could enjoy the journey.

When we worship God as our Almighty, all-powerful Lord, we begin to see that His awesome power is there for us as one of the many signs of His love.

A good father uses his strength and power to protect his children. He uses it to lift them up, to transport them, to sweep them out of harm's way, to help them do things they could not do on their own, and to give them advantages they wouldn't have without him. (Mothers do those things too, but for the sake of this analogy, ladies, please go with me on this.) Our heavenly Father uses His power in the same way. He doesn't use it to destroy us, although He could. He uses it to benefit us.

I remember when I was about four years old, I went to visit my Aunt Jean and Uncle

Jack. I loved visiting them because Aunt Jean was fun and funny and always made me feel loved. Uncle Jack was tall and strong and always made me feel secure. Whenever he picked me up it was swift and deliberate, and it was quite a thrill to be transported to so great a height in a moment of time. From his shoulder I saw the world from a new perspective. His strength impressed me. His strength could have crushed me in an instant, but that possibility never entered my mind because I felt loved and accepted by him.

God has the power to crush and destroy. But because of His love, He uses His power for our benefit.

Waiting for the Power to Come On

One of the most wonderful things about God is that He shares Himself with us. He gives us a portion of all that He is. He even shares His power, and He gives us a way to do and be what we couldn't do and be on our own. Who else would do that but Him? And He does that because He loves us.

God loves us enough to be strong on our behalf. To be strong where we are the weakest. "He gives power to the weak, and to those who have no might He increases strength . . . those who wait on the LORD shall renew their strength . . . they shall run and not be weary" (Isaiah 40:29-31).

> Worship transcends our weakness while acknowledging God's power.
> — Jack Hayford

The thing about God's power is that we have to wait on Him for it. We don't just throw it on like a light switch. *We* don't control it. *He* does. It's *His* power, and He dispenses it at will. He wants us to wait on Him for it. But the problem is, we don't like waiting. We want what we want when we want it. And what does it mean to wait anyway? How exactly are we supposed to do that?

Waiting doesn't mean doing nothing. It's not like waiting for a bus or a cab. We aren't tapping our fingers and looking at the clock. While there can be desperation in prayer when we are seeking God for what we need, when we are waiting on the Lord our soul finds rest in Him. We find peace in the midst of strife.

The way we wait on the Lord is to spend

time with Him in praise and worship. It means focusing and meditating on the greatness of God and praising Him for who He is and all that He has done. It's drawing close to God and telling Him how much we reverence Him. It's praising Him for being our all-powerful Lord. That's how we can run the course and not grow weary. And as we continue to do that, He will lift us up and we will fly.

Paying the Price

God's power is not cheap. Just like the electric power that comes into our homes, there is a price to pay for it. Only the price is not monetary. The price is spending time filling ourselves with God's Word so we can *understand* the power. It's praying so we can *access* the power. It's living in obedience so we can *maximize* the power. It's praising and worshiping God so that we *open up the lines* through which God's power flows into our lives.

You see people everywhere who will not even acknowledge the power of God because they don't want to pay the price for it. They want to live life *their* way and not God's. They want to hang on to their domain and not have to surrender anything to Him. But they live supernaturally powerless lives.

Paul said, "Know this, that in the last days perilous times will come: For men will be lovers of themselves, lovers of money . . . lovers of pleasure rather than lovers of God, *having a form of godliness but denying its power.* And from such people turn away!" (2 Timothy 3:1-5, emphasis added). We don't want to be people who deny the power of God in our lives. We want to fully acknowledge His power, and the best way to do that is by praising Him as the Almighty, all-powerful God of the universe.

Ask God to show you "what is the exceeding greatness of His power toward us who believe, according to the working of His mighty power which He worked in Christ when He raised Him from the dead and seated Him at His right hand in the heavenly places, far above all principality and power and might and dominion, and every name that is named, not only in this age but also in that which is to come" (Ephesians 1:19-21).

Doesn't that sound like the kind of power we can't live without?

Jesus wasn't resurrected from the dead just so we could have a nice, happy life. He was raised up to save us from death and hell so we could live a life of *power*. That same power which parted the Red Sea, opened blind eyes, broke the curse of death, and created heaven and earth can transform your life and the lives of others around you. None of us wants to live a life without power. God doesn't want us to live that way either. He wants to empower us to live the life He has for us. It's worth whatever price we have to pay for it.

Unlimited Power, Limited Access

The most exciting thing about God being all-powerful is that it means *with God, all things are possible*. There is nothing too hard for Him. Gabriel told Mary that "with God nothing will be impossible," and look what happened to her (Luke 1:37). Jesus said, "With God all things are possible," and look what He accomplished (Mark 10:27). There is nothing that God cannot do. God's power is not limited.

When my family and I were living in Los Angeles, we endured some very powerful earthquakes. The power of an earthquake is overwhelming and frightening. If you have ever lived through a disastrous tornado, hurricane, or earthquake, you understand what I mean. Yet God has absolute power over all those things. May I suggest that we don't really *want* to experience the *full* magnitude of God's power?

Suffice it to say that He has far more power than is necessary to meet your needs and lift you above your situation. He has more than enough power to rescue you from your circumstances and help you do things you could not do without Him. If God is so powerful that He can create something from nothing or give life to the dead or "call those things which do not exist as though they did" (Romans 4:17), then think what He can do in your life. He has the power to do whatever is necessary, and He doesn't want you to doubt it.

In spite of all that Job went through, he never doubted God's power. He knew it was without limit. He said, when referring to God's ability to calm a raging storm, "Indeed these are the mere edges of His ways, and how small a whisper we hear of Him! But the thunder of His power who can understand?" (Job 26:14).

"Mere edges"? "Small whisper"? Who, then, can even imagine the mightiness of His power? If God not only created the universe, but upholds "all things by the word of

His power" (Hebrews 1:3), what could be too hard for Him?

When you come in contact with God's awesome power, you can't help but prostrate yourself before Him. You can't help but give Him the glory He is due. That's why God's power is something you should praise Him for every day, no matter what is going on in your life or in the world around you.

God uses His power according to His will. That's why we can't ask Him to strike someone we don't like with lightning. (In fact, you could get hurt doing that.) "Power belongs to God" (Psalm 62:11). So we can't just call up God and demand more power for our own purposes. We only have access to His power as He wills it, for His glory and in His time. He does with it what He wants.

You may be thinking, *If God is all-powerful, why doesn't He do something about my situation now?* The answer is, maybe you haven't been waiting on Him. Or perhaps He is waiting on *you* to pay the price . . . in prayer . . . in praise . . . in the Word . . . in obedience. Maybe intervening is not His perfect will right now. Maybe what you're experiencing is for your own good.

Have you ever had a child want to know *why* you wouldn't let them do something?

And your reason was because it would ultimately be bad for them or that they need to learn self-control, patience, humility, compassion, responsibility, or any number of character building lessons? How happy were they with that answer?

"No problem, Mom. I've been wanting to learn self-control anyway."

"Great, Dad. I, too, feel I need to increase my ability to be patient."

I have never heard my children say anything like that. And we don't say those things to God either.

"Lord, I'm so glad You haven't answered my prayer for provision this month because I really do need to work more on my faith."

"Lord, thank You for not allowing me to get that promotion I prayed for because I really want to learn how to be more humble."

When was the last time any of us said something like that?

We don't always see the value and necessity of the things God teaches us through our waiting times. But *He* certainly does.

The greatest thing about knowing that God is all-powerful is understanding that even though you cannot see a solution to your problem, *He* can. He not only can see it, but He is powerful enough to make it happen.

I've been told by many single women, "I want to be married and have children, but I'm getting older by the minute and there is not a single person in sight whom I can marry. What can I do? Why is God not answering my prayer for a husband?"

I tell them, "You just do what God is telling you to do, go where God is telling you to go, and be what God wants you to be, and all God has for you will come into your life. As long as you are still living, there is still hope. I've seen people appear seemingly from out of nowhere. They practically drop out of the sky or materialize out of thin air. One day they just walk through the door, and you've met your destiny. But that doesn't happen without prayer, praise, faith, obedience, *patience,* and the Word of God. In other words, living God's way."

And if what you desire is *not* God's will for you, as you seek Him about it and praise Him in the midst of it, He will give you peace and the power to live the life He has for you. You never know what God is going to do, because He is a God who can do anything.

When you worship the all-powerful God of the universe for whom nothing is impossible, the hidden power of praise will cause things to happen in your life that you never dreamed possible.

> . . . surrendering your life to God so that He can be powerful in you and demonstrate His power through you.

I Give God My Praise

Lord, I praise Your holy name this day. You are Almighty God. You are the all-powerful, omnipotent Lord of heaven and earth. There is nothing too hard for You. There is nothing You cannot do. Great are You, Lord, and mighty in power; Your understanding is infinite (Psalm 147:5). I know that because You can do anything, no plan or purpose of Yours for my life can be held back.

Lord, I thank You that You have redeemed me "by Your great power, and by Your strong hand" (Nehemiah 1:10). "You have a mighty arm" (Psalm 89:13), and You rule by Your power (Psalm 65:6). You are the potter and I am the clay (Isaiah 64:8), and I give You full power over my life to mold me as You see fit. I surrender my life to You and release it into Your hands. You are "wise in heart and mighty in strength. Who has hardened himself" against You and prospered? (Job 9:4).

Lord, You have said more than once that power belongs to You (Psalm 62:11). "Yours, O LORD, is the greatness, the power and the glory, the victory and the majesty; for all that is in heaven and in earth is Yours" (1 Chronicles 29:11). I know that by the power of Your Spirit, all things are possible. I know that when I come to the end of my life, You who raised up the Lord Jesus will also raise me up by Your power (1 Corinthians 6:14). I give You thanks, "O Lord God Almighty, the One who is and who was and who is to come, because You have taken Your great power and reigned" (Revelation 11:17). "Be exalted, O LORD, in Your own strength!" (Psalm 21:13). To God my Savior "be glory and majesty, dominion and power" (Jude 1:25). I praise and exalt You as the all-powerful Lord of my life. Yours is the kingdom and the power and the glory forever (Matthew 6:13).

God Gave Me His Word

Jesus looked at them and said to them, "With men this is impossible, but with God all things are possible."

Matthew 19:26

For the eyes of the LORD run to and fro throughout the whole earth, to show Himself strong on behalf of those whose heart is loyal to Him.

2 Chronicles 16:9

For though He was crucified in weakness, yet He lives by the power of God. For we also are weak in Him, but we shall live with Him by the power of God toward you.

2 Corinthians 13:4

Your faith should not be in the wisdom of men but in the power of God.

1 Corinthians 2:5

Behold, I am the LORD, the God of all flesh. Is there anything too hard for Me?

Jeremiah 32:27

Giving It Some Further Thought

1. Is there a situation in your life now where you know you cannot do what needs to be done without the miraculous intervening power of God? Explain it in a prayer to God and ask Him to move in power on your behalf.

2. Can you recall a time in your life when God moved powerfully on your behalf? Describe it in a prayer of praise to Him.

3. Read Isaiah 40:28-31 in your Bible. Describe in a prayer of praise everything in these verses which inspire hope that God will give you the power you need for your life.

4. Read Jeremiah 5:22 in your Bible. What should the awesomeness of God's power cause us to do?

5. What is your greatest dream, no matter how impossible it seems? Write it out as a prayer to God and tell Him that you know He is powerful enough to make that happen. Then praise Him for it and release it into His hands saying, "Nevertheless, not my will, but Yours be done."

11

Because He Is
with Me

You know the feeling. That empty longing. That deep hunger in your heart for something more. That languishing need to be fulfilled at the deepest level of your being.

Many people try to fill this vacuum with things they *think* will work. They turn up the music. Attend more social gatherings. Watch all the latest movies. Turn on the TV. Indulge in fantasies of the mind. They buy things. Lots of things. Clothes, cars, vacations, houses, and toys. They strive for success and recognition in their work. They seek satisfaction in relationships, and then they drain people dry trying to make them fulfill all their needs. But none of these things ever really fill that empty place. That's because the empty place in each of us was designed by God to be filled with only

Him. This great hunger in our hearts and our souls can only be satisfied with the presence of God.

I look at unbelievers — people who don't know God, don't *want* to know Him, and say that they don't *need* Him — and I wonder how they do it. They *appear* to not have an awareness of something lacking in their lives. They *seem* totally happy doing the things that, to me, are meaningless without God. Yet I, too, have been there and done that.

I have seen how there comes a time when the music has to be turned off, the party is over, the movie ends, the TV grows boring, the clothes and toys become meaningless, the vacation time is up, the success fades, the relationships don't turn out the way you thought they would, and the fantasies are still just fantasies. There are only so many things you can buy, and you can only work so hard. Then one day you still wake up with that empty feeling. As much as you mask it, it's always there haunting you.

Eventually everything comes down to just you. Alone. And there is nothing you can grasp on to that is lasting — except the presence of God.

You may be thinking to yourself, *What do you mean by "lasting"? The presence of God seems more elusive than anything. How do you hold on to the wind? How do you grasp a moon beam?* But the truth is, the presence of God is more attainable than any of those other things.

That's because He is Immanuel, which means "God *with* us." What other god on earth promises that? Before I met Jesus I involved myself in many other religions, searching for the answer to my emptiness and a way out of my pain. None of them involved a god who promised his presence. Who wanted to be *with* me. Who promised to draw *near* to me whenever I drew near to him.

While it's true that God is everywhere, that wonderful, fulfilling, all-encompassing presence of God we need so much can only be found when we search *after* Him. God wants us to *want* Him. To *seek* Him. To *long* for Him. His presence is with us in varying degrees according to how much we want Him and how far we are willing to go to seek Him out.

If it seems to you that God's presence is elusive, it's because He wants you to go further to find Him. To look deeper. To search for Him. To long for more of Him.

You know how it is when you are in love with someone. You want them to *long* for you. To miss you. So you make yourself a little scarce. Not so available. To see if they will really pursue you. You don't call them; you wait for *them* to call *you*. And when they do, it means they care. But if they don't, it indicates that you weren't that important to them.

God does that with us. Sometimes He waits to give us the portion of His presence that He would like to give us in order to see if we will deem Him important enough to put all else aside and pursue *Him*. He wants us to *come after* Him because He wants us to want Him.

And He does that because He loves us.

What Satisfies Your Hunger and Thirst?

I consider myself an expert on loneliness. Being locked in a dark closet by yourself on an isolated ranch miles away from the nearest human, with no friends and no one to be with except a mother who is so mentally ill that she is disconnected emotionally, tends to make you lonely. And deep loneliness is devastatingly painful. It hurts all the time. You are always looking for something to take away the pain. It becomes a survival thing. It causes knee-jerk reactions to life. It causes you to get involved with people and things you shouldn't just to stop the aching inside. Just to ease the longing.

If you were lost in the desert without anything to eat or drink, you would seek food and water anywhere you could find it, even if it wasn't good for you. You wouldn't care how many impurities it had in it or how bad it tasted. But God has so much more for us than just survival rations.

What do *you* hunger and thirst for?

When King David hungered and thirsted for the Lord he said, "As the deer pants for the water brooks, so pants my soul for You, O God. My soul thirsts for God, for the living God. When shall I come and appear before God?" (Psalm 42:1-2). He wanted the Lord more than anything else. God's presence was food and water to him.

He said, "O God, You are my God; early will I seek You; my soul thirsts for You; my flesh longs for You in a dry and thirsty land where there is no water. So I have looked for You in the sanctuary, to see Your power and Your glory" (Psalm 63:1-2).

Have you ever been that thirsty for God?

David looked for God. He *went after* Him. He *searched Him out until He found Him*. And then he laid his feelings and longings bare. "Lord, all my desire is before You; and my sighing is not hidden from You" (Psalm 38:9). He covered up nothing of his soul.

David found God because he sought Him.

The way we draw near to God and seek out His presence is to worship and praise Him. It's the first step in letting go of everything else in the world. It's the way we dissociate ourselves from the things we normally cling to so we can cling to Him instead. We can't have it both ways. We can't hang on to God with one hand and the world with the other and find deep, rich fulfillment in our soul.

You don't have to be perfect to come to God. If that were true, then who could ever approach Him? I'm saying, *Come as you are.* I mean *really* as you are. Let go of all the trappings, tricks, thoughts, fears, hopes, dreams, possessions, activities, and means of identity preservation, and fall into His arms. You don't have to be anything more than who you are at this moment. With all of your imperfections, He will receive you fully. Then let His river of living water flow over your being and into your soul.

In order for water to remain fresh, it has to flow. If it doesn't, it stagnates. When we praise God, a fresh flow of His living water pours into our souls. Jesus said, "If anyone thirsts, let him come to Me and drink. He who believes in Me, as the Scripture has said, out of his heart will flow rivers of living water" (John 7:37-38). When we have living water flowing out of our hearts, we will never thirst.

Becoming God's Friend

God wants to be with you like a friend. Moses was God's friend. "The LORD spoke to Moses face to face, as a man speaks to his friend" (Exodus 33:11). When Moses wanted to know the way he should go, he said to God, "If I have found grace in Your sight, show me now Your way, that I may know You" (Exodus 33:13). His desire was to know *God,* not just get someplace. And God promised that His presence would go with him and give him rest (Exodus 33:14).

Don't you love that? Don't you want that more than anything else in your life? That God would always go with you and give you rest?

After God made that promise, Moses said one of the greatest lines in the Bible. "If Your Presence does not go with us, do not bring us up from here" (Exodus 33:15).

Moses didn't want to go anywhere if God's presence wasn't going with him. He hungered for God. Not just for what God could do for him. He hungered for His presence. That is our hunger as well, whether we know it or not. We hunger to know *God* and the fullness of His presence.

God is searching for someone who understands that the palace is just a big empty house without the king . . . He is searching for a passionate worshiper who is not as interested in inhabiting the palace and enjoying its royal perks as in abiding in the presence of the King Himself.

— Tommy Tenney

God knows that we cannot contain all of His presence. We couldn't handle it, so He only gives us what we can handle. When King Solomon built a place for God to rest — the temple — he dedicated it to the Lord and praised Him, and asked for His presence to live in their midst. Then he said, "But will God indeed dwell on the earth? Behold, heaven and the heaven of heavens cannot contain You. How much less this temple which I have built!" (1 Kings 8:27). Solomon knew that nothing on earth could contain God's presence, let alone this magnificent temple, but he also knew it was God's mercy that allowed His people to experience as much of His presence as they could. God has so much more He wants to give us of Himself. He desires closeness with us. Worship is the way we grow close to Him.

The more we worship God and praise Him for His presence, the more we have of His presence in our lives. Our very praise makes a place for Him to dwell and to rest. And that is the hidden power of praise.

No matter how much we achieve in life, we will always have a hunger for something more. That's because "Our soul waits for the LORD" (Psalm 33:20). That's why the greatest gift God gives us is His presence. Our deepest desires can only be satisfied by Him alone. Our Creator. Our Father. The true love of our life.

If you don't sense His presence in your life, praise and worship Him until you do. That's not trying to manipulate God, it's breaking down your own barriers in order to allow Him access to your waiting heart.

... coming to God and inviting His presence to dwell with you in greater measure than ever before.

I Give God My Praise

O Lord, I worship You and praise You as Immanuel, my God who is with me. I long for more of You. I seek after You and thirst for You like water in a dry land. I want to stand under the gentle waterfall of Your Spirit and feel the soothing mist of Your love showering over me. I want to be immersed in the center of the flow of Your Spirit. I want to be close enough to You to feel Your heartbeat. You are the only answer to the emptiness I feel when I am not with You. The fullness of Your being is what I crave. The intimacy of Your embrace is what I long for. I know there is nothing or no one in the world that can do for me what You do. I want to feel Your presence in my life in a new and powerful way. You are far and above anything on earth I might long for. You are all I desire.

Just being with You changes everything in

me. Longing for You makes me long to be free of anything that would draw my attention away. Lord, I draw close to You this day. Thank You that You promise to draw close to me. With You I am never alone. I love Your holiness, Lord. I love Your beauty. With joy I draw water from the wells of Your salvation (Isaiah 12:3).

Thank You that You have *chosen* to be with Your people. I am grateful that I don't have to strive to be with You, I only have to *long* to be with You. Help me to make You the first place I run to when I have longings in my heart. I don't want to waste time turning to other things that will never satisfy the need I have for intimacy with You. My soul waits for You, Lord (Psalm 33:20).

God Gave Me His Word

The LORD searches all hearts and understands all the intent of the thoughts. If you seek Him, He will be found by you; but if you forsake Him, He will cast you off forever.

1 Chronicles 28:9

LORD, I have loved the habitation of

Your house, and the place where Your glory dwells.

Psalm 26:8

Behold, the virgin shall be with child, and bear a Son, and they shall call His name Immanuel, which is translated "God with us."

Matthew 1:23

When You said, "Seek My face," my heart said to You,
"Your face, LORD, I will seek."

Psalm 27:8

The poor shall eat and be satisfied; those who seek Him will praise the LORD.

Psalm 22:26

Giving It Some Further Thought

1. Read 1 Kings 8:22-23 in your Bible. How does Solomon begin his prayer dedicating the temple to the Lord? What does he say about God?

2. What is the greatest longing of your heart? Write it out in detail as a prayer to God and then praise Him for all the ways His presence meets that need.

3. Read Psalm 27:4 in your Bible. What is the one thing you desire of the Lord? Write it out as a prayer to Him.

4. Read 1 Chronicles 28:9 in your Bible. Have you been able to lay your heart bare before the Lord? Have you been able to reveal all aspects of how you feel to Him? If not, tell Him now. If you have, tell Him again.

5. Write out a prayer of praise for His presence in your life. Tell Him all the ways you worship Him.

12

Because He Has a Purpose for My Life

No one wakes up in the morning wanting to be insignificant that day. No one likes to feel as if they have no purpose for their life. As if what they do does not matter. I felt that way for years, and I couldn't live with the pointlessness of my existence. When I saw no future for myself, except one of constant pain, futility, and brokenness, it drove me to the brink of suicide.

We all need a sense of purpose. We all need a vision for our future. We don't have to know the exact details of it; we just need to know we have one and that it is good.

Whenever I was around other believers on Christian recording sessions, I could see a sense of destiny in their faces. I saw their fullness in stark contrast to my emptiness. Their lives seemed clear, uncomplicated, simple, and livable. Mine was confusing, complex, difficult, and unbearable. Now I know that being a believer doesn't mean life is suddenly easy or simple, but it is *made* a lot easier and simpler because of the presence of the Lord. That's because no matter what you go through, you don't ever have to go through it alone. You always walk with Him and He carries the burden. The issues aren't confusing because He brings clarity. You don't have to wonder what's right and good because He reveals them to you. Your life has purpose and value simply because you are His.

What has happened to you does not define how valuable you are. The fact that God loves you gives you value.

Everything in God's creation has purpose. That's how you can be sure God has a purpose for *you*. We were created for God's pleasure. "For the LORD takes pleasure in His people; He will beautify the humble with salvation" (Psalm 149:4). He saved us and put His Spirit in us for a reason. Our main purpose is to love Him and glorify Him with our worship and praise.

Every time you worship God, you are fulfilling one of your purposes on earth and you are giving Him pleasure.

When you spend time in God's presence

in praise and worship, He gives you revelation for your life. It is at this very point of revelation, as God reveals Himself to you, that you begin to sense your purpose and your calling. Each time you are in His presence, You will sense it more and more. Your future is determined one day at a time as you seek first the kingdom of God. By all means pray about your future and ask God to lead you into it, but most importantly praise Him for it in advance.

The main thing to remember is that your purpose and your future depend entirely on the Lord. *He* is your future. *He* gives you purpose. And He will fulfill your purpose and lead you into the future He has for you as you trust Him daily. He *is* and *has* everything you need in order to do that. You can work to establish your life, but it must be *built* on a foundation of worshiping God.

Fulfilling Your Purpose Affects Others

Another one of our main purposes is to extend the life of the Lord to others in a way that draws people to Him. We can't do that unless we become *like* Him. God wants us to become more like Christ every day. God chose us "to become like his Son, so that his

Son would be the firstborn, with many brothers and sisters" (Romans 8:29 NLT). He wants you to reveal Him to people. Reveal His presence. His reality, His nature, His attributes, His salvation, His love, His peace, His restoration, and His joy.

One of the best ways to secure your future is to receive all God has for you and then do what you can to share Him with other people. He wants us to tell them about Him and explain why we love Him. But it is hard for us to explain if we are not clear about it ourselves. When we worship and praise God, things become clear. And He gives us His heart for the lost. He shows us what we've been given to share with others, and if we don't share it, *we* are the poorer for it.

Those who have a sense of purpose are better equipped to help others. Queen Esther knew her purpose because she knew her God. Her guardian, Mordecai, taught and prepared her to move into the purpose God had for her. He is like the Holy Spirit in our lives, who prepares our heart and guides us. Esther knew that "for such a time as this" she was born (Esther 4:14). And that sense of purpose enabled her to do what she had to do, which was to save her people from destruction, even though she risked her life doing it.

God wants you to have that same kind of certainty about your purpose. When you do, it will strengthen you to be able to step out in boldness to do His will. That doesn't mean losing all sense of humility. It means you know who you are in the Lord and what He has called you to do.

Worship will only make *complete* sense when we understand its place in God's *complete* plan. He did not give worship as a test of the wills but as the source of our potential. He did not create man as a pawn or a plaything, but to become a partner in His highest purpose.

— Jack Hayford

One of the reasons God wants us to rise up as a body of believers to worship together at His throne is so He can draw all people to Himself. There is a great harvest to be had in the world, and our worship — in purity, truth, and holiness, inspired by the Holy Spirit — will pave the way for each of us to do our part.

Once you have those ultimate purposes clear in your head and your heart — that you are to worship God and share Him with others — the specifics of them, as they are to be worked out in your life, will become more and more clear.

What if I Don't Have What It Takes?

Don't worry if you have doubts about whether you can accomplish what God has called you to do. I would be worried if you didn't. God always calls us to something greater than ourselves — something bigger than we can accomplish on our own. That's because He wants us to rely on *Him*. As long as you think you can easily pursue your calling on your own, you are not ready. It's when you are *convinced* that you *can't* do it on your own that God says, "I can use you now. You're ready to move into what I have for you." Your gifts will make a place for you if you are humble and submitted. If you aren't, God will wait until you are. Or else He will get you humble real quick.

If you think you can handle all God has for you to do on your own, then you are thinking too small.

Every time you feel you are unable to do what God has called you to do, when you feel as though you don't have what it takes to move into the life God has for you, wor-

226

ship is the way to respond. First of all be grateful that you feel the way you do because that means you are humble and dependent on God. Rejoice if you feel inadequate to the task because that means you are going to have to depend on God to enable you or do it through you. And He *will* because "He who calls you is faithful, who also will do it" (1 Thessalonians 5:24).

You don't have to *make* your life happen; you just have to worship God and let *Him* make it happen. You don't have to strive to figure out your purpose. You have to strive to know *God. He* knows your purpose. Your praise will illuminate the path by which God will guide you into your future and the purpose He has for you. *You* won't accomplish it. *He* will. "Not by might nor by power, but by My Spirit" (Zechariah 4:6).

How to Move into a Life of Purpose

Seek God to find out what He has called you to do. As you worship Him, He will come to you in silence like a sunrise in your heart. Once you sense His purpose for you being realized, be careful in all you do. Don't let yourself become distracted from what He has called you to. That will keep you preoccupied with what is not important. Stay focused on Him.

When the anointing of the Lord is upon you, you cannot be careless with any part of your life. Remember, it's all about *Him*, not you. This takes the pressure off you in one respect because you don't have to be the one to *make* it happen. You have to *let* it happen. But there *is* pressure on you to keep certain things from happening that will dilute the impact of your purpose. Things like sin, disobedience, not being in the Word, not praying, not being watchful or diligent, and especially not living a life of worship and praise. We can never find our purpose apart from the presence of the One who gave us purpose in the first place.

When we worship God, He makes us ready to go where He wants us to go and gives us the ability to do what He wants us to do. That's the hidden power of praise.

Remember to keep it simple. You don't have to do everything. You don't have to be everywhere. You don't have to please everyone. You can't do all those things and stay focused anyway. Don't let your mind "be corrupted from the simplicity that is in Christ" (2 Corinthians 11:3). Simply worship God. Get to know Him intimately. Do what He tells you to do and don't worry about what you haven't done. Do what you can and let the rest go.

Every time you are weary of the race, stop where you are and worship God. Get your mind off of yourself and onto Him. Don't *try* to be good; turn to *Him* who *is* good. Don't *try* to be perfect; turn to *Him* who *is* perfect. And because He loves you, He will lead you into the purpose for which you were born. Satan will always try to stop the purpose of God from being realized in your life. When that happens, draw even closer to God. He will instruct your heart and strengthen you as you grow closer and closer to Him in worship.

Parents who love their children guide them, teach them, help them discern their gifts, and lead them on the path toward their future. Because they see great purpose for their children's lives, they do all they can to help them move into it. That's what God does for *us*, and He does it because He *loves* us.

God gives us satisfying work. If you have never felt that, perhaps you are not doing what He has for you to do. Every kind of work has its downside — the difficult, unpleasant, and uncomfortable aspect of it. No work is wonderful every moment of the time. But it is God's gift to us that we can enjoy our work. "Every man should eat and drink and enjoy the good of all his labor — it is the gift of God"(Ecclesiastes 3:13). And we can enjoy the fruit of our labor more knowing it comes from Him. When you are doing the Lord's work, and doing your work for the Lord, even the most unpleasant part of it has meaning. Bring worship into your work and thank Him for everything you can think of with regard to it. Thank Him especially for the opportunity to work for *Him.*

All that being said, however, if you cannot find anything good about the work you are doing, and the people who work with you and over you are demeaning and make you feel so bad about yourself that it hurts your spirit, ask God to move you into something else. Praise Him that He has better things for you. He has called you to a higher purpose than that.

When you worship God, a path is carved between you and Him, and He travels it in an instant to bring all that He is into your life and heart and situation. You can never see His purpose for your life fulfilled apart from your worship and praise of Him.

You have great purpose and a high calling. Don't worry about whether other people recognize it yet or not. And don't let them or any circumstance you happen to find yourself in convince you otherwise. You must have that sense of purpose all the time because it will help you make right decisions and do what you otherwise might not think of doing. If you don't have a sense of purpose, ask God to reveal it to you and worship Him until you do.

WORSHIP IS

... fulfilling your purpose. When you are praising God, you are not just fulfilling a duty, putting in time, doing what is expected of you. You are entering into all He has for you. You are opening a door, behind which you will find His purpose and destiny for your life.

I Give God My Praise

God, I worship You as my Lord and King. I praise You that You are all-knowing and can see the end from the beginning. That You uphold all things by Your power. That You hold my life in Your hand. That You see my past and my future. I lift up to You all that I am and offer my life to You. Make me an instrument through which Your will is accomplished on earth. Use what I have for Your glory. Lift me up to see things from Your perspective, and help me to rise above my limitations. I don't want to limit what You can do *in* me and *through* me because I don't have an adequate vision of what Your heart desires to accomplish.

Lord, I thank You for the work You have given me to do for Your kingdom. Thank You for the opportunities that You have provided and will provide in order to do it. I pray that You will continue to reveal to me what I am to do and enable me to do it well.

Lord, I pray that You would empower me to do something great for You and Your glory. Give me the strength and abilities I need to see it through to completion. Help me to stand strong against any opposition. Help me to recognize the lies of the enemy and strengthen me to resist them. I want to press forward and beyond them to Your highest calling. Help me to reject anything that keeps me from doing what You have given me to do. I praise You that You are all-powerful and there is nothing too hard for You.

I don't want my own dreams and plans for the future to get in the way of what *You* have for me (Ecclesiastes 5:7). I know You desire mercy and knowing You more than sacrifice

(Hosea 6:6). I long to know You more and to conform to the image of Your Son. May Your goodness, holiness, and beauty be upon me and establish the work of my hands (Psalm 90:17). Move me into the future You have for me as I walk in Your presence each day. Thank You that You created me with a purpose, and every time I worship You, I am fulfilling that purpose.

God Gave Me His Word

Share with me in the sufferings for the gospel according to the power of God, who has saved us and called us with a holy calling, not according to our works, but according to His own purpose and grace which was given to us in Christ Jesus before time began.

2 Timothy 1:8-9

For we are His workmanship, created in Christ Jesus for good works, which God prepared beforehand that we should walk in them.

Ephesians 2:10

That the God of our Lord Jesus Christ, the Father of glory, may give to you the spirit of wisdom and revelation in the knowledge of Him, the eyes of your understanding being enlightened; that you may know what is the hope of His calling, what are the riches of the glory of His inheritance in the saints.

Ephesians 1:17-18

Therefore, my beloved brethren, be steadfast, immovable, always abounding in the work of the Lord, knowing that your labor is not in vain in the Lord.

1 Corinthians 15:58

Therefore we also pray always for you that our God would count you worthy of this calling, and fulfill all the good pleasure of His goodness and the work of faith with power.

2 Thessalonians 1:11

Giving It Some Further Thought

1. Read Romans 12:1 in your Bible. What is the first step you must take in your service for the Lord so that you can begin to understand your purpose?

2. Read 2 Timothy 1:9 in your Bible. According to this Scripture, has God called you because of something you have done? If not, why has God called you?

3. Read 2 Thessalonians 1:11 in your Bible. According to this Scripture, how should you pray with regard to your calling?

4. Read Psalm 90:17 in your Bible. What is this Scripture a prayer for? Write this verse out in your own words as a prayer to God for the work you do, or *want* to do. Include praise for the purpose God has for your life in the work you do, and *will* do in the future.

5. Read 1 Peter 4:10 in your Bible. What gifts do you have that would be a blessing to others? How could you use the gifts God has given you in your ministry or work? Write your answer out as a prayer asking God for that to happen and then praise God that He has a purpose for your life and gifts and will use them for His glory.

13

Because He
Redeems All Things

What have you lost in your lifetime? Have
you lost hope? Love? A relationship? A marriage? A friend? A family member? A sense of
purpose? A dream? A child? An ability? A
part of your body or soul? Have you lost your
way? Your will to live? Your mind? Your
home? Your financial security? Your willingness to trust?

Whatever you've lost, God will restore.
He won't necessarily replace it with the
exact same thing, but He will redeem the
situation in some way. He will replace your
loss with something only He can give.
That's because God is a Redeemer.

God's most important act of redemption
was when He redeemed our lost relationship with Him through His Son, Jesus. It
was lost a long time before you and I were

born, and Jesus paid the price to redeem it. But God redeems our life in many other ways too.

One of God's greatest works of redemption in my own life, other than my salvation, was when He redeemed my greatest loss. That loss was never having had a real mother-and-daughter relationship. I believe it's the most foundational relationship a person can have. Because it was missing in my life, I had a hole in my soul that kept me looking for a mother for many years, even well into my thirties. I developed great relationships with the mothers of my friends — especially the men I dated. Long after I had broken up with the son, I still stayed close to his mother.

When I married my husband, Michael, I immediately developed a great relationship with his mother. She and I talked on the phone together nearly every day for close to an hour. She already had two wonderful daughters, Michael's sisters Linda and Annette, and she certainly didn't need another one. But she welcomed and accepted me, and she was so wonderful that I believed I had finally found the mother I had been missing all my life. Tragically, she died of cancer the first year we were married. It was a devastating loss for all of us.

In that following year as I grew in the Lord, I came to understand the far-reaching effects of God's redemption. It extends to every aspect of our lives. So I began to pray fervently again that He would redeem my lost mother-and-daughter relationship. But I never saw the answer to my prayer the way I prayed it.

My mother only became progressively worse in her mental illness. She violently refused any kind of medicine or help, and she even disappeared one time for two weeks at the mere suggestion by my father and aunt that she allow them to check her into a mental hospital. My father would not sign the papers to have her picked up and committed because he thought she would never forgive him if he did. He had antiquated ideas about what mental institutions were like and didn't believe she could be helped there. So he waited for her to "snap out of it," which she never did. Instead, she became increasingly unbearable.

One day as I was praying to God about this yet again, He spoke to my heart saying that He *would redeem* my mother-and-daughter relationship, but it would be through my own daughter, not my mother. That really shocked me, for one very important reason. I didn't have a daughter.

And we all know what that means!

My pregnancy with my first child, my son, was extremely difficult, and I was so sick the entire nine months that I didn't think I would ever go through that again. Yet now I knew God was asking me to cast "precaution" to the wind.

God impressed upon my heart that every time I worshiped Him, I should lift up praise to Him as *my* Redeemer and thank Him that He redeems all things. And it seemed the more I did that, the more I grew to understand this aspect of His nature. And my faith grew in the process, to the point where I believed God's redemption of this part of my life could actually happen.

When I did become pregnant again, I thought it surely meant that this pregnancy would be far easier. (This was God's idea, after all.) I was wrong. It was worse. I even ended up in the hospital trying to keep the baby and me alive and well.

about seven months into the pregnancy, one Sunday evening after I had just been released from the hospital again, Pastor Jack called the entire church to pray for me. He and many other people had been praying for me all along, but he said he had been especially impressed by the Lord to pray with the entire congregation right then. At the same time as those prayers were being prayed in church, I was miserable at home in bed. And suddenly the worst of the symptoms lifted. It was miraculous. There is no other way to explain it. And I went on to carry the baby to full-term.

My daughter was born healthy and whole, and right away the redemption process began. Being her mother fulfilled so many of the longings in my own heart, and every day I sensed the healing of longtime hurts from that missing relationship filling the hole in my soul.

Today my daughter, Amanda, is in her twenties, and we consider each other to be our best friend. God has redeemed that relationship beyond what I ever dreamed, and we both recognize that the closeness we have is a gift from God. I know it is a result of God's redemption.

God's redemption doesn't always happen in the way we expect. But isn't that often how the Lord does things? He doesn't do what we *think* He's going to. He always does something *greater*.

What Do You Need Redeemed in Your Life?

God is all about redemption and restoration. We look for perfect things in our lives.

Perfect situations. Perfect work. Perfect people. Perfect relationships. Perfect marriages. Perfect timing.

God is all about taking the imperfect and injecting His perfection into it.

So often we are willing to throw things out because we think they are unredeemable. Things like relationships, marriages, situations, hopes, dreams, people, even our own lives.

God wants to redeem things we never dreamed possible.

His redemption is one of the most beautiful and touching things about the Lord. It is nothing less than solid evidence of His love for us. When you understand that, it'll change your perspective on things. You'll see possibilities for your life like never before. It will cause you to be expectant and hopeful about what God can do in difficult situations.

God's redemption is all about His love for us.

God is *your Redeemer* too. What do you need God to redeem in your life? He has redeemed you from *hell* (Job 33:28), from *death* (Job 5:20), from *condemnation* (Psalm 34:22), from your *enemies* (Job 6:23), from your *troubles* (Psalm 25:22), from *sin* (Psalm 130:8). *And He wants you to trust Him to be* your Redeemer for all time and in all things. He asks, "Is My hand shortened that it cannot redeem?" (Isaiah 50:2). He says, "I will deliver you from the hand of the wicked, and I will redeem you from the grip of the terrible" (Jeremiah 15:21).

Whatever has been lost or stolen from you, God will restore in some way. He will take all the broken and missing pieces of your life and put them together again. And there will come a point when you no longer feel the pain of loss. "The LORD redeems the soul of His servants" (Psalm 34:22). But it has to be done in *His* way and in *His* time. And worshiping and praising God as your Redeemer is a big part of seeing Him accomplish that. He does it most visibly in an environment of praise. He comes into our worship to infuse our situation with Himself and cause it to be transformed.

Every time you worship God for who He is and praise Jesus as your Redeemer, the hidden power of praising God will open up the avenue by which His redemption flows into your life.

When Adam and Eve chose the lie of the enemy over the truth of God, death entered their lives. But God immediately had a plan to provide for their redemption. That's because God has no intention of giving His creation over to the enemy. There had to be a blood sacrifice for their sin, so animals were killed to provide for it. Jesus did the same for us. He was the innocent one who sacrificed Himself, and *His* blood was shed to cover our sins. Our sacrifice to Him now is our worship. As we lift up a sacrifice of praise, He works further redemption in our lives.

God has given worship as a means for man's recovery, restoration, reviving, redemption, and refreshing.

— Jack Hayford

You may wonder, *Why didn't God just create us to be perfect so we wouldn't need redeeming?* It's that old love story again. He wants us to love Him. How loved would you feel if you had a robot following you around saying "I love you"? That's what makes the film *The Stepford Wives* so ridiculous. The men in that town made their wives into robots so they could have sex whenever they wanted and a spotless house at all times. It didn't bother them that they would not have love for themselves or their children. If your computer popped up an "I love you" sign on the screen periodically, how loved would that make you feel? It wouldn't do it for me. It doesn't do it for God either.

Why does God want our love anyway? Why does He care about us so much? I have no idea. But if there is ever a question-and-answer session in heaven and I still care about the answer to those questions by then, I will ask Him and try to send word back. But for now, I believe it is because love is best when it is returned.

Because God loves us so much, He wants to totally restore, repair, rebuild, recover, renew, and redeem our souls and our lives. No matter how much damage has occurred, we cannot experience a loss so great that He cannot restore or redeem it in some way.

I don't want this to sound materialistic, and forgive me if it does, but I now live in a house with a lot of windows and tall ceilings. While that might not mean as much to anyone else, to me it is a sign of God's redemption. I grew up being locked in a small, cramped, dark closet under the stairs. Need I say more?

I thank God every day for this house. The windows and ceilings give me joy and the light feeds my soul. I see them as a gift from God, and I praise Him that in eternity heaven will be a big place with a lot of light

— *HIS* — and the ceilings, if any, I'm sure are very high.

The more I have been restored, the more I want to see restoration happen in others. People who are hurting, who feel forgotten, who believe there is no one on their side, who are devastated and hopeless because of the tremendous losses they have suffered, need to know about their Redeemer and the restoration He has for their lives. The more I worship God and praise Him as my Redeemer, the more I find it impossible to do nothing. It will be the same for you. Praising your Redeemer will inspire you to want to be an instrument of His redemption.

WORSHIP IS

. . . drawing near to God, your Redeemer, knowing that even as you do, He is redeeming your life in ways you can't even imagine.

I Give God My Praise

Lord, I worship You as my God and Savior. I praise You, Jesus, as my precious Redeemer. Thank You for redeeming my soul from the pit of hell. Thank You for redeeming me from death (Hosea 13:14) and from the power of the grave (Psalm 49:15). Thank You for redeeming my life from oppression (Psalm 72:14).

Thank You for love so great that You desire to restore my life in every way. Redeem me and revive me according to Your Word (Psalm 119:154). Thank You for Your goodness and mercy. "Draw near to my soul, and redeem it" (Psalm 69:18). "Redeem me and be merciful to me" (Psalm 26:11). Thank You for all the redemption You have already worked in my life. I pray that You will continue to redeem my life in ways I never dreamed possible. I lift up this particular situation that badly needs Your redemption power to flow into it (name the situation before the Lord).

Lord, I thank You for all the times You have redeemed my life from destruction. For all the times You have shown Your lovingkindness and tender mercies to me (Psalm 103:1-5). Everything in me blesses Your holy name, for You are the Lord, my Redeemer, who has made all things and made my life to be a testament to Your glory and redemption. You, O Lord, are my Father; my Redeemer from everlasting is Your name (Isaiah 63:16). "Let the words of my mouth and the meditation of my heart be acceptable in Your sight, O LORD, my strength and my Redeemer" (Psalm 19:14).

God Gave Me His Word

The LORD redeems the soul of His servants, and none of those who trust in Him shall be condemned.

Psalm 34:22

For your Creator will be your "husband." The Lord Almighty is his name; He is your Redeemer, the Holy One of Israel, the God of all the earth.

Isaiah 54:5 TLB

They remembered that God was their rock, and the Most High God their Redeemer.

Psalm 78:35

I know that my Redeemer lives.

Job 19:25

Thus says the LORD, your Redeemer, and He who formed you from the womb: "I am the LORD, who makes all things, who stretches out the heavens all alone, who spreads abroad the earth by Myself."

Isaiah 44:24

Giving It Some Further Thought

1. Read Titus 2:11-14 in your Bible. How does God want us to live? Why did Jesus sacrifice Himself for us?

2. Read Galatians 4:4-5 in your Bible. Why did Jesus come? What can we become because of His redemption?

3. Read Psalm 103:4 in your Bible. From what does God redeem our lives? Write out a prayer of praise to God listing all the reasons to praise Him in this verse.

4. Read Psalm 130:7 in your Bible. Where should we put our hope? Why should we put our hope there?

5. Read Colossians 1:13-14 in your Bible. In whom do we have redemption? How did we get it? From what has He set us free?

14

Because He Is the Light of the World

When God moved me and my family from California to Tennessee, I thought my life was over.

This is it. I've been put out to pasture. God has taken me out of Mars and dropped me on Pluto. My life is finished.

It wasn't that California was perfect and Tennessee was bad. It was that I left everything I knew — the people I loved, the church and pastor I adored, the lifestyle I understood, the beauty of the ocean that I didn't think I could survive without, and the best restaurants and produce in the world.

My children were older and didn't seem to need me much anymore. My husband was gone all the time establishing himself in a new town and didn't seem to need me at all. The church was new, and I didn't know anyone very well. Plus, it seemed much more difficult to get acquainted in this new place. I was a fish out of water, the new kid on the block, and I had a hard time feeling accepted.

I sank into a darkness of despair. The only thing that kept me afloat was my relationship with God and my children, who were trying as hard as I was to adjust to their new planet.

I felt as though I had lost everything familiar to me. I couldn't get my bearings. The dark and narrow two-lane roads were frightening at night. And everything was hills and curves, which meant I never knew which way was north, south, east, or west. It summed up my entire life. I felt as though I were lost on a treacherously dark, narrow road in the middle of nowhere, not knowing what direction I was going in. Or if I was, in fact, actually going anywhere.

Yes, I knew the Lord. Yes, I prayed. Yes, I read the Word. Yes, I had faith. That's what kept me alive. But I was still in a dark season of my soul. I thought I would either drown in my own tears or disintegrate into nothingness and be blown away.

One day as I was clinging to God and His Word, I read a verse that I had seen countless times before. But this time the sun rose in my heart and the profound truth of it dawned on me. My understanding was illuminated, and I saw for the first time the true meaning of Jesus' words: *"I am the light of the world. He who follows Me shall not walk in darkness, but have the light of life"* (John 8:12).

So simple. Yet I never really got it before.

If I am following Jesus, which I definitely am or I wouldn't even be where I am in the first place, I thought, *then I really can't be in the dark. If Jesus has come as a light into the world, so that whoever believes in Him should not live in darkness, then I don't have to live in the dark. If I believe in Him, then His light is in me and nothing can put it out* (John 12:46).

It was a revelation to me.

I had walked through many dark times in my life after I became a believer thinking, *I must have really done something wrong, otherwise, why is God allowing me to suffer like this?* But that day, when I finally began to truly see Jesus as the Light of the World, I learned to trust that even in the darkest times of my life, His light is still there. I just have to open my eyes to see it.

I also learned that worshiping God and exalting Jesus as the Light of the World changed things in me. The more I worshiped and praised Him, the more I sensed His light in my life. It wasn't as though I were persuading Him to turn up the light. It's that every time I praised Him, *my* capacity to see and contain His light increased.

Beginning to See the Light

God allows us to go through dark times so that we will reach out for Him and find His light in them. He wants us so sure of His light in us that we never doubt it.

God says there are treasures hidden in darkness (Isaiah 45:3). Let me tell you that the treasure I've found hidden in darkness is *Him*. I know this because every time I'm in a dark situation and I reach out for God, I find Him waiting for me. And His light, which is a reflection of His glory, is who He is. His light is already there. We have to open our eyes and hearts to see it.

Worshiping Jesus opens up the channel through which His light increases in our lives. He is the light source. We are the avenue through which it shines. Praising Him increases our capacity to reflect His light.

The hidden power of praising God is that His light increases in us and in our lives as we worship Him for who He is and praise Jesus as the Light of the World.

Whenever *you* reach out to God in the dark times of *your* life, you are always going to find His hand waiting for *you*. When you praise Him in the midst of whatever is happening, it turns on the switch that allows His light to flow freely through you and shine a light on your path.

But so often we don't reach out.

So often we don't praise Him.

We look for other sources of light instead, or we try to make light happen on our own. But that kind of light doesn't last.

Could it be that if we turned our faces toward the light of heaven, we would be molded to the image of Christ more swiftly and surely? Could it be that if we finally placed all that we have, all that we aspire to, all that we are before God on the altar of worship, that He would return it to us filled with His light and transformed by His glory?

— David Jeremiah

You know how it is when a person is around someone they love? Their face lights up. They have a sparkle in their eyes and a radiant glow to their smile. And if that love is returned, their entire soul is illuminated. Love always lights up our lives. God's love does that for us. He loved us enough to not let us sit in darkness. Jesus gave it all so we could have His light forever (Matthew 4:16). There is no greater love than that. The light He brings into each of our lives is a reflection of His love for us, and it gives *us* a sparkle and glow.

Once you begin to see God's light in the midst of your darkest times, darkness will never be the same to you. It will never have the same foreboding. It will never bring with it the same fear. You will perceive things differently. When bad things happen in your life, you won't react with the same despair. You will be able to say, "Praise You, Lord. I worship You in the midst of this situation. I know that You are the Light of the World who lives in me, and Your light can never be put out. I know that You are with me now, and You will shine Your light on this situation. Your glory is over heaven and earth, and it is over my life today."

In the darkest times of your life, your praise to God should be the loudest. It will not only turn on the floodlights, but it will strengthen your faith and let the enemy know you're not afraid of the dark.

Traveling at the Speed of Light

People are attracted to the light. Otherwise, why would they lay out half naked in it every time they get a chance? We who have the light of the Lord *in* us can bask in it as well whenever we come before Him in worship and praise. When we do, He will shine His light into the dark places of our souls and burn them out of us. That in turn makes room for more of His light, which He then shines *through* us to others. And that glorifies God. "If you extend your soul to the hungry and satisfy the afflicted soul, then your light shall dawn in the darkness, and your darkness shall be as the noonday" (Isaiah 58:10). "Let your light so shine before men, that they may see your good works and glorify your Father in heaven" (Matthew 5:16).

One of God's ultimate purposes for our lives is that His light will shine through us to others.

Just as the light we see from the moon is a reflection of the sun's light, the light people see from us is also a reflection of the Son's light. The more time we spend with the Son, the more we will reflect and radiate His light. Just as Moses' face shone so brightly after being with God, ours will too (Exodus 34:29-30).

Well, maybe not quite *that* bright. But bright.

Every time we worship God, the light in us grows brighter. And it's not possible to have so much of the Lord's light *in* us and not have it shine *through* us. It happens instantaneously. It travels at . . . well . . . the speed of light. People are attracted to it immediately, even if they don't recognize what it is. And when they don't know what that light source is, it's our job to tell them.

Learning to Trust the Light

Often when we get into dark circumstances we think we must have stumbled into the cheap motel of life where they only use 15-watt bulbs. You know, the ones that give you just enough light to keep you from killing yourself by running into things. The ones that obviously believe the people staying there don't read. But God's light is not like that. It is never dim or limited. It is more brilliant and penetrating than we can handle. If it seems dim, it's because our perspective is off.

Our problem, sometimes, is that even though we have His light, we don't trust it.

God says, "For you were once darkness, but

now you are light in the Lord. Walk as children of light" (Ephesians 5:8). How do we do that? How do we walk as a child of light?

First of all, we keep plugged in to our light source. We walk with Him and in His ways. We look to Him for everything. We praise Him in all situations.

I wrote a book entirely about this subject called *Just Enough Light for the Step I'm On.* In it I talk about walking step-by-step through life with God and how He gives us the light we need for the moment we're in. It's a day by day, moment by moment life of faith in the Lord.

"We need to be walking so closely to the Lord that we hear His voice in the midst of any upheaval in our lives. We have to trust Him so thoroughly that we will follow Him wherever He leads us. We must walk perfectly within the revealed light God has given us, not running ahead, not lagging behind, not striving to go somewhere else. When we allow God's light to shine through us, no matter how imperfectly we feel we do that, it not only shines on those around us, but it illuminates our own path as well."*

*Stormie Omartian, *Just Enough Light for the Step I'm On* (Eugene, OR: Harvest House Publishers, 1999), p. 94.

That's exactly how I got through that extremely difficult transition from one planet to another. I walked through it one step at a time, holding God's hand, and He gave me the light I needed for the moment I was in. It was a walk of faith, and my life will never be the same. It is how I will travel the rest of my days and into eternity as well.

The move to Tennessee turned out to be the best thing for our whole family, even though it was the most difficult time we have ever gone through. We now have wonderful new friends and pastors and a great church. The beauty of this new place is so exquisite that it gives me life just to be here. And there can be no more kinder people in the world. I travel those same dark roads at night now and know many of the neighbors who live along them. I know they would never hesitate to help me if I needed it. I thought my life was over, and God was actually leading me into my future. I thought I was free-falling in the dark, but He was wanting me to see and trust His light in a deeper way. And now I praise Him every day for it.

I'm still looking for an ocean view, however, because I know that nothing is impossible with God.

Praise Jesus as the Light of your World,

and He will give you the light you need for the step you're on.

WORSHIP IS

. . . embracing God in all His glory. When you do, His radiance will illuminate the dark places of your soul, warm the cold places of your heart, and shine a light on your path.

I Give God My Praise

Lord, I worship You for who You are. I praise You, Jesus, as the Light of the World. You are the Light of my life that shines in me. I know that there is no darkness so great that Your light cannot penetrate it. There is no situation or circumstances that can ever eclipse Your light in my life. Your light is *in* me because *You* are *in* me, and nothing will ever change that.

Lord, help me to trust Your light in my life. I look to You to be my treasure in darkness. I know that You are light and in You is no darkness at all (1 John 1:5). "Send out Your light and Your truth! Let them lead me; let them bring me to Your holy hill"

(Psalm 43:3). Lord, You see what is in the dark (Daniel 2:22). And when I am in darkness, You will be my light (Micah 7:8). I know that when I fall, You will lift me up again. I worship You as the Light of my life and thank You that You will enlighten the dark for me (Psalm 18:28).

Shine Your light on any area in my life where I am not walking in full obedience to Your ways. I don't want to do anything that would in any way dim Your light in my life. Take any dark place of rebellion in me and illuminate it with Your truth. Lord, I know that "the darkness shall not hide from You, but the night shines as the day; the darkness and the light are both alike to You" (Psalm 139:12). You are the true Light who gives light to everyone (John 1:9). I pray that my light will so shine before others that they will see it and glorify You (Matthew 5:14-16).

Lord, thank You that I don't have to fear the darkness because even in dark times You are there. I know that "if one walks in the night, he stumbles, because the light is not in him" (John 11:10). But Your light is in me, Jesus, because You have come as a light into the world so that I don't have to live in darkness (John 12:46). The enemy wants me to dwell in darkness, but You have given me light. I choose to walk in the light You have given me. I need no other light but Yours.

Whatever is good and perfect comes from You, the Creator of all light, and You will shine forever without change (James 1:17 TLB). Lord, I thank You for Your guiding light on my path. Even when I can't see exactly where I am going, I know *You* can and You will lead me. Thank You, Lord, that You will always give me just enough light for the step I am on and provide what I need in every situation.

God Gave Me His Word

Arise, shine; for your light has come! And the glory of the LORD is risen upon you. For behold, the darkness shall cover the earth, and deep darkness the people; but the LORD will arise over you, and His glory will be seen upon you.

Isaiah 60:1-2

Who walks in darkness and has no light? Let him trust in the name of the LORD and rely upon his God.

Isaiah 50:10

The sun shall no longer be your light by

day, nor for brightness shall the moon give light to you; but the LORD will be to you an everlasting light, and your God your glory. Your sun shall no longer go down, nor shall your moon withdraw itself; for the LORD will be your everlasting light, and the days of your mourning shall be ended.

Isaiah 60:19-20

But the path of the just is like the shining sun, that shines ever brighter unto the perfect day.

Proverb 4:18

You are a chosen generation, a royal priesthood, a holy nation, His own special people, that you may proclaim the praises of Him who called you out of darkness into His marvelous light.

1 Peter 2:9

Giving It Some Further Thought

1. Read Exodus 34:29-30 in your Bible. Why did Moses' face shine so brightly? Who had he been with? Who noticed his radiance? What was it a reflection of?

2. Read Revelation 22:4-5 in your Bible. Why will we not need light from the sun in heaven?

3. Read 1 John 1:5-7 in your Bible. Is there any darkness in God? If we say we are in God but continue to walk in darkness, what does that say about us? What do we have to do to have fellowship with one another? What happens when we do?

4. Read Revelation 21:23 in your Bible. Why did the city have no need of light? What was their light source? Write out a praise to God telling Him how

thankful you are that because of His presence in your life, you need not be afraid of the dark.

5. Read Daniel 5:13-14 in your Bible. What had the king heard about Daniel? Write out a prayer to God asking that those same qualities be seen in you by those around you.

15

Because He Is

Parents enjoy giving good things to their children. We give them love, food, a safe and comfortable place to live, and as good a life as we can provide. We protect them, help them to learn, discipline them, take care of them when they are sick, and guide them in the right direction for their lives. We try to give them some of the things they want as well as what they need.

We do this all because we love them.

We don't, however, want our children to take the good things we give them for granted. We want them to be grateful and appreciative. We don't want them to only come to us for money or things. While we enjoy giving these things to them, we don't want that to be the biggest part of our relationship. We want them to *want* to *be with* us just because they *love* us. And we, in turn, want to simply be with *them*, so we can *impart* ourselves and our love into their souls.

God wants that too. And sometimes He withdraws the fullness of His gifts and presence so we will seek after Him. Just to be with Him.

A number of years ago one of my children — who was in junior high at the time, which explains a lot of this story right there — began taking their good life for granted and disobeyed Michael and me by doing some things that were forbidden. When it started getting out of hand, in order to make a point, I removed everything from that child's room except the essentials — five very basic and unexciting school outfits, shampoo, soap, a toothbrush and toothpaste, a Bible, school books, and school supplies. When the child came home from school and found everything gone, they knew immediately that they had been "busted." We confronted them with what they had done and the subsequent consequences of their disobedience.

"As parents we are only required to feed you, clothe you, and give you a place to live," I said. "Everything else you had was extra because we love you and wanted you to have it. You don't realize the price of disobedience, but it can cause you to lose everything.

It appears that you don't appreciate us as parents or all that God has given you, so everything has been taken out of your room except the essentials. It may or may not all come back to you depending on how you react. If you are sorry for what you have done and stop all disobedience immediately, every day you may ask for one thing back and we'll give it to you."

As it turned out, that child was so completely and totally repentant that I wanted to give everything back right then. But I knew that when I had prayed to God asking Him what to do about this situation, this is how I believed we should proceed. Every morning my child was allowed to choose one thing to be returned. And what was chosen each day revealed so much to me about that child's character. I was extremely impressed with what was most treasured and valued.

The first day the request was not for the CD player or the computer. It was for a special Bible that had been given as a gift. The second day it was not for a piece of clothing deemed critical to maintain a certain social status; it was for an article that had belonged to a close friend of the family before their death. The next number of things were equally special. The value of everything had been carefully assessed, and what was most important were these priceless treasures.

I had made it clear that this disciplinary measure was not a taking *away* of love, but a *deeper reaffirmation* of it. I didn't discipline my child because I was mad, but because I loved that child so much that I wanted to make certain they were on the right path. So I took every opportunity to *show* love in any way I could that didn't involve material things. I thought of creative ways to *convince* that child more than ever of how much I loved them.

With my child's diversions gone — the CD player, the games, the phone — we were able to spend more quality time together than we would otherwise have had. We did things like just sitting outside on the front porch talking or taking long walks around the neighborhood. We were able to express our love for one another in ways that I know we would not have taken the time to do otherwise. We each began to sense an amazing depth of love from the other.

The result was that my child changed completely, stopped all disobedience, developed a more humble attitude, and became highly appreciative and grateful for everything, taking nothing for granted. And is *still* that way today. Our relationship is as strong as it could possibly be. I know my child loves me, not for what I can give, but just because I am alive. And the feeling is mutual.

God wants us to value *Him* that way too.

God wants us to value *Him* more than anything He can give us. He delights in giving us things. It's His nature. It gives Him pleasure. But He will withhold when it's necessary, when it seems that we desire the gifts more than the Giver. He wants us to love Him enough to simply be with Him. To seek *Him* as our greatest gift. Just because *He is*.

> Fully to enjoy is to glorify. In commanding us to glorify Him, God is inviting us to enjoy Him.
>
> — C. S. Lewis

It takes faith to come to God simply to be *with* Him. It proves, first of all, that we believe He exists. And that *He* is our greatest gift. We're not just throwing a prayer out in the universe to see if God might pick up on it and do something. "Without faith it is impossible to please Him, for he who comes to God must believe that He is, and that He is a rewarder of those who diligently seek Him"

(Hebrews 11:6). When we go to God just to "be" with Him, *He* is our reward. When we come before Him in worship for no other reason than because we value Him above all things, He rewards us with Himself.

What greater reward do we need when every-thing we need can be found in Him?

God is waiting for us to seek His presence (Psalm 14:2). He wants us to love and appreciate Him simply because He *is.*

How to Maintain a Passion for His Presence

When you love God and want to be with Him simply because He *is,* one of the things that happens is that the joy of the Lord rises in you like a spring of pure water. It happens every time you praise Him. It is instantly felt in His presence. This joy comes from a source that never runs dry and becomes your strength (John 4:14). No matter what else is happening, it's that underlying feeling that everything is going to ultimately be good.

Just being with God fills us with joy. We can experience the joy of the Lord in the midst of any situation because it's found in His presence. Does that mean people will never die, everyone will always be healed, and we will have our prayers answered every time just the way we prayed them? Of course not. It means that in the midst of whatever happens, He will never leave us or forsake us. He will always be everything He is. And we will have the joy of His presence, even when passing from earth to be with Him in heaven forever.

The way to maintain a passion for His presence is to be in His presence often. His presence is addictive. The more we experience Him, the more we want.

Moses asked God what he should tell the children of Israel when they asked who sent him, and He said, "Thus you shall say to the children of Israel, 'I AM has sent me to you' " (Exodus 3:13-14).

That is about as basic and bottom line as it can get. He *is*. We can worship Him because He *is*. Because He *is*, I can live today. Because He *is*, I can get through tomorrow. Because He *is*, I can have joy.

We can read in the Bible about the many times God had to bring destruction into people's lives so they would know that He is God. He had to take away everything. Whenever He warned the people about what He was going to do, He said, "Then they shall know that I am the LORD." He wants us to recognize that too. He says, "I

273

am God, and there is none like Me" (Isaiah 46:9). We don't need to lose everything or have a disaster happen in order to realize this. We just need to praise Him and it will become clear.

The hidden power of praising God opens up the pathway by which all that He is affects all that we are.

"Be still, and know that I am God" (Psalm 46:10). It's not that He is necessarily trying to get us to shut up. Or perhaps He *is*, but God's ultimate goal is to get us to know *Him*. And we can't know Him fully unless we spend time with Him quietly. Just "being" in His presence. Just letting Him "be" in yours.

Have you ever talked with someone who was asking for advice but wouldn't stop talking long enough to hear what advice you had to give them? That's often the way we are when we come before God. It's not that we have to be still *all* the time, but perhaps *some* of the time. We need times when we simply come before Him quietly in worship. To be still before Him. To simply rest in His presence.

When you let all else go and just "be" with God, when you simply worship Him because He *is*, He will elevate you to His perspective and give you His joy and His rest.

. . . coming before God and telling Him you love Him just because He is and that you want to simply be in His presence.

I Give God My Praise

God, I worship You. I believe that You have always been and always will be Lord over everything. How lovely is Your dwelling place. My soul longs for Your courts. My heart and my flesh cry out for You, the living God (Psalm 84:1-2). Lord, I pray that "You will show me the path of life" because I know that "in Your presence is fullness of joy" and at "Your right hand are pleasures forevermore" (Psalm 16:11).

Lord, I long to know You in a deeper and more intimate way. My soul hungers to be close enough to You to feel Your heartbeat and sense Your love flowing into my being. I want to know everything there is to know about You. Fill my heart with such great knowledge of You that praising You becomes like the air I breathe. I want to show my love for You by embracing You with my worship. All honor, glory, and majesty belong to You,

Lord, for You are worthy to be praised. You are holy and righteous, and I have no greater joy in life than entering into Your presence to exalt You with worship and praise. I will bless You at all times; Your praise shall continually be in my mouth (Psalm 34:1). I welcome Your presence now. And I thank You that because You *are,* I can *be* too.

I will praise You, Lord, with all my heart, and I will tell everyone of Your greatness. You make me glad, and I rejoice in You (Psalm 9:1-2). I know that in Your presence I will find everything I will ever need. I know that when I worship You, it is the closest I can be to You this side of heaven.

God Gave Me His Word

The LORD looks down from heaven upon the children of men, to see if there are any who understand, who seek God.

Psalm 14:2

All who seek the LORD will praise Him. Their hearts will rejoice with everlasting joy.

Psalm 22:26 NLT

Whoever offers praise glorifies Me; and

to him who orders his conduct aright I
will show the salvation of God.

Psalm 50:23

By Him let us continually offer the sacrifice of praise to God, that is, the fruit of
our lips, giving thanks to His name.

Hebrews 13:15

Blessing and honor and glory and power
be to Him who sits on the throne, and to
the Lamb, forever and ever!

Revelation 5:13

Giving It Some Further Thought

1. Read Revelation 21:6 in your Bible.
    Who is God in this Scripture? What
    will He give to you when you long for
    His presence?

2. Read Psalm 14:2 in your Bible.
    According to this Scripture, what is the
    Lord looking for? What can you do to
    be what God wants?

3. Have you ever just gone before the Lord and sat in His presence and simply worshiped Him? If so, describe what that was like. If not, write out a prayer asking God to help you do that often.

4. Read Matthew 11:28 in your Bible. What happens when we simply come to God?

5. Read Psalm 45:11 in your Bible. Why are we to worship God? Write out a

prayer of praise to God, thanking Him
for simply being in your life and living
in your heart.

Part 2

Fifteen Times
When Praise Is
Crucial

Why We Need to Praise God More

Worshiping God is not just about singing praise songs in church once a week. Although there is great power in that, and it is vitally important to our lives to do it on a regular basis, there is still more to it than that.

Worship and praise is what we do in the car on the way to work, to school, or to the store. It's what we have in our heart when we're in the mall, the airport, or the doctor's office. It's what we do when the kitchen sink stops up, the car has a flat tire, we become sick, or we've lost our keys for the millionth time. It's what we speak fervently when we are in the emergency room, at a loved one's burial, or in the middle of a tornado. It's an ongoing attitude of the heart. An attitude that doesn't change, no matter what else in your life does.

I'm not talking about some kind of positive thinking. This is not a plunge into denial that says, "This isn't really happening" or "I'm going to pretend that I'm not actually feeling this way."

I'm talking about looking at the *reality* of your life *straight on* and declaring an *even greater reality* straight *over* it.

I'm saying that instead of letting yourself sink to the level of the problem, make yourself rise to the level of the solution.

One of the secrets of experiencing the power of praise is to make a decision that you will worship God no matter what your circumstances are. When you get to the place where praise comes automatically, no matter what is going on, you will come to know God more intimately. And when you do, you won't be able to *stop* yourself from praising Him.

It's easy to praise God when great things happen or when you see answers to your prayers, but what about when everything is going wrong? What is your first reaction to difficult or bad things that happen? If you blame others, yourself, or God, this only compounds the problem. It leads to more distress, misery, and difficulty. If you, instead, refuse to react to your problems in the flesh and move immediately into the realm of the spirit by praising God, things will turn out differently.

When we make our first reaction to what happens in our lives a reaffirming praise to God for who He is, we invite His presence to inhabit the situation and His power to come and change things. This is the hidden power of praising God.

A woman recognized who Jesus was and came to Him wanting help for her demon-possessed daughter. But before pleading her case, she *worshiped* Him. Seeing the woman's faith, He commended her for it and healed her daughter immediately (Matthew 15:24-28). We should approach our Lord the same way. We should come to God in worship *first,* declaring who He is and the great things He has done. That clears the path for God to flow His life into ours and for miraculous things to happen.

The purpose of the second half of this book is to help you learn how to make worship and praise your *first* reaction to everything that happens in your life and not a last resort. I want to show you how to align your will with God's in *every* situation and open your arms and heart to embrace Him, even when your heart hurts and your first tendency is to embrace your difficult situation instead.

In the following chapters, I have given you 15 times in our lives when praise is crucial.

There are many more situations than this, but I believe these are the most common times when praise is often the last thing we think about doing. If we learn to praise God in the midst of each of these situations — and eventually in *every* situation — we will experience greater victory, success, joy, and peace.

God wants you to exalt *Him* and not your problems. The more you praise Him, the more you are centered on Him and the more you will be relieved of the burden of those problems. This doesn't mean you are pretending they don't exist. It means you are saying, "Although I have these problems, I know that You, Lord, are greater than they are. You created me. You are my heavenly Father. You are a good God. In You is everything I need for my life, and I choose to exalt You above all."

When you become convinced of the power of praise in every situation, and understand all that is accomplished when you are a true worshiper of God, your life will be changed forever.

16

When I Am Troubled by Negative Thoughts and Emotions

I am the queen of negative emotions. Name a negative emotion, and I have had a struggle with it. I was taught them. I inherited them. I entertained them. I practiced them. And I was good at it. Negative emotions were so thoroughly entrenched in my life, in fact, that I believed they were me. *Depressed, sad, hurting, and lonely is just the way I am,* I always thought.

When I came to know Jesus, I wasn't suddenly free of all negative emotions. It wasn't until my pastor and my Christian counselor both said to me, "You don't have to live this way. God has more for you," that I saw I could actually have a life without those feelings and thoughts. I saw I could actually have a *life*, period! From then on it was a layer-by-layer peeling away of depression, sadness, self-pity, loneliness, anxiety, hopelessness, and feelings of futility as I learned to walk with God in prayer, praise, and His Word, and as I learned to receive His love.

We all need to be loved. We would love to be able to choose *who* loves us and *how much* they love us, but we can't. There are a few people who are attractive and wonderful enough to be able to manipulate that, but the vast majority of us are not. And although I have never done a scientific study on this, from what I've seen and heard I believe there are more people in the world who don't feel loved than those who do. For many of us, the negative thoughts and emotions we entertain in our hearts and souls are there because we don't believe the important people in our lives really love us. Or at some time in our past, the love we desired and needed was missing.

That's why the first place to start getting free of negative emotions is to immerse ourselves in the love of God. No matter what we do, we can never *make* other people truly love us. But we never have to try and make *God* love us — He already does. He loved us before we knew Him. Now that we know Him, it's a matter of *trusting* in His love.

When we are able to receive and trust God's love completely, I'm convinced our negative emotions will be gone.

But how do we do that? How do we really receive God's love, more than just knowing it in our mind? How does His love get past our defensive barriers and into our heart? It happens when we read God's love letter — *His Word*. It happens when we talk to Him — *in prayer*. And it happens when we reach up to Him — *in praise and worship*.

Whenever we express our love for God through praise and worship, we open up the channel through which His love flows into our heart. We invite His presence to come into our lives in a powerful way that, in the process, breaks down the strongholds of negative emotions. That is the hidden power of praising God.

Worship breaks down barriers in our heart and puts up a protective wall around it that keeps negative thoughts and emotions away.

I'm sure there is not a person on earth who has never experienced the negative emotions I mentioned at some point in their life. You are not abnormal or alone if you are experiencing them now. (Anxiety, fear, and discouragement are so common they have their own chapter.) But you must know these emotions are not God's will for your life. God has a way to transform your mind and set you free from negative emotions so that you don't ever have to be controlled or tormented by them.

How to Transform Your Mind

I was on a runaway horse once. You have absolutely no control over it. It carries you at a frightening and violent speed anyplace it wants, and you have no choice but to hang on tight and go with it.

I was only seven at the time. The uncle who was with me later told me it was a snake that frightened the horse. I'm certainly glad I didn't know that then.

The only way my uncle was able to get the horse to stop was to ride ahead of it on *his* horse and then jump out in front of my horse while waving his arms in the air. My horse stopped abruptly and I went flying over his head and into the dirt. Fortunately it was freshly plowed dirt, so I wasn't hurt except for a few bruises.

Our mind can get out of control like a runaway horse. We like to think we have perfect control over it, but too often it starts racing and runs wild, affecting our emotions more than we think. Too often we just hang on and go where it leads. But God wants to step in front of our runaway mind so it can be brought under *His* control.

Our mind is also like a sponge soaking up all that flows into it on a daily basis. We can have thoughts and images we don't want to entertain inside our head, yet because of what we have inadvertently seen and heard, they are there. Sometimes we allow negative thoughts from the past to play over and over in our mind like an old tape recording just because we haven't known how to turn them off. We remember things we want to forget. We forget things we think we will remember. And even though we want to think clearly and soundly, our mind can become a place of confusion and torment.

I used to think that whatever thought came into my mind was just me, as if I had absolutely no control over it. My thoughts could make me feel rejected or sad. Fearful or depressed. When the voices I heard in my head said things like, "You're no good," "You will never be worth anything," "You will always fail," "No one will ever love you," I used things like drugs and alcohol to try and quiet them. At one point I sank into such an abyss of depression that the only voice I heard was, "There is no way out of your misery." And so I tried to kill myself.

All because I couldn't control the thoughts in my head.

After I came to know Jesus, the voice of hope and reason became louder than the voices of futility and confusion. I learned how to gain control over my mind and distinguish the lies in my head from the truth in God's Word. I learned to communicate with God in prayer and experience the freedom of living *God's* way. And I learned about worship and the hidden power of praise. I discovered that every time I praised God, the negative voices in my head were silenced. They not only had no power; they could not be heard.

Even now, whenever I worship and praise God I find that my mind becomes clearer and I am better able to hear God speaking to my heart. I can see myself and my life from His perspective, and I can better understand the truth about my own situation.

Worship is the secret place that hides the heart from the advances of the enemy.
— Michelle McKinney Hammond

We are all capable of becoming weak in our thinking, no matter how long and well we have known the Lord. We each have the ability to get a little crooked, a little askew, somewhat off the path, a touch messed up in our thought processes if we don't focus our mind on Him. Just thinking good thoughts is not enough to get your thoughts right. I tried that and it doesn't work. You can't overcome negative thoughts with good thoughts. The battle between the two will rage on forever. You have to combat bad thoughts with the Word of God, prayer, and praise.

God wants us to take charge of our mind and not permit thoughts to take hold that are opposed to what He says in His Word. Instead of allowing negative thoughts to torment you, drown them out by speaking the Word of God and praising Him. Clap your hands and say, "I worship You, Father God. You are my Lord and King." Focus on God's greatness and His love for you, and praise Him for it. If you do that every time negative thoughts come to mind, they will eventually disappear.

Each time I became afraid I would end up like my mother, I quoted the verse that says God has given us a sound mind (2 Timothy 1:7). I praised God and said, "Thank You, Lord, that You have given me a sound mind." You can do the same. If you have torment of any kind in your mind, stop everything and worship God for who He is, and then praise Him for the sound mind He has given you. Thank Him that "He heals the brokenhearted and binds up their wounds" (Psalm 147:3). Praise and worship is extremely important in order to maintain a sound mind.

The enemy of your soul will constantly try to remind you of your faults and shortcomings. But when you are praising God, his voice is drowned out and he has to leave. Praise and worship will clear your mind, silence the voices, straighten out your path, and make you better able to hear God speak to your heart.

We don't want to think futile thoughts that lead to darkness and misery. "Although they knew God, they did not glorify Him as God, nor were thankful, but became *futile* in their *thoughts,* and their foolish *hearts* were *darkened*" (Romans 1:21, emphasis added). We want to have the transformed and renewed mind God has for us (Romans 12:2). Praise and worship is where it begins.

How to Get Free of Negative Emotions

Our mind — where we think, reason, and

perceive — is part of our soul along with our emotions and will. It's great when we can get them all lined up together, working on the same page, observing the same guidelines, and functioning in unity, but they don't always cooperate. Even if we have an unsentimental, pragmatic, analytical, and objective mind, we can still be laid to waste by an emotion that says, "I've been rejected." Or, "I'm lonely." Or, "I can't do anything right." How do we keep our emotions from getting the best of us and causing us to do, say, or feel something we don't want to?

Have you ever been kept awake at night by a heavy heart? By oppressive and tormenting thoughts swirling in your mind? By feelings of dread, sorrow, or hopelessness overtaking your soul? Have you ever felt on some days as though you were sinking into an abyss of despair? Have you ever felt disconnected from other people when you were around them? As if you could not be 100 percent in the moment because a big part of you was being sucked dry with negative thoughts and emotions? You are not alone. Those kinds of feelings are epidemic. I've spent countless nights like that in my past.

Listen to how King David, an expert on

"heavy heart syndrome," described it. He said, "My soul melts from heaviness; strengthen me according to Your word" (Psalm 119:28). "Have mercy on me, O LORD, for I am weak; O LORD, heal me, for my bones are troubled. My soul also is greatly troubled" (Psalm 6:2-3). "I am weary with my groaning; all night I make my bed swim; I drench my couch with my tears. My eye wastes away because of grief" (Psalm 6:6-7). "My spirit is overwhelmed within me; my heart within me is distressed" (Psalm 143:4). "How long shall I take counsel in my soul, having sorrow in my heart daily? How long will my enemy be exalted over me?" (Psalm 13:2). "My God, my God, why have You forsaken Me? Why are You so far from helping Me, and from the words of My groaning? O My God, I cry in the daytime, but You do not hear; and in the night season, and am not silent. I am poured out like water, and all My bones are out of joint; my heart is like wax; it has melted within Me. My strength is dried up like a potsherd, and My tongue clings to My jaws; You have brought Me to the dust of death" (Psalm 22:1-2,14-15).

That definitely sounds like negative thoughts and emotions to me.

If you have ever felt the way David did,

you need to know about the power of worship and praise, and how it can bring down strongholds of sadness, hurt, loneliness, rejection, hopelessness, and depression.

ATTENTION ALL READERS! I am not talking about *clinical depression* here. Nor am I telling anyone who is clinically depressed to get off of their medicine. I am talking about a wounding of the soul. Whether you take medicine or not is between you and your doctor. If you need it, take it. Some people feel that if they have to take medicine they have failed in some way. Nothing could be further from the truth. Take your medicine and praise God that He has provided it for you.

Medicine, however, does not solve the problem for everyone. Pills did nothing for my sadness and depression. They made me feel worse, in fact. Only worship, prayer, and the Word of God set me free. Praising God in the face of my negative emotions completely dissipated the strength of them.

One great worship song talks about trading our sorrows for the joy of the Lord. What a wonderful way to think about it. We have a choice. We can either keep our negative emotions, or we can trade them in for the joy of the Lord by worshiping God, the source of all joy. God said He came to give us "beauty for ashes, the oil of joy for mourning" and "the garment of praise for the spirit of heaviness" (Isaiah 61:3). Let's trade in all the old stuff for that wonderful new garment, shall we?

We were created to worship God, but it is often the last thing we feel like doing when we are oppressed in our souls. We can become so distracted and preoccupied with our pain and sadness that we don't set our hearts on Him. But we can't wait until we *feel* like it to worship God.

There were times I used to feel so locked up that I didn't think I could praise God at all. Usually it was because I had been deeply hurt in my soul. But when I finally determined to resist those negative emotions and praise God no matter what I felt like, I broke through that barrier and *did* get free. Praise releases us from negative thoughts and emotions.

David asked God to "bring my soul out of prison, that I may praise Your name" (Psalm 142:7). We need to do the same. And we need to thank God that we are "a new creation" in Christ, that "old things have passed away" and everything has become new (2 Corinthians 5:17). When we make praising God our *first* reaction to the hurt we feel, He can lift us above it.

One of the most powerful things you can do when you are being weighed down with negative thoughts and emotions is to sing songs of worship to the Lord. I know that may be the *last* thing you feel like doing. It's hard to open up your mouth and sing when your heart is heavy. But that is exactly what you need to do. And it is the most crucial time to do it.

Remember, you don't have to have a perfect heart in order to come to Him in praise. And you don't have to have a perfect voice either. If that were true, how many people could come to Him? The great thing about the hidden power of praise is that God can purify your heart in the very process of you praising Him. And He can make you forget about your voice too. Your voice will come from a deeper place than your body, or even your soul. It will come from your spirit. It will be inspired and sustained by the Spirit of God in you. And it will be beautiful.

Negative emotions are never God's will for you. Knowing that is half the battle. Praise and worship is one of your greatest weapons against them.

... lifting your hands to God in surrender, lifting your voice to God in songs of praise, and lifting your heart to God in love, reverence, and devotion.

I Give God My Praise

Lord, I worship You. You are my Lord and King, my precious Redeemer. There is no other God like You, entirely full of goodness, grace, and mercy. Thank You, Lord, that You heal us when we are brokenhearted and bandage our wounds. You build us up when we are weak in our soul (Psalm 147:1-4). You are great and powerful, O Lord, and You understand all things, even what is in my heart (Psalm 147:5).

Lord, I praise You and thank You that You have given me a sound mind. I lay claim to that this day. Thank You that You are "not the author of confusion but of peace" (1 Corinthians 14:33). I choose peace this day, and I worship You, the God of peace. Thank You that I have the mind of Christ (1 Corinthians 2:16). Thank You that You enable me to cast down every argument and high thing that exalts itself against the knowledge of You and bring every thought into captivity to the obedience of Christ (2 Corinthians 10:5). Help me to be renewed in my mind and put on the new person You created me to be in righteousness and holiness (Ephesians 4:22-24).

Lord, thank You that I don't have to live with sadness, hurt, or depression. I know that "weeping may endure for a night, but joy comes in the morning" (Psalm 30:5). Thank You that "You have put gladness in my heart" (Psalm 4:7). This day I put on the garment of praise in exchange for the spirit of heaviness (Isaiah 61:1-3), and I glorify You as Lord of all.

God Gave Me His Word

You have turned for me my mourning into dancing; You have put off my sackcloth and clothed me with gladness, to the end that my glory may sing praise to You and not be silent. O LORD my God, I will give thanks to You forever.

Psalm 30:11-12

Let this mind be in you which was also in Christ Jesus.

Philippians 2:5

You have heard Him and have been taught by Him, as the truth is in Jesus: that you put off, concerning your former conduct, the old man which grows corrupt according to the deceitful lusts, and be renewed in the spirit of your mind, and that you put on the new man which was created according to God, in true righteousness and holiness.

Ephesians 4:22-24

If anyone is in Christ, he is a new creation; old things have passed away; behold, all things have become new.

2 Corinthians 5:17

For though we walk in the flesh, we do not war according to the flesh. For the weapons of our warfare are not carnal but mighty in God for pulling down strongholds, casting down arguments and every high thing that exalts itself against the knowledge of God, bringing every thought into captivity to the obedience of Christ.

2 Corinthians 10:3-5

Giving It Some Further Thought

1. Read Isaiah 61:1-3 in your Bible. What did Jesus come to earth to do for His people? Whom did He come to comfort? What will He give them? Write out a prayer of praise to God for all the things listed in these verses for which you are grateful. Describe what you are *most* thankful for, especially with regard to any negative emotions you may be feeling or have felt. (For example, "Lord, I praise You and thank You that You came to earth to heal those who are brokenhearted . . .")

2. Read Psalm 9:9-10 in your Bible. What can we do when we feel oppressed with negative emotions? What will happen when we do that?

3. Read Isaiah 65:2 in your Bible. Do you have any negative thoughts and emotions troubling you right now? How long have you had them? Have you ever accepted those kinds of thoughts and feelings as "just the way you are"? Write out a prayer below giving those emotions and thoughts to God. Ask Him to set you free from them and give you His thoughts.

4. Read Hebrews 4:12 in your Bible. How can the Word of God help us in our thinking and feelings?

5. Read Philippians 4:8 in your Bible. What are we supposed to think about instead of negative things? Write your answer out as a prayer to God and praise Him for His answer and His Word. (For example, "Lord, I pray that You would help me to think only thoughts that are true . . .")

17

When I Have Anxiety, Fear, and Discouragement

What if I lose my job? What if I can't pay my bills? What if I never marry? What if I fail at what I'm doing? What if I can't pass the test? What if my relationship falls apart? What if things never get any better? What if something happens to my child? What if I become seriously ill? What if my loved one dies? What if terrorists bomb the building I'm in or the plane I'm on?

Much of our anxiety comes from "what if" thoughts.

But God says to not be anxious about anything (Philippians 4:6).

Anxiety comes from fear. All of our worry, uncertainly, distress, dread, and panic comes from fear. Fear can come on us with heart-stopping suddenness. It can distort our thinking. It can control our lives. It can paralyze us.

But God says fear doesn't come from Him (2 Timothy 1:7).

When we suffer from anxiety and fear over a long period of time, we can become discouraged. You know how it is when you get a crack in something, and it weakens it just enough so that it can eventually be broken. As with a package that has been sealed in protective plastic wrap, all it takes is one tiny hole in the plastic to create enough of a weakness to rip that thing apart.

It's the same with our lives. If the enemy can get a tiny crack in our courage, he can rip it away from us. Discouragement happens a little at a time.

But God says to not be discouraged (Deuteronomy 1:21).

Anxiety, fear, and discouragement are epidemic in our world today, yet God has promised us a way out of all three.

At the First Sign of Anxiety

When God tells us not to be anxious about anything, it's not the same as someone telling us to "cheer up." It's not the same as when something terrible happens and a friend says, "Don't worry." God is not just saying, "Forget about it." He is giving us the solution. He says we should pray about everything and give praise and thanks to Him. When we do that, He promises to give us His peace that is beyond all comprehension. That means we will have peace even when it doesn't make sense. That kind of peace will protect our heart and mind (Philippians 4:6-8).

We are instructed to "rejoice in the Lord" (Philippians 4:4). That means that we are to find our joy in Him. So many times we think our fear and anxiety are connected to God. We think we feel that way because of something He didn't do or may not do for us. *What if He doesn't provide for us? What if He doesn't protect us? What if He doesn't give us what we want or need?* When we anticipate the worst or have a sense of foreboding, we create anxiety and mental distress that interfere with our ability to function.

This kind of anxious unrest can come into our soul at any time. It often happens in the middle of the night when your home is quiet but your mind is not. Pills can give temporary relief, but when they wear off the anxiety is still there. The problem has only been masked. That anxiety can only be quieted by the peace of God. And the moment we receive Jesus, we have access to peace that is beyond all understanding (Philippians 4:7).

Today we have television, newspapers, and magazines telling us about all the reasons we should feel anxious. Not only are we reminded of the *dangers* around us, but we are constantly bombarded with images of how we should *look, talk, walk,* and *be.* There is tremendous pressure, especially for young people, to live a certain way, look a certain way, wear certain clothes, accomplish certain things, go along with certain behavior, and mold to a certain image in order to fit in and avoid rejection. We are constantly being reminded of how we are falling short. We are losing the freedom to just be and not have to look constantly in the mirror to see whether what is reflected there lives up to a high enough standard.

Praising God is the way to combat all anxiety, and it's best to do it the moment you sense anxiety over *anything.* And then *continue* to praise God until all anxiety leaves.

When you *worship God* for all that He is, *praise Him* as your mighty Prince of Peace, and *thank Him* that in His presence you can find peace for your soul, then you will experience that peace that passes all understanding. The more you praise Him, the more you will sense His peace flowing over you.

You need to have total peace about who you are, what you are doing, and where you are going in your life. You need peace about your past, present, and future. You need to have peace about the circumstances you're in, no matter what they are. The lack of such peace in your heart and mind can make you miserable. The strife, torment, anxiety, and stress can make you sick.

When we are fearful, apprehensive, worried, alarmed, or terrified, only the peace of God can restore us to a calm, assured confidence. Even though life is unpredictable and sometimes full of fearful things, God says we don't have to live in fear.

At first sign of anxiety, seek the peace of God. In His Word. In prayer. And in praise and worship.

At the First Sign of Fear

Job was considered by God to be a righteous man, yet he had fear. He feared something happening to his children. He feared failing health. He feared losing everything. When each one of these fears came true, he said, "For the thing I greatly feared has come upon me, and what I dreaded has happened to me. I am not at ease, nor am I quiet; I have no rest, for trouble comes" (Job 3:25-26). The things that happened to Job even made him wish he had never been born (Job 3:3-16).

Who can criticize Job for his reaction? How many of us have lost everything — including our children, health, and possessions? How would we respond to such a horrible situation?

When the thing we fear and dread most comes upon us, the only way to react is to praise God in the midst of it. I'm not saying we have to act as though nothing bad has happened. I've seen people do that to the point that they actually seemed happy their loved one died. We don't have to go that far. But we can still recognize the things about God that are always true no matter what is happening and how afraid we are.

Whatever your deepest fears are right now, bring every one of them to God. Thank Him that He is greater than any of them. Enter His "gates with thanksgiving" and His "courts with praise" (Psalm 100:4), and thank Him that in His presence all fear is gone.

The precious thing about the Lord is that

it is His love that takes away our fear. It is His love that gives us the power to stand against the enemy of our soul when He comes in to bring fear upon us. And even when our worst fears do come upon us, it is God's love for us that assures us He will bring good out of the situation.

The first thing the people of Israel did when they were faced with an enemy was to offer sacrifices day and night. "Though fear had come upon them . . . they offered burnt offerings . . . and they sang responsively, praising and giving thanks to the Lord" (Ezra 3:3-11). There is that singing of praise again. I'm telling you, it is powerful. Don't just read about it. Do it. Make praise your *first* response to fear.

I used to be afraid to fly. But when I began to walk step-by-step with God and knew I was *called* places to which I would *have* to fly, I turned to God in my fear. He assured me that I was not traveling alone. He was going with me. Whenever I became afraid I would worship God and say, "Thank You, God, that You are always with me. Thank You that You have not given me fear, but rather You have given me Your love, Your power, and a sound mind." There were many flights when I quietly sang praise to God while sitting in my seat. (Don't worry,

311

the engines were loud and no one heard.) Worship made the difference because God lived in my praise and His presence took away my fear.

God wants us to praise Him at all times, but especially when we are afraid or discouraged. When we do, not only will He take away our fear, but He will make our faces radiant because we were with Him (Psalm 34:1-5).

True worship will set us free from the bondage of twisted belief and a fake religious system. Only as we truly worship God is our spirit released from captivity to soar into the presence of God.

— Sam Hinn

Fear will lie to you. It will tell you things that are not God's truth for your life. Fear denies that God's presence is fully active, and it cancels all hope and faith in God's power to work in your behalf. But faith, prayer, praise, and the Word of God will conquer every fear.

At the First Sign of Discouragement

God is a God of encouragement. That's because He is a good God. His encouragement comes through His Word. It comes when we pray. It comes through His presence when we are with Him in worship and praise.

We can be encouraged by others, but we can't depend on that. Most people want to be encouraged themselves, and they are not thinking about whether *you* need to be unless you come right out and tell them. But if you are around someone who is constantly discouraging you day after day, you need to ask God to help you find some other *encouraging* people to be around.

When Joshua went into the Promised Land, God told him over and over, "Do not be afraid, do not be discouraged." He also said, "Don't let My Word depart out of your mouth." In other words, keep speaking God's Word. If you are not speaking God's Word, your courage will dissipate.

When you start to enter the Promised Land of your life, the place God is leading you into, there will be things to be afraid of and things that will be discouraging. But don't be worried or anxious by what you see. Just know that the greater the future

313

you have, the greater the attack on you will be. Right when you are entering into your destiny you will be faced with the biggest challenge you have ever faced. You can count on it.

Discouragement happens a little at a time. The courage you have to face your problems and challenges is chipped away bit by bit. The enemy wants to convince you that you can't make it, so you might as well give up. And the closer you come to your destiny or time of victory, the harder the enemy will try to discourage you. He will attempt to strip you of your confidence. And when you don't see the success or fruit you want in your life in the time you thought it would happen, you may become discouraged.

Sometimes we are so discouraged about our future that we don't even have the faith to ask God about it anymore. So we withdraw from Him. We don't pray. We don't go to His Word. We think we must have done something wrong and God is mad at us or disappointed in us. But until we deal with our discouragement first, we won't have the strength to face what opposes us or to walk into all that God has for us.

In your career, marriage, ministry, or relationships you may be right on the brink of breakthrough when something comes to shatter your hope. You may be steps away from walking over the threshold of your future, and you are struck down. That is the very time you need to praise God. Make yourself do it. Tell your mind, emotions, and will to stop worrying about everything and put your hope in the Lord (Psalm 130:7). Say, "I'm going to praise God whether I feel like it or not, and no matter what is happening. Praise the Lord, O my soul, and don't forget all He has done for you" (Psalm 103:2).

When the enemy starts breaking you down and saying, "You don't have what it takes," "You're over the hill," "You're too weak," "You can't do it," then praise God that He renews your strength like the eagles. And what you praise Him for every day will become one of the weapons of your deliverance.

At the first sign of discouragement, worship God and find your encouragement in Him.

When you praise God in the face of your anxiety, fear, and discouragement, you open up the channels through which God's peace, love, and encouragement flow to you. That is the hidden power of praise.

> . . . entering into God's presence ex-
> pecting His love, peace, and joy to over-
> take you no matter how you feel at that
> moment. It's proclaiming that He is
> bigger than anything you face.

I Give God My Praise

O Lord, I worship You above all else. You
are my Creator, my heavenly Father, my Almighty God. You are my light and my salvation; whom shall I fear? You, Lord, are the
strength of my life; of whom shall I be afraid?
(Psalm 27:1). I cast my burden on You,
knowing You will sustain me and I will not be
shaken (Psalm 55:22). I thank You that
"though an army may encamp against me, my
heart shall not fear" (Psalm 27:3). In You,
Lord, "I have put my trust; I will not be afraid.
What can man do to me?" (Psalm 56:11).
"Whenever I am afraid, I will trust in You"
(Psalm 56:3). Thank You, Lord, that when I
seek You, You hear me and deliver me from all
my fears, that You save me out of all my troubles. Thank You that Your angel camps
around me to deliver me (Psalm 34:4-7).

Lord, I give all of my anxiety and fear to You. I surrender my hold on them and release them into Your hands. Instead, I lift my eyes to You, for You are my help in time of trouble. I will praise You in the midst of all that happens in my life. I know that in Your presence I don't need to be anxious or afraid of anything. I refuse to entertain discouragement and instead choose this day to find my encouragement in You. Your love comforts me and takes away all my fear. Your power in my life gives me strength and makes me secure. Thank You that You have given me a sound mind that is able to see the truth and discern what is happening around me. Thank You for giving me the courage to go forward and fulfill the destiny You have for me.

God Gave Me His Word

Be anxious for nothing, but in everything by prayer and supplication, with thanksgiving, let your requests be made known to God; and the peace of God, which surpasses all understanding, will guard your hearts and minds through Christ Jesus.

Philippians 4:6-7

I cried to the LORD with my voice, and He heard me from His holy hill. I lay down and slept; I awoke, for the LORD sustained me. I will not be afraid of ten thousands of people who have set themselves against me all around.

Psalm 3:4-6

There is no fear in love; but perfect love casts out fear, because fear involves torment. But he who fears has not been made perfect in love.

1 John 4:18

This poor man cried out, and the LORD heard him, and saved him out of all his troubles. The angel of the Lord encamps all around those who fear Him, and delivers them.

Psalm 34:6-7

Let all the earth fear the LORD; let all the inhabitants of the world stand in awe of Him.

Psalm 33:8

Giving It Some Further Thought

1. What are the things you fear most right now? What attributes of God are you most grateful for with regard to the things you fear most? Write your answer out as a praise to God.

2. Read John 6:18-21 in your Bible. Why were the disciples afraid? What did Jesus tell them that comforted them? How did the disciples respond to Jesus? What happened immediately after that? Do you think that by receiving Jesus into your own circumstances it would calm your fears and get you safely to where you need to go too?

3. Read Psalm 34:1-10 in your Bible. How much and how often are we to praise God? What does it do for others

319

when they see us praising God in the midst of our fear? Write out a prayer of praise for the things you are thankful for in this section of Scripture.

4. Read Psalm 34:17-22 in your Bible. Write out a prayer of praise to God for all that you are thankful for in these verses, especially with regard to your life right now.

5. Read Psalm 103 in your Bible. Write out a prayer of praise to God for all that you are thankful for in this psalm.

18

When I Become Sick, Weak, or Injured

She is one of the most beautiful and inspiring women I have ever met. That is how I would describe her. When she was only a teenager, she suffered a spinal cord injury in a diving accident and became a quadriplegic. She prayed as fervently as anyone could for total healing, along with millions of other people who prayed as well, and still she was not healed. At least not in the way we wanted her to be. Yet there were countless miracles along the way — the fact that she is alive being the greatest miracle of all.

At one point, Joni Eareckson Tada became so despondent she didn't want to live anymore, but she couldn't even kill herself. In her greatest moment of despair, in the midst of unimaginable suffering, she began to praise God, and things changed in her heart. It was a turning point in the middle of her agony when she started to see hope for the first time. She saw that even if God never healed her, she still had a great purpose.

Since that time Joni has accomplished much more than most of us could do in a lifetime. She prayed for a miracle, but she *is* the miracle.

Joni and I have appeared and spoken at the same events. I know how hard it was on my body to get there and do it. I can't imagine how difficult and complicated it was for her. Yet she sparkles. She glows. She is radiantly beautiful. Her eyes are effervescent pools that your spirit can swim in when you look into them. When I look into Joni's eyes, I see Jesus. That's because Jesus is what Joni is all about. He sustains her. He gives her breath. He motivates her life and gives her direction and purpose.

During the last conference we spoke at together, Joni told me that when she wakes up in the morning she doesn't think she can make it through the day. But she perseveres. Even with all the wonderful people around her, without whom she could not do all that she does, it is still *her* body that has to be ready to go. It is still *her* mind and voice that have to function to full capacity. It is still *her* spirit and soul that have to give out to others what she came to impart. There is no way she could do all that she does and still have the warm, joyful, vivacious, and magnetic personality she has without an infusion of God's Spirit. It is her attitude of praise and worship of God that pervades her life.

Every time I talk with her she gives me strength and hope and encouragement. So often when I felt I couldn't make it, I would think of Joni, and she inspired me to not give up.

I have often thought, *If Joni can do what she does, surely I can endure what I'm going through and be praise-filled in my attitude too.*

Joni is too humble and pure a person to know the full extent of the powerful impact she has had on the lives of millions. Especially me. I love her. She is my hero. She has taught me more about Jesus than she can ever imagine. Although Joni has not been healed as far as walking, she has been healed in so many other ways in the three decades since her accident. And she is still alive and well and touching millions of people every day. We have seen the face of Jesus in hers, and He is beautiful, radiant, sparkling, vibrant, and loving.

Praise in the Midst of Suffering

I have had many near-death experiences, one of which I recounted in an earlier chapter. Why didn't God heal me so that I wouldn't have had to go through such life-threatening agony? I don't know. All I know is that I trust Him, whether I am healed or not in answer to my prayers. There were times when I *have* been healed. There were times when I *haven't*. But it is God who has kept me alive. I am grateful for His will in my life, whatever that might be.

Jesus is a healer, but He heals His way and in His time. When we pray for healing — as in all other prayer requests — we aren't telling God what to do. He is sovereign and He knows what to do. Though I believe Jesus came to earth as *our* Healer, not all sickness or injury is healed. At least not the way *we* always want it to be. If He doesn't heal us the way we ask Him to, it's because He has a greater plan and His glory will be seen in it.

Some sickness comes from the enemy. God allowed Job to be made sick by Satan. "And the LORD said to Satan, 'Behold, he is in your hand, but spare his life.' So Satan went out from the presence of the LORD, and struck Job with painful boils from the sole of his foot to the crown of his head" (Job 2:6-7). God allowed it for a reason. And even though we don't understand the reason that God doesn't always heal us, we can trust that He will bring good out of our suffering.

Our suffering forces us to draw closer to God.

Even though Job was a very righteous man, there was still more he could learn about the Lord. Job had to repent for questioning God about what had happened to him. He realized that God is sovereign, and we can't know His ways and why He does all the things He does. Job's repentance and restoration are linked together.

The Bible says that. "Is anyone among you suffering? Let him pray . . . and the prayer of faith will save the sick, and the Lord will raise him up . . . Confess your trespasses to one another, and pray for one another, that you may be healed. The effective, fervent prayer of a righteous man avails much" (James 5:13-16). It's very clear that if we are suffering, we are to pray. And we are to pray with passion. That means burning, devout, sincere, wholehearted, and enthusiastic prayer. This means with our whole heart. While we don't have control over God's answers to our prayers, we *can* control how we pray.

Praying passionately and fervently for our own healing is not a problem because we are never apathetic about that. We feel very strongly about it, in fact. And the sicker, the more miserable, pained, and incapacitated we are, the more fervently we pray. There is no doubt that Joni's prayers were some of the most fervent ever prayed. And likewise those that were prayed *for* her by the many people who love her. But God had other plans. He has made her to be an amazing testimony to His sustaining goodness, grace, and love. The good that she has accomplished for so many on this planet cannot even be measured in this lifetime.

Joni learned to praise God in the midst of her suffering. I have learned that too. Praise brings healing one way or another. I have been in the shadow of the valley of death many times, but I found that the name of Jesus is deeper. I've been on the mountaintop of health, but I know the name of Jesus is higher. Whether I am healed or not, I have learned to praise Him in both places.

I think God is especially honored when we offer a sacrifice of praise. He is glorified when we offer words of adoration wrenched from a pained and bruised heart . . . Most of the verses written about praise in God's Word were penned by men and women who faced crushing heartaches, injustice, treachery, slander, and scores of other intolerable situations.

— Joni Eareckson Tada

Jesus took the penalty for our sins when He suffered and was crucified on a cross. And it is through the suffering that He bore in His own body that allows for our healing (1 Peter 2:24). But it is all up to God. We are not dictating to Him when we pray. He is our Healer, but not all of us find the healing we want when we want it. Sometimes the healing is delayed. And we can grow weary in the waiting. Time passes slowly when we are in pain or are suffering. But praising God will sustain us through that time.

When we praise God in the midst of our sickness, pain, weakness, or misery, our act of worship opens up a channel through which His healing presence can penetrate our lives to heal us or to sustain us as He sees fit. That is the hidden power of praising God.

Once when I was enduring tremendous physical suffering, I randomly opened my Bible for comfort. Instead of turning to where the ribbon marked my place of ongoing reading, I found myself at Psalm 102. What I read there was written thousands of years ago, yet it could have been written for me right then in terms of what I was experiencing. The writer was honest before God about the way he was feeling and all that he was suffering, and he cried out to God to hear his prayer and give him a future. After reading the psalm, I did the same thing. Like the writer, I recognized that God will be forever and will never change, and I have an eternal future with Him. No matter how bad it is down here, I have the hope that whether God chooses to heal me or not, I have a life forever with Him that is free of pain, and I praise Him for that.

I have found that no matter how bad I feel, when I praise God I feel better. I have enjoyed much healing in worship services where many people are worshiping God together. I have also found healing when worshiping God by myself. Things happen when we worship God, because praising God is the prayer that changes everything.

Whether we acknowledge it or not, we are all alive today because God has healed us in some way at some time. But not everyone glorifies God as their Healer.

Ten lepers cried out to Jesus to heal them and He did. But only one of the ten returned and glorified God (Luke 17:15). How often are we like the other nine? God does something great for us, and we just take it in stride and don't fall down on our face at His feet and thank Him for it. We often do that with healing, even when it is an answer to a specific prayer we prayed. Many people think, *Well, this would have happened anyway.* We take the blessings of our health for granted instead of praising Him every day and giving thanks that He is our Healer.

God's healing is one of the greatest demonstrations of His love. When we praise God, it invites His presence into our life in a powerful way. "The power of the Lord was present to heal them" (Luke 5:17). In His presence there is healing.

. . . a sacrifice because it is not something we naturally do. We have to *want* to do it. We have to *decide* to do it. We have to *take time* to do it. We have to make the *effort* to do it.

I Give God My Praise

Lord, I worship You. Almighty God, I praise You. Jesus, I exalt and thank You that You are my Healer. Thank You for dying for me on the cross, for bearing the consequences of my sin in Your body. You are greater than anything I face or suffer, and I thank You that in Your name I can find healing. You are my strong tower, You are my strength. Your power is unlimited. I know that if You heal me, I will be healed completely. Thank You that You will rise up with healing for those who fear Your name (Malachi 4:2). "Be merciful to me, O God, be merciful to me! For my soul trusts in You; and in the shadow of Your wings I will make my refuge, until these calamities have passed by" (Psalm 57:1). "Have mercy on me, O Lord, for I am weak; O

Lord, heal me, for my bones are troubled" (Psalm 6:2).

Lord, I praise You and thank You that You never change and my life in eternity with You is secure. I lift up to You my affliction this day (name it before the Lord), and I ask You to take it away. I know You are able to do this, and I know You are a God of mercy. Have mercy upon me, Lord. Thank You for Your grace and mercy toward me. "I will extol You, O LORD, for You have lifted me up . . . O LORD my God, I cried out to You, and You healed me" (Psalm 30:1-2). "Bless the LORD, O my soul, and forget not all His benefits: who forgives all your iniquities, who heals all your diseases" (Psalm 103:2-3). I know that it is Your will that shall be done, and I trust You in that too. Should You decide not to heal me in the way and time I desire, I trust that You will bring good out of my suffering and that it will glorify You.

God Gave Me His Word

Heal me, O LORD, and I shall be healed; save me, and I shall be saved, for You are my praise.

Jeremiah 17:14

331

He sent His word and healed them, and delivered them from their destructions.

Psalm 107:20

But He was wounded for our transgressions, He was bruised for our iniquities; the chastisement for our peace was upon Him, and by His stripes we are healed.

Isaiah 53:5

He Himself took our infirmities and bore our sicknesses.

Matthew 8:17

Is anyone among you suffering? Let him pray. Is anyone cheerful? Let him sing psalms. Is anyone among you sick? Let him call for the elders of the church, and let them pray over him, anointing him with oil in the name of the Lord. And the prayer of faith will save the sick, and the Lord will raise him up. And if he has committed sins, he will be forgiven. Confess your trespasses to one another, and pray for one another, that you may be healed. The effective, fervent prayer of a righteous man avails much.

James 5:13-16

Giving It Some Further Thought

1. Read 2 Corinthians 5:1 in your Bible. What is our ultimate hope when we are not healed as we prayed?

2. Read Isaiah 58:6-12 in your Bible. According to these verses, what are some of the things that can happen when we observe the fast God has chosen and pray?

3. Read Psalm 102:1-12 in your Bible. In this prayer David is afflicted and over-whelmed with his condition. What did he do in the midst of it?

4. Have you ever felt the way David did in the above verses? Do you feel that way now? What can you praise God for in the midst of your suffering?

5. Read Exodus 15:26 and Jeremiah 30:17 in your Bible. What are the promises of God in these verses? How do they give you hope?

19

When I Struggle with Doubt

I doubt there is anyone who never struggles with doubt at one time or another. How many of us *always* "walk by faith, not by sight" (2 Corinthians 5:7)? But I have discovered that having doubt is not the greatest sin. Not having faith is.

We can have doubt and still step out in faith. I have doubt about my abilities, but I still step out in faith to do the things God has called me to do. My doubt about what *I* can do increases my faith about what *He* can do. I know that "I can do all things through Christ who strengthens me" (Philippians 4:13). I know that "all things are possible to him who believes" (Mark 9:23).

We can have doubt. Just not about God. With God we need unwavering faith.

Too often we don't give God the benefit of

the doubt but immediately assume the worst. That's sin. Whatever is not of faith is sin (Romans 14:23). When we fail to use our spiritual eyes to see God's love in every aspect of our lives, when we don't give thanks to Him in all things, and when we don't look for His goodness and mercy in all that happens to us, we must grieve Him.

You know how it is when you love someone and all you see is the good in them, yet whenever you give them a compliment, they don't believe you. They only see what they perceive as their faults and refuse to be swayed by your perspective. Or when you tell them not to worry because you will take care of them and handle things for them and they don't trust you. It makes you sad.

It makes God sad when we don't trust *Him*. He wants to provide for our needs, deliver us from the enemy's plan for our lives, show us our purpose, and help us move into it. He wants us to trust Him in all things at all times. It makes Him sad, I'm sure, when we don't.

Faith is a gift. God gives us a certain amount of faith to live our lives. Faith for the future. Faith in His power to guide us. Faith in His ability to take care of us. "God has dealt to each one a measure of faith" (Romans 12:3). Sometimes God also gives us a *special measure* of faith for the moment we are in. When He does, we need to act on it.

The Bible tells of a widow who told the prophet Elisha that creditors were coming to take her sons as slaves. When Elisha asked her, "What do you have in the house?" she answered that she had nothing but a jar of oil. Because God uses what we have, Elisha then told her to borrow as many empty vessels as she could. "Do not gather just a few," he said (2 Kings 4:2-3).

In other words, don't think too small about what God could do in your life. Be prepared for God to do a big thing.

The widow did as Elisha instructed her and then "shut the door behind her and her sons, who brought the vessels to her" (2 Kings 4:5).

When we offer all that we have to God and prepare for Him to do something great, we then must close the door and shut out the doubt of the world.

When the widow poured her oil into the vessels she had gathered, she filled every one of them. When all the vessels were full, "the oil ceased" to flow (2 Kings 4:6).

God poured out as much as she was able to contain.

The widow then sold the oil, paid her

debt, and had enough money to live on. It doesn't say that God did this every month for the rest of her life — it was a special thing He did at that time. And He provided in proportion to what this woman was able to receive.

God will pour out to us as much as we have faith to receive.

There will be times when we need more faith in order to receive what God wants to give us. The problem is that often when times are the toughest for us — times when we need the biggest miracle because we know that if God doesn't do something, we are sunk — those are the very times we become scared and start to doubt. And if our prayers haven't been answered, or we haven't prayed about it as much as we should have, this *increases* our doubt. And if we haven't been reading God's Word as we should have, then our faith has not been strengthened as it should be (Romans 10:17).

I'm not talking about putting faith in faith. I'm talking about putting faith in God and His ability to do what is impossible for us to do.

I have found that worship and praise increases our faith and not only lifts our sights to see who God really is and all that He has done, but also enables us to see what He is capable of doing. Praise increases our ability to receive a gift of faith beyond what we already have. It increases our awareness of the grand things He wants to do in our lives and the lives of other people. It gives us vision for new possibilities.

Praise is a declaration, a victory cry, proclaiming faith to stand firm in the place God has given you. Praise is a proclamation that the enemy's intent to plunder you will not rock you. Praise declares that you will not be moved by the enemy's attempt to snatch you away.

— Darlene Zschech

God doesn't like complaining. When the people of Israel complained that they were out in the wilderness and they doubted that God had anything good in mind for them, He sent fire to destroy some of them (Numbers 11:1). We need to come before God and see if some of the fires in our lives are for the same reason. Maybe we get burned too often because we let doubt take over instead of faith.

Complaining instead of praising and worshiping is a sign that we are not grateful to God and doubt His goodness and faithfulness. It shows that we do not believe God is really who He says He is. When we complain, we indicate we don't trust God and fear He won't come through for us. We doubt that nothing is impossible with Him. Our lack of faith puts up a barrier between us and Him, and we cut off the avenue by which He can bless us.

Praising God in the midst of times of doubt opens up the avenue by which a fresh infusion of faith comes into our souls. That is the hidden power of praise.

Some people have faith in faith and not faith in God. When that happens, it doesn't matter what God wants; it's only what the person exerting the faith wants. Then there is the opposite extreme, which are the people who won't even allow you to mention the word "faith" because it means you are a part of a "faith movement," whatever that is. They look at faith as a dirty word. We have to stay with *God's Word,* which is between those two extremes. According to His Word, He wants us to have faith. He gives us a measure of faith. Hearing God's Word gives us faith. God wants us to have faith in Him and what He says. He wants us to know what is true about faith.

1. **Having faith pleases God.** "Without faith it is impossible to please Him, for he who comes to God must believe that He is, and that He is a rewarder of those who diligently seek Him" (Hebrews 11:6). It's important to make God happy.

2. **Having faith keeps us from sin.** "Whatever is not from faith is sin" (Romans 14:23). It is sinful to not have faith.

3. **Having faith protects us from the enemy.** "Above all, taking the shield of faith with which you will be able to quench all the fiery darts of the wicked one" (Ephesians 6:16). We need that kind of protection every day.

4. **Having faith helps us find peace.** "Therefore, having been justified by faith, we have peace with God through our Lord Jesus Christ" (Romans 5:1). When we let doubt come in and swallow our faith, we lose our peace.

5. **Having faith helps us find healing.** "Then Jesus said to him, 'Receive your sight; your faith has made you well'" (Luke 18:42). We all need

healing at one time or another in order to stay alive.

6. **Having faith helps us to live successfully.** "For in it the righteousness of God is revealed from faith to faith; as it is written, 'The just shall live by faith'" (Romans 1:17). We don't want to just get by in our lives, we want to have lives with impact. And that can't happen without faith in the power of God to help us to be all He has called us to be.

7. **Having faith breaks down walls in our lives.** "By faith the walls of Jericho fell down after they were encircled for seven days" (Hebrews 11:30). The only way we can break down the obstacles that are erected in our lives is by faith in God to do what we cannot.

With God, All Things Are Possible

Miracles happen because people have faith. Not faith in miracles; faith in God, who performs miracles.

When a woman who had had a flow of blood for 12 years touched the hem of Jesus' garment, Jesus turned around and said, "Be of good cheer, daughter; your faith has made you well." The woman was made well from that hour (Matthew 9:20-22). Jesus healed blind men after He touched them and said, "According to your faith let it be to you" (Matthew 9:29). It is by faith the Israelites passed through the Red Sea as though it were dry land, while the Egyptians drowned trying to do the same thing (Hebrews 11:29).

In order to see miracles in our lives, we have to touch Jesus and have faith in His ability and desire to touch us. Praise and worship enables us to do that. Our worship will influence what emanates from our life — whether it be great faith or great doubt.

What do you do when you receive bad news? How do you react when you receive a bad report from the doctor after your test results are in? Does it cause your heart to sink and fear to rise? Does depression settle over you like a dark blanket of dread? If that ever happens to you for any reason, begin immediately to praise God. Praise Him out loud if you are in a position to do so. Sing praise and worship songs to Him until the grip of sadness or shock is broken. Thank Him that because of who He is, anything is possible. Pray about the specifics. Tell Him your needs, requests, concerns, and fears. Tell Him all the reasons you love Him.

Thank Him for His Word. Quote His Word in your prayers. As you do all that, you will find your faith increasing. The more it increases, the more you will be able to face your doubts and fears and say, "With God, all things are possible. Blessed be the name of the Lord."

The fact that God responds to our faith is a sign of His love for us. He rewards us for believing in Him. For trusting Him. For loving Him. It is His great love for us that causes us to have faith in Him. You know how it is when you fall in love with someone. Their love for you causes you to trust that person. It's the same with God. The more you realize how much He loves you, the more you will have faith in Him. The more you worship Him, the more you will understand and trust His love for you.

WORSHIP IS

. . . a place where we can drown out the voices of fear and doubt with a flood of adoration and praise. And as we come before the Lord, He reminds us of all that He is, and that increases our faith.

I Give God My Praise

I worship You, Almighty God, and give You all the glory that is due Your name. I praise You, Lord of heaven and earth, and thank You that with You all things are possible. The things that are impossible with men are possible with You (Luke 18:27). Thank You that You give faith as a gift to those who ask. Because of You, I don't have to live in doubt. I ask You to increase my faith to believe for bigger and greater things. Help me to always "ask in faith, with no doubting." May I never be like a wave of the sea driven and tossed by the wind because I have doubt (James 1:6-8).

I know it is by faith we stand (2 Corinthians 1:24). I want to have so much faith that I am fully convinced that whatever You have promised to me, You will also be able to perform it in my life (Romans 4:21). Specifically, Lord, I would like to have increased faith in this area (name the area of your life in which you would like to have increased faith). I know that faith is a gift from You and it gives me hope to believe for the things I have not yet seen (Hebrews 11:1). I pray that my faith, no matter how it is tested by fire, will glorify You and bring all the praise and honor and glory that belong to

You. Thank You that You have given me Your Word whereby my faith can be increased. Help me to grow in my understanding of it. May Your Word be so mixed with my faith that it will glorify You (Hebrews 4:2).

God Gave Me His Word

If you have faith as a mustard seed, you will say to this mountain, "Move from here to there," and it will move; and nothing will be impossible for you.

Matthew 17:20

In this you greatly rejoice, though now for a little while, if need be, you have been grieved by various trials, that the genuineness of your faith, being much more precious than gold that perishes, though it is tested by fire, may be found to praise, honor, and glory at the revelation of Jesus Christ.

1 Peter 1:6-7

Now faith is the substance of things hoped for, the evidence of things not seen.

Hebrews 11:1

So then faith comes by hearing, and hearing by the word of God.

Romans 10:17

The gospel was preached to us as well as to them; but the word which they heard did not profit them, not being mixed with faith in those who heard it.

Hebrews 4:2

Giving It Some Further Thought

1. Read James 1:6-8 in your Bible. How are we to live? How are we to ask for things from God? What happens when we don't live that way?

2. Read Hebrews 10:38 in your Bible. How are we supposed to live? What happens when we don't?

3. Has anything happened to you recently or in the past that has caused you to feel doubt about God's ability or desire to help you and take care of you? Do you truly believe that God always has your best interests in mind? Why or why not?

4. In what area is your faith weakest? Write it out as a prayer of confession to the Lord. (For example, "Lord, I confess that my faith is weakest when it comes to my finances . . .") Then write out a prayer of worship, praise, and thanksgiving to God for the things about Him that most encourage you in this area where your faith is weakest. (For example, "Lord, I praise You that You are my Provider. Thank You that You are a God of restoration and blessing . . .")

5. Read Hebrews 11 in your Bible. What of the things these great people did by faith do you most want to emulate? (For example, "I would like to have the faith to follow God wherever He leads me the way Abraham did mentioned in verse 8.")

20

When I Don't See Answers to My Prayers

Have you ever prayed and prayed and prayed about a situation, a person, a need, or a dream and still have not seen an answer to your prayers? Perhaps you have been hurt again and again by someone who never changes no matter how hard you pray. Or maybe you've prayed over and over for financial breakthrough, yet you still live with the threat of losing your home every month. Or you've prayed countless times for healing, but you can never seem to rise above your health problem. When it seems as though our prayers have gone unanswered for a long time, we may feel like giving up or becoming upset with God or losing heart instead of standing strong in the waiting time.

Losing heart means that you have been hurt deeply enough that you no longer have the strength, ability, motivation, or hope to keep on praying. Losing heart means being disappointed for so long that you start to believe nothing is ever going to change. There is no known cure in the *world* for losing heart.

Actually the *world's* coping methods for losing heart are found in things like alcohol, drugs, affairs, or expressions of anger. And the anger is usually at God. Because people can't strike out at God, they look for opportunities to strike out at someone else instead. A man may yell at his wife, a woman may abuse her child, or a person may take his anger and frustration out on one of his friends. The man who goes into his place of employment and shoots his coworkers is probably more angry with God than he is with the people he shot. He just doesn't know it.

Have you ever been mad at God because your prayers were not answered? Someone might respond to that question by saying, "I have been upset that nothing ever changed with a situation I prayed for over a long period of time, but I wasn't mad at *God*."

The truth is if you are upset because your prayers were not answered, then you are upset with God for not answering those prayers.

Believe me, I know what I am talking

about here. I have been there and done that. And I found that the only way out of that frustration and bitterness and loss of heart is through praise. Every time I start to become impatient about the lack of an answer to a particular prayer, I stop everything to worship the Lord as the all-knowing, all-powerful God of the universe. I praise Him for being faithful and trustworthy.

When we worship, we ascend, when we ascend we gain revelation from God.
— Chuck D. Pierce

When I praise God, it becomes easier for me to recognize my sin of doubt and disappointment so I can confess it. Worship helps me recognize that God is greater than any of the things I am praying about. It helps me trust that God has heard my prayers and *will* answer in *His* way and in *His* time. It helps me release that situation to God and trust *Him* for the outcome. It gives me renewed faith to believe again.

When we praise God at the first sign of disappointment and loss of heart, He will open our eyes to the truth and help us see things from a perspective closer to His own.

What to Do While You're Waiting

One of the worst things that could happen to a woman in Bible times, aside from the death of her husband, was to be unable to have children. At that time, infertility was always blamed on the woman, and it was seen as the woman being punished by God for her sin. It was *her* failure, and she was scorned because of it. Childless women were belittled, disenfranchised, disrespected, and even divorced. The social stigma was devastating.

When the prophet Isaiah foretold of Jerusalem's coming restoration, he likened its condition to a barren woman. He told the Israelites to sing in the face of it. He said, "Sing, O barren, you who have not borne! Break forth into singing, and cry aloud, you who have not labored with child!" (Isaiah 54:1).

This is how we should respond to unanswered prayer or to the barren or unfruitful situations in our own lives. We are to sing praise to the One who can bring to life the places in us and our situations that are dead. The One who can birth something new in us and our circumstances. The One who hears our prayers and answers in His way and His time.

353

The Bible tells of a number of women who could not conceive, yet God heard their cry and answered their prayers many years later. Elizabeth and Sarah were even way beyond the age when it was even humanly possible. All hope was gone completely. Yet even though they thought their prayers had not been answered, they did not become bitter toward God. For a woman of long ago to sing when she was barren is the same as you or me singing praise to God in the midst of our unanswered prayers. It means that we refuse to become discouraged, hopeless, or bitter.

Whenever we have a dream in our life that seems to go unfulfilled year after year, and there is no way possible to make it happen, we need to worship God in the face of it. When hope that this thing can ever be brought to life completely dies, we need to praise God for His resurrection power. The Bible tells us that not only can God bring to life things that are dead, but we are to prepare for that possibility because of who He is and what He does.

Even when all hope for our situation seems to be dead, praising God releases His resurrection life to flow in us. This is the hidden power of praise.

At first the thought of singing in the face

of terrible disappointment may seem like a cruel thing to ask of someone. *But the very act of singing praise and worship to God releases His blessings to us.* When we become discouraged or defeated over unanswered prayer, we can turn our sorrow into joy through singing praise. When we do, heavy chains of despair are broken. When we sing, we indicate that our faith and focus are in God's goodness and power and not in our circumstances.

Praising and worshiping God doesn't guarantee that our prayers will be answered exactly the way we pray them. That doesn't happen to anyone all the time. Again, prayer is not telling God what to do. It's sharing our heart and making our requests known to Him. He then answers in accordance with His will.

We are not worshiping God to *obtain* His blessings. That's not really worshiping *God;* that's worshiping the *blessings.* But whenever we fully acknowledge who God is and worship Him as such, our praise unleashes the blessings that are *with* Him and *in* Him and *because* of Him. Praise brings us into the presence of God and invites His presence to dwell in us in a deeper way. And in His presence it is impossible not to be blessed.

We also have to remember that *His* timing

355

is not ours. God's timing is perfect and His ways are perfect. Praising Him helps us to rest in that. Often He holds off answering our prayers for a time so that we can know with absolute certainty that it is *He* who is making things happen. He holds back until all hope in anything else but *Him* is dead.

Our Sovereign God has decreed that His will is for you to pray. Your prayers ensure that His will is done on earth. Not praying can keep God's perfect will from happening. Not praising can do the same. When we don't praise God, we shut off the possibilities that He can birth something new in us. Jesus said that men always ought to pray and not lose heart (Luke 18:1). He wanted to remind us that we should not allow ourselves to become discouraged in praying when our prayers have not been answered. If we do get discouraged, we should be even *more* persistent in prayer and praise. So if your prayers haven't *been* answered, it doesn't mean they won't *be* answered. In fact, they may already have *been* answered, but just not the way you wanted or expected them to be, so you're not seeing the answer yet.

A widow came to a judge to ask him for justice against her adversary. Even though the judge didn't care about her or God, he helped her because he saw that her continual asking would wear him out. How much more will God answer His beloved sons and daughters who pray with perseverance? "Shall God not avenge His own elect who cry out day and night to Him, though He bears long with them? I tell you that He will avenge them speedily. Nevertheless, when the Son of Man comes, will He really find faith on the earth?" (Luke 18:7-8).

How often do we stop praying when we should pray harder? How often do we lose faith to believe that God is listening to our prayers and will answer when that should not be even a question? Don't let that happen to you. Remember that sometimes you have to wait a long time, and then God will do something suddenly. So while you're waiting on the Lord, press into Him more and more in worship and praise. Tell Him that you will wait on Him no matter how long it takes or what is happening in your life.

How to Maintain the Right Attitude

Paul and Silas were having a very bad day. They had been arrested. Beaten. Thrown in jail. Locked in stocks. They could have had a very bad attitude about this treatment. They could have complained. But they didn't. They sang praise to God instead (Acts 16).

Every day in every situation, we always have two attitudes available to us. We can complain and make things worse, or we can praise God and watch Him turn things around. While it's always easy to find something to complain about, we can always find something to be thankful to God for too. God Himself is worthy of praise no matter what is happening to us or around us. If we don't see it that way, it is because we are blaming God for the situation. That always keeps us away from worship.

When we become mad at God, a wall goes up between us and Him. It's not *His* wall; it's ours. We don't think we've constructed this separation, but we have. Any bitterness or unforgiveness we harbor puts up a partition between us and the object of our unforgiveness.

Often our situation won't change until our attitude does.

There have been many times when I have prayed to be healed or to have a good result on a medical test, but it has not turned out that way. I was not healed at that time, and the results of the tests were depressing. I felt sadness, self-pity, and disappointment creeping in. But when I repented of my attitude and sang praise to God in the midst of it, that heaviness lifted and I felt hope and the joy of the Lord again. God didn't heal me right away, and I still had to go through the fire, but I had the peace of His presence going with me, and that made my love for Him increase.

When our prayers are not answered, often we think God doesn't love us or care about us and the things we care about. But the exact opposite is true. Nothing diminishes His love for us. I have witnessed far too many people become mad at God when He didn't answer their prayers the way they prayed He would, and they grew bitter and resentful. They forfeited what God wanted to do in their lives. While we have the privilege of praying, we don't have the right to tell God how to answer. That's *His* job. Our job is to pray and praise. We need to do *our* job and let God do *His*.

WORSHIP IS

... an act of faith where we demonstrate to our heavenly Father that although we don't always see His answers to our prayers, we still know His plans for us are for good.

I Give God My Praise

Lord, I worship and praise You as the all-knowing and all-powerful God of the universe. You are Lord of heaven and earth, and Lord over my life. You are Immanuel, God with us. Thank You, Lord, that You are always with me. Thank You that Your presence frees me from all doubt and gives me increased faith. Thank You that You hear my prayers and will answer in Your time and in Your way. You, Lord, are without limitations. I don't want to limit Your working in my life by my own faithlessness. Help me to "be joyful in hope, patient in affliction, faithful in prayer" (Romans 12:12 NIV).

I know that You have called me to pray. But I also know that answering prayers is Your job. I know that what I may see as unanswered prayer may not be unanswered at all. It means that You are answering according to Your will. Whether I understand Your will or not doesn't affect the fact that I trust it and praise You for it. Thank You for Your unfailing Word and that You always keep Your promises to me.

I praise You for Your perfection. I thank You that Your power is infinite. Your judgments and Your will are perfect, and I trust them. Whether or not my prayers are answered the way I pray them, I will praise and worship You above all things. For You are my Wonderful Counselor, my Everlasting Father, my Stronghold in the Day of Trouble, and my Resting Place. I rest in You today.

God Gave Me His Word

Let us not grow weary while doing good, for in due season we shall reap if we do not lose heart.

Galatians 6:9

Continue earnestly in prayer, being vigilant in it with thanksgiving.

Colossians 4:2

Do not throw away your confidence; it will be richly rewarded. You need to persevere so that when you have done the will of God, you will receive what he has promised.

Hebrews 10:35-36 NIV

Sing praises to the LORD, who dwells in Zion! Declare His deeds among the people. When He avenges blood, He remembers them; He does not forget the cry of the humble.

Psalm 9:11-12

Though the fig tree may not blossom, nor fruit be on the vines; though the labor of the olive may fail, and the fields yield no food; though the flock may be cut off from the fold, and there be no herd in the stalls; yet I will rejoice in the Lord, I will joy in the God of my salvation.

Habakkuk 3:17-18

Giving It Some Further Thought

1. Is there anything you have been praying about for quite some time that you have not seen an answer to yet? How do you feel about that? Are you discouraged or hopeful? Write it out as a prayer again. (For example, "Lord, I lift up my marriage to You again and ask You to heal it and make it good and solid . . .")

2. Write out a prayer of praise and worship to God for the things about Him that most pertain to your greatest needs. Tell God what it is about Him that inspires you to trust Him to answer in His way and His time. (For example, "Lord, I praise You that You are a God of love, redemption, forgiveness, and restoration . . .")

3. What do you know about God that gives you the most peace regarding what you have been praying about?

4. Read Hebrews 10:23 in your Bible. What should you do while waiting for God to answer your prayer?

5. Read Psalm 13 in your Bible. What did David say to the Lord about his struggle with unanswered prayer? Even though his prayers were not answered, what did he do? Write in your own words the praise David spoke to the Lord.

21

When I Have Problems
in a Relationship

The moment you acknowledge God as your heavenly Father, you become part of His family. He has lots of kids. And you may not like all of them. But maintaining good relationships with your brothers and sisters in the Lord is vitally important to your well-being.

A parent hates it when his children fight. And when sibling relationships are broken, it grieves a parent's heart. God feels that same way. It grieves Him when we can't get along with others and our relationships have strife. That's not to say we can't disagree; it's just that we can't lose our ability to love in the process.

Nothing is more stressful than having problems in a relationship. Especially if the relationship is between you and someone you live with on a daily basis. Or between you and a close friend or family member. The most miserable situation is strife between a husband and wife. The pain of it is inescapable. But the good thing about being in a committed relationship like that is, in order to be able to stay in the relationship and live, you *have* to work it out. You *have* to solve the problems. You have to *talk* them through. You have to *communicate*. You have to *humble* yourself. You have to *compromise*.

The cause of so much strife in a marriage, or in any important relationship, is that usually someone has a hard heart. One of the best ways to soften a hard heart is through praise.

When you focus your entire attention on God and welcome His presence into your soul and life through praise, your heart melts before Him and becomes more like *His*. You are infused with His love because you are worshiping the God of love. You are becoming like what you worship.

When we praise and worship God, it helps us to release *control* over our relationships. When we lift our heart, hands, voice, soul, and mind up to the Lord in love, it's impossible to hang on to things and people around us. That's because *true love* creates an environment of freedom and release, not control. *Control* demands all the *externals* of love without the *heart* of love.

There were so many times in our marriage relationship when Michael and I had strife between us. But we would go to church, and by the time the worship part of the service was finished, the hardness of heart that we had toward one another was completely gone. We could feel it lift. I finally learned to praise God in the early signs of "hard-heart syndrome," and I would watch praise change not only my heart but Michael's too.

While you can't control someone else's heart, you can control your own. When you worship God, the love in your heart increases and the hardness melts away. When your heart is full of love, it can melt another person's heart toward you.

Praise Unlocks Love in a Relationship

God is in the business of changing hearts if we will give Him the opportunity to do so. When we praise and worship Him and appreciate fully all that He is, and express thanks and gratefulness to Him for all He has done in our lives, and tell Him how much we love Him, we open up a channel through which more of His love pours into

367

our heart. Then His love will overflow us and spill onto everyone with whom we come in contact.

Though the best relationships have the common root of God's Spirit and are built on a foundation of love, unity, and trust, every relationship improves when at least one of the people involved develops an ongoing attitude of praise and worship toward God in their hearts. The reason for that is when you worship God, you are communing with Him, connecting to Him, and opening the channels through which His love flows. When *His* love enters into the midst of two people, the relationship is transformed. God's love overflows us by the power of His Spirit and gives us peace and enables us to have restored relationships.

When you praise the God of love, His love pours into you like a holy osmosis, and you end up having an abundance of His love flowing through you to others. This is the hidden power of praising God.

Immediate family relationships — husband and wife, parent and child, brother and sister — all respond positively and immediately to a home filled with worship and praise. These relationships are especially strengthened when worship and praise happens with each other. This can either be at home alone or in a large group setting, such as at church or in a prayer meeting. Both are vital to good family unity and peace. I have also found that just putting on a worship album to play in the house can change the atmosphere in the home immediately because it changes the attitude of each person listening to the music. If you play it long and loud enough, people will even find themselves singing along to it, if only in their heart. Praise changes things.

Worship is giving God the best that He has given you. Be careful what you do with the best you have. Whenever you get a blessing from God, give it back to Him as a love gift. Take time to mediate before God and offer the blessing back to Him in a deliberate act of worship.
— Oswald Chambers

When we work or live with someone on a daily basis, it's easy to fall into the habit of not making eye contact or looking at them closely anymore. How many couples have you seen who never look at each other? God doesn't want that to happen. When we have longtime relationships with people, we need to ask God to help us see them in a fresh way. Just as He wants you to see *Him* with fresh eyes every day, He wants you to see other people with fresh eyes too. The benefits of being in a mutually loving relationship is the comfort, help, love, peace, health, happiness, purpose, and fulfillment that are so vital to our well-being and success in life. That's why we must protect and nurture our relationships in every way we can. The way to do that is through praise and worship.

When you take time to focus on the Lord's attributes and tell Him the things you appreciate most about Him, you establish His position in your heart as a top priority. This allows His Spirit to be poured in you in a fresh way, and He will pour *through* you and into your relationships in a fresh way too.

God says we are to love and honor one another as well as reverence and honor *Him* (1 Peter 2:17). We are to be humble and submissive toward one another (1 Peter 5:5) just the way we are to be to Him. We are also to pray with and for one another (Romans 1:9). We are to esteem one another as God's beautiful creation. And we are not to grumble and complain against one another or there will be consequences (James 5:9).

Nothing is worse than having someone

say something bad about you — especially if it is a family member, a close friend, or a brother or sister in the Lord. And it hurts terribly when what they are saying about you isn't true. When people say untrue and vicious things about you, praise God that He is a God of truth and the truth will be revealed. Thank Him that you will see His goodness prevail in the situation (Psalm 27:11-13).

The Bible says, "Do not take to heart everything people say" (Ecclesiastes 7:21-22). Don't take the unloving or inconsiderate things people say to you or about you too seriously. When that happens, come before the Lord in worship and wait on Him to strengthen your heart and give you peace in the midst of it (Psalm 27:14). Focus on the love and goodness of God instead. That's where you will find the power to transform your relationships.

What to Do With a Problem Relationship

I once had a relationship with someone very important to me that became severed for several years. She suddenly stopped speaking to me, and there seemed to be no way to reconcile the problem. I didn't even

371

know what the problem was, and that person did not want to tell me. Because she was very important to me, I continued to pray fervently about the situation and asked God to bring restoration. Every time I prayed, I thanked God for her. I praised Him for creating her and allowing me to be part of her life. I released her to the Lord and let go of my desire to want to fix the situation. As I continued doing that, I began to see things from God's perspective and hers as well.

In the process, God did a major work in each of our hearts and grew us up in Him. We were eventually able to see the other's needs, vulnerabilities, perspectives, frailties, hurts, and personalities with new eyes. We were also able to see where we ourselves had been at fault. I saw how I had been insensitive to her needs, not knowing or fully understanding what were her hurts and desires and feelings. I expected her to want the same things I did, and she didn't at all. And she saw how she had blamed me for things that I had absolutely no control over.

One day, in an entirely unplanned meeting, we had the opportunity to apologize for anything we had done to offend the other. Our hearts were completely open to talking everything out, and the reasons the breach happened seemed so minor because now we had perspective on the bigger picture. We saw how our relationship was far more important than the reasons that had divided us. It has now been restored to be stronger than it ever was before.

The enemy of your soul wants to destroy your relationships. He realizes how vital they are to your success and well-being. He knows that "every kingdom divided against itself is brought to desolation, and a house divided against a house falls" (Luke 11:17). That's why we can't allow our house of relationships to crumble. We must take a stand against his schemes. It is our personal responsibility to see that our relationships are brought under the lordship of Jesus Christ by lifting them up in prayer and thanking God for each one of them.

If you have a serious problem in a relationship, ask God to repair and heal it. Then every time you think of that person, praise God for him or her. Thank Him for bringing them into the world and for all the good things you can think of about them. Praise Him that He is a God of restoration and redemption, and thank Him that He can redeem anything. He can even redeem the words you shouldn't have said or the damaging and hurtful things someone did to you.

Thank God that *He* is in charge of your relationships and *not* the enemy. Thank Him that *His* will is going to be done in your relationships and not the enemy's. Thank Him that even when someone tells lies about you, His truth will prevail. Thank Him that He enables you to forgive frequently and completely.

We all want someone to say, "I love you completely just the way you are. You don't have to perform for me, strive for me, or turn yourself inside out trying to please me. You don't ever have to be insecure about my love for you. It is eternal and will always be there for you. I will love you completely, and my love will make you feel complete. Because I see the beauty in you, my love will make you feel beautiful. My love will give you the confidence you need to do anything you need to do. My love will help you move into your destiny and fulfill your purpose."

I finally realized that God is the only one in the world who can ever say those things and back them up.

It's only when we open up our heart to receive all of God's love that we can stop putting so much pressure on other people to love us the way we want to be loved. It's only when we start loving Him with all of our being that we can receive all the love He has for us. And then we can start loving others the way He wants us to.

Keep in mind that the only things that last forever are God, His Word, and His people. We need to be very careful with all three.

WORSHIP IS

. . . letting go of all else and lifting our hands to God in an act of love, surrender, and exaltation, and letting His love flow into our heart.

I Give God My Praise

Lord, I worship You. I praise You, precious God of love, and thank You that You have poured out Your love on me. I lift my heart to You and ask You to fill it so full of Your unfailing and unconditional love that it overflows onto others. Thank You, Lord, that You are the God who makes all things new, even our relationships. You can put new love in our heart. You can revive love that has died and make love live again.

I give all of my relationships to You and thank You for them. For those who are closest and most important to me, and those that are most challenging and difficult, enable me to love them the way You do. I especially want to thank You right now for my relationship with (<u>name of person or persons you are most concerned about now</u>). Help us to draw closer to one another. Help me to fulfill Your Word and love them as I love myself (Matthew 19:19). Enable me to honor them (1 Peter 2:17) and be humble and submissive before them (1 Peter 5:5). I praise You as the God of restoration, for I know You can restore my relationships to complete wholeness. Help me to be in unity with others and to be compassionate, loving, tenderhearted, and courteous, "not returning evil for evil," but rather only giving blessings to them (1 Peter 3:8-9).

I praise You as my Creator and recognize that You created all the people with whom I am in relationship. You are their heavenly Father just as You are mine. They are my brothers and sisters, and You love and forgive them as You love and forgive me. You laid down Your life for them as You laid it down for me. You have a purpose for their lives just as You have for mine. Help me to love them as You love me.

God Gave Me His Word

A new commandment I give to you, that you love one another; as I have loved you, that you also love one another.

John 13:34

Owe no one anything except to love one another, for he who loves another has fulfilled the law.

Romans 13:8

No one has seen God at any time. If we love one another, God abides in us, and His love has been perfected in us. By this we know that we abide in Him, and He in us, because He has given us of His Spirit. And we have seen and testify that the Father has sent the Son as Savior of the world. Whoever confesses that Jesus is the Son of God, God abides in him, and he in God. And we have known and believed the love that God has for us. God is love, and he who abides in love abides in God, and God in him.

1 John 4:12-16

Let us love one another, for love is of

God; and everyone who loves is born of
God and knows God.

1 John 4:7

Since you have purified your souls in
obeying the truth through the Spirit in
sincere love of the brethren, love one another fervently with a pure heart.

1 Peter 1:22

Giving It Some Further Thought

1. Read Ecclesiastes 4:9-12 in your Bible.
   Describe in your own words why relationships are important according to
   these verses.

2. Read Psalm 27:12-14 in your Bible.
   How did David respond when people
   said bad things about him? What kept
   him from losing heart? How should we
   respond?

3. Read 1 John 3:16 in your Bible. How are we to treat our relationships? Why? In what ways can we lay down our lives for others? (Remember Jesus paid the ultimate price, so John is not talking about *us* dying. He is talking about us making a sacrifice for others.)

4. Do you have a relationship in your life that is especially difficult or troubling for you right now? What is the condition of that relationship? What good seeds have you sown into that relationship in the past? (For example, "I have spent a lot of time or resources on them. I have encouraged them. I have kept in close contact with them. I have been kind and loving toward them. I have told them how much I care about them. I pray for them often . . .") What could you praise God for in that relationship right now?

5. What good seeds could you sow into all your relationships that would make a big difference in each of them? (For example, "I could call them more often to see how they are or if they need anything. I could tell them how important they are to me. I could pray for them every day . . .") Write out a prayer of praise to God for those people in your life, and ask Him to fill you so full of His love that it overflows onto them.

22

When I Need to Forgive

Four hundred and ninety times!

That's a lot of times to forgive someone. Yet that's what Jesus said to do.

When His disciples asked Jesus if seven times were enough to forgive a person, He told them *seventy times seven* was more like it (Matthew 18:21-22).

I don't think Jesus is saying we should keep a close count, and then once we reach four hundred and ninety-*ONE* we can stop forgiving. He knows we would probably be ready to strangle the person about the fiftieth time we had to forgive them anyway. What Jesus is saying is just keep on forgiving as many times as necessary. Because that is, after all, what He does with *us*.

Jesus illustrated this with a story about a man who owed a king a huge sum of money. It would be like you or me owing a half billion dollars to the IRS. It is such an enormous amount that it would be unpayable. This happened back in the days when there was a debtor's prison. If you couldn't pay your bills, you were thrown in jail until you could. How impossible is that?

This man who owed the money humbled himself before the king and begged him to have compassion. When the king saw his humility, he had mercy and completely forgave him the huge debt. That would be like you or me going to the IRS office and asking them to release us from our half billion dollars of debt. What are the chances of that happening? How grateful would you be if the IRS forgave whatever you owed in taxes for the rest of your life? You would want to celebrate. You would take your family and friends out to dinner. You would tell everyone how much you loved them, even people you didn't know. And you would forgive anything anyone had ever done to you or owed you.

But not this man.

After he was forgiven by the king for his huge debt, he went immediately to find one of his coworkers who owed him a tiny amount of money and said, "Pay up now or I'll sue you and make sure you go to prison."

Even though his coworker begged the

man for more time to pay off his debt, the man refused to wait and had him thrown in jail.

That would be like you or me leaving the IRS office and, after just having a half billion dollars in back taxes removed completely from our bill, calling up one of the people we work with and saying, "Pay me the $2.35 you owe me for lunch last week or I will have you arrested." And when our coworker begged us to wait until Friday when he received his paycheck, we said no and called the police.

When the king found out this man had done that to his fellow worker, he was very angry. He said, "Should you not also have had compassion on your fellow servant, just as I had pity on you?" (Matthew 18:33). The king was so angry, in fact, that he had this selfish man put in prison and tortured.

Listening to this story we might think, *What is the matter with a man who is forgiven such a huge debt and yet won't forgive his coworker such a small one? He deserves to be punished. I certainly would never do that!*

But Jesus drops the bomb when He says that it is the *same* with forgiveness. "So My heavenly Father also will do to you if each of you, from his heart, does not forgive his brother his trespasses" (Matthew 18:35).

383

If we don't forgive others when we have been for-
given so much, we too will be locked up and tor-
tured in our own soul.

There is torture in not forgiving.
Unforgiveness imprisons us. It shuts off
lines of communication between us and
God. It makes us miserable. It's too easy for
us to forget all that God has forgiven us and
get petty with others. I am by no means sug-
gesting that all unforgiveness is for petty
reasons. Far too often the things that
happen to us are serious, and their impact
and consequences are major. Forgiving at
these times doesn't come easy or naturally.
But, thank God, He helps us in that too.

Praising God Helps Us Forgive Others

When we worship God and praise Him
for how much He has forgiven *us,* it makes
forgiving *others* easier. When we come in
contact and connect with the One who is the
Forgiver, forgiveness rubs off on us. That's
because we become what we worship.

When we worship God, our merciful Forgiver,
we come under the influence of His Spirit of for-
giveness, and He gives us the capacity to forgive
others. This is the hidden power of praise.

When we *don't* forgive others, it ties us to

them. We are never free of them or the memory of the situation. And our unforgiveness tortures us by making us miserable and sick in our minds, emotions, and bodies. When we have hatred, anger, or bitterness toward someone, we have a hard time facing God. There is nothing that hinders intimate relationship with God more than unforgiveness. It separates us from Him, and He won't listen to our prayers. "Your iniquities have separated you from your God; and your sins have hidden His face from you, so that He will not hear" (Isaiah 59:2). When our heart is filled with unforgiveness, our relationship with Him doesn't feel warm, open, and full.

As long as there are other people in our lives, forgiveness will be an ongoing issue. If we don't realize that, we can be fooled into thinking we are the most forgiving person in the world. Until one day God shows us what we have been harboring in our heart. Perhaps someone has hurt us in the past — intentionally or not — and we think we have forgiven them and let it go. That is, until one weak moment when the truth comes out.

Don't feel bad if that happens to you because it happens to *all* of us. Unforgiveness is a natural human emotion. Forgiveness is supernatural. Of course, you have to be *willing* to forgive, but in order to *truly* forgive, you need the Lord's enablement. That's why you should praise God for His forgiveness and ask Him to show you any unforgiveness in you so you can confess it as sin.

Forgiving someone is easier when we understand how much God has forgiven us. The more we praise God for His forgiveness, the more we understand its magnitude. The more we think seriously about where we would be *without* it, the more grateful we are *for* it.

There was one particular time when I needed to forgive someone who had done something wrong to me. It wasn't just an insignificant mistake; it was a major violation. I actually could have had the person arrested. But I saw that my response to this situation was key. Would I act in forgiveness and the love of God, or would I have to set things straight, express my anger, hurt, and disappointment? And then make sure there was retribution? My response would set the tone that would affect everyone with any knowledge of the details. I knew I didn't have it in my flesh to just let it go, but I also knew God could help me. As I praised Him for His forgiveness toward me, I felt the release I needed to just let *Him* take care of it. And I'm glad I did, because that person later came to know the Lord and told me it was my love and mercy toward them during that time that opened their heart to receive Jesus.

We all have to learn to forgive on a *daily basis.* Not only do we have to forgive *others* for offenses against us, we have to forgive *ourselves* for not being perfect. And we have to forgive *God* when we blame Him for things that happen — or *don't* happen.

Often we blame God for things we think He should have done or could have prevented. We don't like to think we have anything in our heart against Him, but we are better at holding things against God than we realize. Ask God to show you if you are blaming Him for anything. Don't shut off what He wants to do in your life by having less than a forgiving heart.

True worship can only take place when we agree to God sitting not only on His throne in the center of the universe, but on the throne that stands in the center of our heart.

— Robert Colman

Forgiveness is a decision we make. It's something we choose to do. We don't *accidentally* forgive someone without realizing it. But we certainly *are* able to *not* forgive someone without realizing it.

The first time I asked God if there was anyone I needed to forgive, it was because my Christian counselor, Mary Anne, was teaching me about the freedom and power of forgiveness. She had instructed me to forgive every person I needed to forgive so that nothing would stand in the way of all God had for me. I especially forgave my mentally ill mother for being abusive to me when I was young. I had years and layers of not forgiving her to bring before God in order to be set free.

The day I asked God about whether there was anyone else I needed to forgive, I did it more as a mere formality. Mary Anne told me she thought I needed to forgive my dad, but I didn't agree. (Though I shared this story earlier, let me share it again here in the context of this chapter.)

"Forgive him for what?" I said. "He wasn't the abuser."

"Just ask God about it. If there is anything there, He will tell you," she said, and she let it go at that.

So I did ask God, thinking He would

surely say, "There is absolutely no one you need to forgive, my good and faithful servant, but what a wonderful person you are to ask."

I was wrong. Instantly I was struck through my heart with the truth. In that moment I suddenly saw the whole picture. I had never forgiven my dad for not protecting me from my mother. And he was the only one who could. In all those years, my father had never rescued me from my mother's insanity, and I had held this against him without even realizing it.

That realization caused me to convulse with sobs, and I immediately confessed my lack of forgiveness toward my dad. I thanked God for releasing me from all the bitterness I had kept inside. When I did that, I felt a freedom and peace in my spirit like I had never known before. In retrospect, I believe that if I had not asked God to reveal any unforgiveness in my heart, I might never have seen this on my own.

We all can be blind when it comes to our unforgiving attitudes. It's hard for us to see them when we have them, but God will show us the truth if we ask Him. The problem with us is that too often we don't ask.

God's forgiveness is one of His greatest

acts of love toward us. He wants forgiveness to be one of *our* greatest acts of love toward *others*.

WORSHIP IS

... without full impact and power if we have unresolved issues with another brother or sister in Christ. True worship can only take place when we are free from animosity, bitterness, anger, or unforgiveness.

I Give God My Praise

Lord, I worship You for who You are. I praise You, my precious and loving God of forgiveness. Thank You for forgiving me. Where would I be without You setting me free from the consequences of my own sin? Lord, I surrender to You everything that is in my heart. Take away anything that separates me from You and hinders my knowing You better. Pour out Your Spirit upon me in a fresh new way and reveal anything in me that is not of You.

Help me to become the loving and forgiving person you want me to be. Shine

Your light into the corners of my heart and reveal any unforgiveness I have in me toward anyone. Specifically I ask that You would help me to forgive (<u>name of person or persons you need to forgive</u>). I want to be forgiving toward others the way You are forgiving toward me. Show me anyone or any incident I need to forgive that I am not aware of right now. I want to be forgiving so I will always be forgiven (Matthew 6:14-15).

It amazes me, Lord, that You love me so much that You would sacrifice Yourself so I could be forgiven completely. "Your unfailing love is better to me than life itself; how I praise you! I will honor you as long as I live, lifting up my hands to you in prayer. You satisfy me more than the richest of foods. I will praise you with songs of joy" (Psalm 63:3-5 NLT). Thank You that You loved me, even though You have seen me at my worst. I praise You, heavenly Father who is rich in mercy and grace toward me. Thank You that Your love and mercy are everlasting.

God Gave Me His Word

If you forgive men their trespasses, your heavenly Father will also forgive you. But if you do not forgive men their trespasses, neither will your Father forgive your trespasses.

Matthew 6:14-15

The discretion of a man makes him slow to anger, and his glory is to overlook a transgression.

Proverbs 19:11

Judge not, and you shall not be judged. Condemn not, and you shall not be condemned. Forgive, and you will be forgiven.

Luke 6:37

As far as the east is from the west, so far has He removed our transgressions from us.

Psalm 103:12

Be kind to one another, tenderhearted, forgiving one another, just as God in Christ forgave you.

Ephesians 4:32

Giving It Some Further Thought

1. Write out a prayer praising God for all that He has forgiven you. Be specific. Praise Jesus for the tremendous price He paid to secure this forgiveness for you. Thank Him in advance for the times He will need to forgive you again in the future.

2. Read Mark 11:25-26 in your Bible. What is it in these verses that most inspires you to forgive?

3. Is there someone in your life you need to forgive? Is it a family member or friend? Is it someone with whom you do business? Is it yourself? Is it God? Write out a prayer confessing your lack of forgiveness and then ask God to help you forgive that person or those persons completely.

4. Read Matthew 22:38-39 in your Bible. How can we show our love for God? How can we show our love for others?

5. Read Job 42:10 in your Bible. What did God do for Job when he forgave his well-meaning, but hurtful, friends?

23

When I See Things Going Wrong and I Feel Powerless

Do you ever have days when everything seems to be going wrong? Do you have *weeks* like that? *Months?* How many times have you heard someone say, "I'm so glad this year is over!" How often have you said those words yourself?

I have found that there are two main reasons why we go through difficult seasons in our lives:

Reason 1: We are doing something wrong.

Reason 2: We are doing something right.

Sometimes things go wrong because we do wrong things. We've been neglectful. We haven't been taking care of business. We've been stupid or irresponsible. We've made unwise decisions. We've been disobedient.

Usually we can figure out when that's the case. And if we don't know, we can ask God and He'll show us. Then we can bring our mistakes to Him and confess them. We can thank Him that, as our Redeemer, He will get us back on the right path.

Sometimes it's not that we've necessarily done something wrong; it's just that we haven't been doing enough of what we *should* be doing to avoid problems. When that is the case, we can ask God to reveal the truth of the situation and He'll show us.

There are other times, however, when things go wrong even when you have been doing everything right. Sometimes it is *because* you are doing something right. Sometimes the difficult things we are going through are the work of the enemy. So if you are doing something right and the enemy is trying to get you off course, then rejoice. "For it is better, if it is the will of God, to suffer for doing good than for doing evil" (1 Peter 3:17). The enemy of our soul wants to thwart the work of God in our life. He will always challenge whatever we do that is good and right and is for the Lord. Praise God that He is more powerful than anything or anybody opposing you.

If things start going wrong and you're not sure of the reason for it, ask God, "Why is this happening, Lord? Have I done something that has caused this or made way for it to happen? Have I *not* done something I should have? Is this an attack of the enemy?" Keep asking Him and He will show you.

If we are going through difficult situations that are not caused by our own disobedience or neglect, we can know that God has allowed these trials in order to work a greater purpose in us. They will test our faith, patience, and love. And the way to get through them successfully is to stand strong by praising God in the midst of whatever is going wrong.

Trials Test Our Faith

God allows things to go wrong in order to test and perfect our faith. This glorifies Him (1 Peter 1:6-8).

Having faith means that even though you don't see His hand working in your situation, you believe that He is there for you in the bad times as well as the good. It means you find your joy in Him no matter what is happening. If you are still asking yourself, "Does God really *love* me?" "Is He really *with* me?" "Does He have my *best interests* in mind?" "Is He in the midst of my *problems* as well as my *blessings?*" "Can I *trust* His word?" "Is He *always* good?" "Is He *really* all-powerful?" then you need to get the answers to these questions straight in your mind.

Answering these questions with all certainty will be crucial to getting through tough times successfully. Deciding whether you believe God's power will or can quiet the storms in your life is crucial to the strength of your faith. If you doubt God's power or His willingness to use it on your behalf, you will always feel powerless to get through the tough times in your life successfully.

When going through any storm in your life, remember who it is who calms them. When Jesus' disciples woke Him on the boat in the middle of a storm and told Him they were all going to die, Jesus calmly got up and rebuked the wind and the raging water. They stopped completely and there was tremendous calm. Then He said to His disciples, "Where is your faith?" They were afraid, and said in amazement to one another, "Who can this be? For He commands even the winds and water, and they obey Him!" (Luke 8:24-25).

When Jesus was in the boat with His disciples, they forgot who He really was. They became fearful that they would die. If you are in the middle of a raging storm in your life, you have to remember who is in the boat with you. And you have to remember to worship and praise Him for all that He is. When you wake up in the middle of the night with fearful thoughts swirling around you, remember who is with you. Recognize that your help is in Him and all you need to do is call out His name and praise Him in the midst of it.

Faith means that no matter what you are going through, you will believe in God's goodness, righteousness, and love. Faith means you can say as Job did, "Though He slay me, yet will I trust Him" (Job 13:15). In other words, even if He lets me die, He is still my salvation, and I will live with Him for eternity.

Trials Test Our Patience

Times of trial are full of suffering, trouble, distress, affliction, misery, or pain. But God says during those times that we are supposed to "count it all joy" because "the testing of your faith produces patience" (James 1:2-3).

How are we supposed to count it all joy

when we are miserable? How does that work? Why are we being tested anyway? And why do we need patience? Why is it so important? What is the purpose of being patient? In our fast-paced world and fast-lane lives, patience seems like an imposition, and it's difficult to see the value in it. God says patience makes us "perfect and complete, lacking nothing" (James 1:4). How does that happen?

One of the things that patience works in us is that it gets rid of pride. Impatience is caused by pride. And patience burns it out of us. "The patient in spirit is better than the proud in spirit" (Ecclesiastes 7:8).

When we become prideful, our hearts are full of ourselves and not of God. We focus on us and not on *Him*. We want *our* timing and not *His*. We want it *now* and not later. The perfect example of that was Satan, the original worship leader in heaven. He was called Lucifer then, and he was beautiful and perfect until he became proud and arrogant and wanted to exalt himself over God. "I will exalt my throne above the stars of God," he said. "I will be like the Most High" (Isaiah 14:13-14).

His fall from his exalted position before the throne of God was sudden and swift. That's why he doesn't want you rising above your circumstances and growing closer to the Lord. Satan wants you to worship anything but God. Most of all, he would like you to worship *him*, but if you won't do that, he will try to get you wrapped up in yourself.

God allows us to go through difficult times in order to break us of our pride in thinking we can make life work on our own. Difficult times force us to stop looking to anything or anyone else but Him for our help. Not waiting on God reveals a prideful and independent spirit. When we are patient, we are willing to wait on the Lord for as long as it takes. We are willing to stand strong in Him, no matter what comes. We are willing to trust His perfect timing for everything.

God makes it very clear in His Word how He feels about pride. He doesn't like it. We are warned that "pride goes before destruction, and a haughty spirit before a fall" (Proverbs 16:18). When we become prideful or full of ourselves, God will not seem as close as He once was.

Whenever we go through a time of testing, we need to repent of pride. We can tell if we have pride by our reaction to the testing. When things don't go our way, do we get mad at God? Do we become indignant? Do we develop an attitude? Or show anger? Pride makes us think we deserve better than what is happening. Testing times help us to know God better and see ourselves more clearly. He will test us to reveal exactly what is in our heart. "God withdrew from him [Hezekiah], in order to test him, that He might know all that was in his heart" (2 Chronicles 32:31). When He tests us, *we* too will see what is in our heart. The more we realize that it is only because of what Jesus accomplished on the cross that we are able to come before God and commune with Him at all, the more humble we will become.

If pride made a devil out of an archangel, what will it do to us?

God wants to perfect us by teaching us patience. But transformation to perfection doesn't happen in an instant. Or then it wouldn't be patience, would it? It's the *process* that perfects us. What we do in the process is the key. The best thing to do in reaction to our trials is to praise God. Through praise we can gain His perspective instead of depending on our own, which is influenced and tainted by what we are going through. Through praise we can find the joy of the Lord, and that's the way we can count it all joy.

Trials Test Our Love

God always wants to know the depth of our love for Him. In the midst of our time of trial, our love for Him and His love for us are revealed. Will we become mad at God and blame Him for what's happening? Blaming God is not a good idea, unless you are fond of lightning. It will go better for you if you refuse to blame God for things that happen and recognize that problems and difficulties are a part of life. Get used to it. Rather than question God about why He allowed a difficult situation, worship Him for who He is, praise Him as your all-powerful Lord, and thank Him that He is sustaining you through it.

God wants you to love and trust Him enough to say, "I will endure whatever You allow in order to glorify You."

For years, the church has emphasized evangelism, teaching, fellowship, missions, and service to society to the neglect of the very source of its power — worship.

— Robert E. Webber

If your usual reaction to trouble is anger, despair, or hopelessness, try resisting that old habit. The minute something negative happens, meet it with praise to God. Determine that no matter what you are going through, in the midst of it you will exalt the Lord in worship and wait before Him until you will find peace, direction, and hope.

Every time you walk through a difficult time and maintain an attitude of praise and worship before God, you will find your faith, patience, and love becoming stronger, more established, and more settled. That is the hidden power of praise working in your life.

Once your trial is over, remember to praise and worship God immediately. Don't just say, "Love ya, Lord. I'll take it from here," and then not check in with God until the next emergency.

The first thing Noah did when he and his family left the ark was to offer a sacrifice of praise to God. What would have happened if Noah had stepped out of the ark shaking his fist at God, saying, "Why did You let this happen? These floods were over the top! I was miserable in this creaky old boat with these stinking animals. And my family is really getting on my nerves. What are we supposed to do now?"

The human race might have pretty much

ended right then and we wouldn't be here today. But Noah was a man of faith, patience, and love. And he knew to worship God in all times and in all things.

If you go through a time when you feel as if you're going to be washed away, draw close to God and wait patiently on Him. Love Him enough to praise Him all the way through it, no matter what the outcome. Thank Him that He is a good God, and ask Him to show you the good in your situation, because "the earth is full of the goodness of the LORD" (Psalm 33:5). Instead of complaining, look at your life and ask, "What's right with this picture?" Then thank God for everything you see.

As you worship and praise God, you will see Him in all His power and glory. You'll see how much greater He is than what you're going through. Something amazing will be worked in your life because you are praising God through this time. Remember that "our light affliction, which is but for a moment, is working for us a far more exceeding and eternal weight of glory" (2 Corinthians 4:17).

Problems are not a sign that God doesn't love you — they are a sign that He does. And He wants the chance to show you how much if you will let Him love you through them.

Problems are a part of life. "Yet man is born to trouble, as the sparks fly upward" (Job 5:7). We will have trouble in this life, but God has the power to deliver us out of it if we worship Him *in* it.

When we go through storms in our lives, they serve to bring us to a place where God's purposes can be accomplished. Paul was engulfed in a storm that caused his ship to run aground on an island. In that place God did miracles through Paul, and he was able to bring healing, deliverance, provision, and the love and life of Jesus to the people there. In the midst of every trial, God will use you powerfully in ways you can't even imagine. He has a purpose for that storm in your life, and as you praise Him through it, you will see miraculous things happen.

Because there is a time for everything, there will be a time when what you are going through will end. But we can't force God's timing to be any different than what He wills it to be. Just know that when you are being refined in the fire of tough times, it will produce in you something that shines like gold but is far more valuable.

... praising God for who He is, which in turn strengthens and builds our faith and gives us courage in the midst of whatever we are going through.

I Give God My Praise

Lord, I praise Your name. I exalt You above all things. You are my King and Lord. In the midst of everything that is happening in my life and all that I am going through, I know that You are the all-powerful God of the universe. Lord, hide me in Your secret place in my time of struggle. Lift me high upon a rock so that I may rise above the plans of my enemies to surround me with problems. And I will sing and offer You the sacrifice of praise (Psalm 27:5-6). You are my help, and I will hide myself in You, I praise You for all that You are. "My soul follows close behind You; Your right hand upholds me" (Psalm 63:8). No matter what is going on around me, You are in charge of my life, and I trust You to bring good out of it.

Help me to endure any hardship in such a

way that I may glorify You in it. Help me to compete like an athlete according to the rules so that I may attain the victor's crown (2 Timothy 2:3-5). As I go through tough times when everything seems to be going wrong, I draw near to You and disengage from the concerns of this life. I thank You that You are able to do exceedingly abundantly above all that I ask or think, according to Your power that works in me (Ephesians 3:20).

I worship You, God of grace, and thank You that after I have suffered a while, You will perfect, establish, strengthen, and settle me (1 Peter 5:10-11). I praise You for Your power and thank You that You pour power into my life in great measure. I worship You, Father of mercy and comfort, and thank You that You comfort me in my times of trial. Help me to comfort others who are struggling with the same comfort with which You have comforted me (2 Corinthians 1:3-4).

God Gave Me His Word

Beloved, do not think it strange concerning the fiery trial which is to try you, as though some strange thing happened to you; but rejoice to the extent that you partake of Christ's sufferings, that when His glory is revealed, you may also be glad with exceeding joy.

1 Peter 4:12-13

We have this treasure in earthen vessels, that the excellence of the power may be of God and not of us.

2 Corinthians 4:7

In this you greatly rejoice, though now for a little while, if need be, you have been grieved by various trials, that the genuineness of your faith, being much more precious than gold that perishes, though it is tested by fire, may be found to praise, honor, and glory at the revelation of Jesus Christ, whom having not seen you love. Though now you do not see Him, yet believing, you rejoice with joy inexpressible and full of glory, receiving the end of your faith — the salvation of your souls.

1 Peter 1:6-9

Therefore, since Christ suffered for us in the flesh, arm yourselves also with the same mind, for he who has suffered in the flesh has ceased from sin, that he no longer should live the rest of his time in the flesh for the lusts of men, but for the will of God.

1 Peter 4:1-2

My brethren, count it all joy when you fall into various trials, knowing that the testing of your faith produces patience. But let patience have its perfect work, that you may be perfect and complete, lacking nothing.

James 1:2-4

Giving It Some Further Thought

1. Read 2 Corinthians 1:3-4 in your Bible. Where do we find comfort during our times of trial? What is one of the purposes of these difficult times? What good can come out of it?

2. Read Isaiah 41:10 in your Bible. Why do we not need to be afraid or dismayed during a time of trial or struggle? Write out a praise to God for the promises in this Scripture.

3. Read James 1:2-4, Ecclesiastes 7:8, and Proverbs 16:18 in your Bible. Why should we find joy in the midst of our trials? Why is it important to learn to have patience? Write out a prayer asking God to help you have joy and patience in the difficult times of your life.

4. Read Psalm 107:28-32 in your Bible. What happens when we are in the middle of a storm in our lives and we cry out to God? What does God do in response? What should we do in response to Him?

5. Read Romans 8:18 in your Bible. How are we to look at our times of suffering?

24

When I Long to Know God's Will

When my husband wanted to make the big move from California to Tennessee that I described earlier, everything in me did *not* want to go. Of course, I would have made the move if Michael had insisted, but he finally gave the job of convincing me to God. I asked the Lord to show me what *He* wanted, and then every time I started to become worried that we might make the wrong decision, I would praise God for His perfect will, His wisdom, and His revelation.

I joined Michael on a business trip to Tennessee, and in the afternoon after our arrival, I laid down on the guest bed upstairs in the home where we were staying to rest before dinner. As I was at peace there in the soft light of the late afternoon, I again praised God for His perfect will in our lives and for His faithfulness to reveal that to us when we ask Him to. In the middle of that time of worship, I felt a sudden very clear impression in my heart that we were definitely supposed to make the move. I had spent months praying about this, but in that time of praise it was unmistakably revealed to me. Only God could have done that. This was definitely not a conclusion I would have come to on my own.

You may be asking, "Well, couldn't you have just trusted your husband's judgment and made the move?"

Yes, I could have. And I would have, if it came to that. But in a marriage partnership it is far more appealing to make major life-transition decisions together. To be in unity, Michael wanted me to be as enthusiastic about the move as he was. He wanted me to hear from God about it so I would be convinced it was His will.

And we certainly needed that solid knowledge of God's will because of the three years of storms (literally) and trials and monumental challenges that were to come once we moved. Had we not known for certain the move was God's will, we might have entertained the idea of moving back. We would have thought we had made a mistake. And, amazingly enough, *I* was the one who had to convince my husband a few times that we were right where God wanted us.

I've had that same thing happen so many times. I will be in the middle of praising God for His perfect will, and suddenly I will see as clearly as anything the answer to what I should do or the decision I should make. I may not even have been praying specifically about it at the time, although I had prayed much about it before, and suddenly the clouds part and I see the light.

When we praise our all-wise, all-knowing God, the very act of praising Him opens the channel through which He imparts His wisdom and a knowledge of His will to us. That is the hidden power of praising God.

Our All-Knowing God Can Be Known

One of my favorite things about God is that He can be known. Some people know Him better than others. Some people don't care about knowing Him at all. But people who *long* to know Him better can and will.

Along with this ability to know *God* comes the ability to know His *will*. God's perfect will for your life can be known too. First of all, it can be found in His Word. There we

415

can find the things that are *always* God's will for our lives. For example, it's always God's will that we love Him with all our heart, mind, and soul. It's always God's will that we love others as we love ourselves. It's always God's will that we obey Him. It's always God's will that we pray and have faith. In doing those things, we *know* we are doing God's will.

God's will for the specifics of your life can be known too.

When you have to make a decision that you know will greatly affect your life and you need to have God's direction, you can find it. When you need the leading of the Holy Spirit, and the mind of Christ, He will give it to you.

Our greatest happiness and peace will always be found in the will of God.

We may enjoy going to a football game, a film, a concert, an amusement park, or the beach. We may love going on vacation. But the greatest thrill we will ever have will be found in knowing Jesus and living in God's will. Everything else is fleeting. The most important thing is to decide that it's *His* will that we want and not our own. Jesus said, "I have come down from heaven, not to do My own will, but the will of Him who sent Me" (John 6:38). He *wanted* to do God's will.

How much more should *we* want to do God's will in our life?

Another part of living in God's will is *telling* God that you want His perfect will to be accomplished in your life. Even Jesus did that before He went to the cross. He said, "Father, if it is Your will, take this cup away from Me; nevertheless not My will, but Yours, be done" (Luke 22:42). He prayed for what He wanted, but He emphasized that He did not want it at the sacrifice of God's will. We should pray for what we need or desire, but always include, "May Your will be done in this matter."

What happens, however, when you pray and pray about a particular decision and you hear nothing? Time is running out, and you need to know what to do right away; still, God seems silent. What do you do then?

First of all, do what you *know* is God's will. And it is always God's will to pray and praise Him. "Rejoice always, pray without ceasing, in everything give thanks; for this is the will of God in Christ Jesus for you" (1 Thessalonians 5:16-18). How much more clear can our instructions be? Praising and worshiping God is vital when we need to know His will for our lives.

> God is seeking those who hear His call to a life of worship. Those who heed are those who will walk in His presence. They will know Him intimately as He will manifest Himself to them.
>
> — John Bevere

Something always happens when you praise God. Worship softens and opens up your heart to the Holy Spirit's fresh infilling. You become more receptive to His will in your life. You gain the mind of Christ and the leading of the Holy Spirit, so that even if you were predisposed toward doing one thing and that wasn't actually the will of God, your heart would open up to what He wanted for you and your mind would change.

Our All-Wise God Gives Us Wisdom

We can't make ourselves wise simply by wishing, studying, or hoping for it. We can't make wisdom happen on our own. "I said, 'I will be wise'; but it was far from me" (Ecclesiastes 7:23). We've all seen people who have great academic accomplishments but still are not wise. Or people who are extremely intelligent, but have no wisdom. That's because God is the source of all wisdom. We have to seek Him for it. When we have wisdom from God, it functions all the time. It's not just a now and then thing. When you need the wisdom that can only come from God, He says to ask for it.

Haven't there been times when you just *knew* the truth about a situation or a person? Times when you were *sure* of the right decision to make? Times when you sensed strongly what the wrong decision would be? Times when you were aware of danger, although you had no hard evidence, and you knew to get out of where you were, change where you were headed, or get yourself on a different path? Haven't there been times when you knew to leave or avoid the company of certain people? When you knew who could be trusted and who could not? That's the wisdom God gives you. That's the wisdom God wants us to seek Him for.

The Bible says, "Do not be unwise, but understand what the will of the Lord is" (Ephesians 5:17). That means we shouldn't risk making an unwise decision by moving before we understand the mind of God or the leading of the Holy Spirit about it. That means we need to pray — and be *specific* when we pray. "Lord, show me if I am to quit my job and take this other one." "Lord, should I move to this city or that one?" "Lord, is this really the person I am supposed to marry?" "Lord, what is the best use for this money?"

But after you have made your requests known, worship God and praise Him as the Lord of all wisdom. Thank Him that He will reveal His will to you. "If any of you lacks wisdom, let him ask of God, who gives to all liberally and without reproach, and it will be given to him" (James 1:5).

God created us with the capacity to do the right thing, but we have selfishly sought our own way and not His. "God made man upright, but they have sought out many schemes" (Ecclesiastes 7:29). The way to make sure you are doing the right thing is to ask God to show you what it is and to give you wisdom. That means looking to the One who is all-wise and asking Him to impart His wisdom to you. Then praise Him that He has already determined to give it to those who ask. "Wisdom strengthens the wise" (Ecclesiastes 7:19).

God wants us to be in His will because He loves us. Because He knows that is where our greatest blessings will be found. But even though being in God's will is a place of covering and protection for us, it doesn't mean that it will be easy, comfortable, and trouble free. Far from it. Being in God's will can be very uncomfortable, and sometimes even miserable. Ask Jesus. He'll tell you.

When you have an important decision to make, by all means pray to God about it. Ask Him for wisdom, revelation, and clear leading from the Holy Spirit. But then, whether you receive the answer right away or not, worship God for who He is and praise Him for His wisdom and His will. You may not get the answer suddenly. Most of the time it's a slow dawning. Like a sunrise rather than flipping on a light switch. Other times it's even slower, like polishing tarnished brass. It takes a lot of effort, strength, and persistence in order to obtain the results you want, but it's worth the time it takes to do so.

WORSHIP IS

. . . lifting our hearts to God in praise, giving Him permission to have His way in our lives, and surrendering our will completely to Him.

I Give God My Praise

Lord, I worship You and praise You as the all-knowing and all-wise God of the universe. All things are known by You. You know all of my days, and You know the way I should go. Thank You, Lord, that You give wisdom to those who ask for it. And I ask for wisdom today. I know that having mere knowledge apart from You will never be enough to satisfy the longing in my heart. I can never know enough. What I need to know, only You can teach me.

Lord, I know it is Your will for me to give thanks *in* all things, so I thank You this day *for* everything You have done in my life (1 Thessalonians 5:18). Work in me what is pleasing in Your sight (Hebrews 13:21). Thank You for giving me knowledge of Your will in all wisdom and spiritual understanding (Colossians 1:9). Thank You for guiding me and leading me. Thank You for giving me understanding from Your Word and directing my steps so I can stay on the path You have for me. Thank You for revealing to me the way in which I should go regarding every decision I make. I praise You for Your wisdom and knowledge and revelation. Thank You for helping me to stand perfect and complete in the center of Your will (Colossians 4:12). Give me the endurance I need, so that after I have done Your will, I will receive the promise (Hebrews 10:36).

God Gave Me His Word

For this reason we also, since the day we heard it, do not cease to pray for you, and to ask that you may be filled with the knowledge of His will in all wisdom and spiritual understanding; that you may walk worthy of the Lord, fully pleasing Him, being fruitful in every good work and increasing in the knowledge of God.
Colossians 1:9-10

Wisdom is good with an inheritance, and profitable to those who see the sun. For wisdom is a defense as money is a defense, but the excellence of knowledge is that wisdom gives life to those who have it.
Ecclesiastes 7:11-12

Not everyone who says to Me, "Lord, Lord," shall enter the kingdom of heaven, but he who does the will of My Father in heaven.
Matthew 7:21

The world is passing away, and the lust of it; but he who does the will of God abides forever.

1 John 2:17

A man's wisdom makes his face shine, and the sternness of his face is changed.

Ecclesiastes 8:1

Giving It Some Further Thought

1. Read Isaiah 30:21 in your Bible. What are we supposed to do to find God's will? Write out a prayer of praise and thanksgiving for the promise in this Scripture for you.

2. Read Romans 12:2 in your Bible. What do we need to do to realize the perfect will of God in our lives?

3. Read Psalm 16:7-8 in your Bible. Who gives us counsel? What does that guarantee you?

4. What decision do you need to make soon that you must have the mind of Christ about so that you can act according to God's will? Write out a prayer to God asking Him to reveal to you His will in this matter. Be specific.

5. Write out a prayer to God praising Him for who He is and for His perfect will in your life. Thank Him that He is a God who makes His will known to those who seek to know it. Thank Him that He will reveal His perfect will in regard to the matters that concern you.

25

When I Seek Breakthrough, Deliverance, or Transformation

In a movie I once saw, there was an advertisement for an ocean cruise. Only you didn't actually get on a boat. Instead, you were in a small, shiplike structure built over the water. And you weren't really going anywhere because the structure was stationary. It looked a *little* like a boat, but it really wasn't one. The film was a comedy, of course, but after I saw it I thought seriously about how I felt as though I were on that cruise. My life was going nowhere, and no matter how hard I tried to get somewhere, I kept ending up in the same place.

Have you ever felt like that?

Have you ever felt as if you were stuck in one place? As if you are nailed down in some area of your life and you need to get free? As if your life has a lock on it and you can't find the key? You keep coming back to the same problems over and over? The same struggles? As if part of you is imprisoned in your soul and you feel powerless to escape? As if, no matter what you do, you can't move beyond where you are in your life?

Have you ever been overtaken by certain obsessive thought processes that keep playing over and over in your mind and you can't shut them off? Or you've fallen into some kind of destructive habit and, try as you might, you cannot get free of it?

Have you ever thought you were cruising along in life, but actually you were caught in a riptide of circumstances that were taking you adrift? And you didn't even realize your life was floating off course until one day you see how far you were from where you knew you should be? And all your efforts to get yourself back didn't work?

Those are the times when you need breakthrough or deliverance in your life. The times when you or your situation need to be transformed. And you know *you* don't have the power to make it happen. That's when you need the power of God to set you free.

We can become locked up like that in our lives because of our own sin. Sin weaves its tentacles around us in such a subtle way that we don't even realize it has bound us. But God gives us a way to get free by bringing our sin to Him in confession and repentance.

There are also other situations that can arise that are not our fault and are totally out of our control. Situations in which we can't seem to do anything to get our lives moving. You who have been there know what I'm talking about. It may be a ploy of the enemy to put a hold on our lives. And the Lord allows it so we will be forced to rise up and resist it with the Word of God, fervent prayer, and heartfelt worship. It may be something God is allowing to draw us closer to Him.

If you ever find yourself locked up like that, proclaim the Word of God, pray without ceasing, worship God for who He is, and praise Him as your Deliverer. Thank Him that He has the power to break through any barrier that keeps you from becoming all He created you to be. Thank Him that He has the key to any place you are locked up in your life. Rejoice because His will for you is freedom in Him.

What to Do While You're Still in Prison

Remember when Paul and Silas were beaten and thrown in prison? They didn't complain about their terrible circumstances. They didn't say, "Hey what's going on, God? We're here serving You, and, frankly, You're the reason we are in jail. How come You didn't protect us? Why did You let this happen? And how soon are You getting us out of here?"

In fact, they did the exact opposite.

They prayed. They worshiped God. They sang praises to Him. And while they were singing, a powerful earthquake shook the prison and opened the doors of all the cells where they and the other prisoners were locked up (Acts 16).

How many of us *sing* praise to God when we find ourselves imprisoned in our lives? That's usually the last thing we feel like doing. How much do we worship God when we are locked up in our souls? We often feel as though our jaws are locked too. Yet worshiping Him is *exactly* what we're supposed to do.

Paul and Silas were worshiping God because they loved Him more than anything and wanted to glorify Him in all things. They knew that no matter what happened to them, He would be with them every step of the way. It was in the very act of praising God that they were set free. And not only did *their* chains fall off, but the chains of *every* prisoner in the jail as well. Even the prison keeper saw what happened and was saved.

There is freedom that happens just being in the *presence* of people who are worshiping God when our hearts are tuned to it.

Whenever we worship and praise God, things are shaken up around us, chains fall off, and we are set free.

When you praise God, breakthrough, deliverance, and transformation happens. That's because "the Lord is the Spirit; and where the Spirit of the Lord is, there is liberty" (2 Corinthians 3:17). When we praise God, we invite His presence to be with us. And in His presence we find freedom. In His presence we are being transformed from glory to glory by the power of the Holy Spirit (2 Corinthians 3:18).

God told the Israelites to march around Jericho once a day for six days in silence. On the seventh day they were to march around the city seven times and lift up a shout of praise to God. Then He would give them the city. They did just as He said, believing in His word and the greatness of His power, and the wall around Jericho fell down (Joshua 6:1-20). It didn't just *kind* of fall down, or *mostly* fall down. The enormous, impenetrable wall fell down *flat*.

It is the same for our lives. We can look at the walls that have been erected around us to keep us from moving into our destiny, and they may seem impenetrable and impossible. But when we listen to God, do what He says, and lift up powerful praise to Him, the walls *will* come down. And they will come down completely.

God can do anything. Nothing is impossible for Him. But that doesn't mean He will choose to do everything possible. He does His will. So when you are praying for the impossible, it doesn't mean He will do it. He may. Or He may not. But praising Him invites Him to do what He *wants* in your life, which is always greater than anything we can imagine anyway.

The Bible says that God keeps us from trouble by surrounding us with songs of deliverance. "You are my hiding place; You shall preserve me from trouble; You shall surround me with songs of deliverance" (Psalm 32:7). Does this mean God sings songs over us? Or does He send angels to sing over us? Do the praise songs of others deliver us? Or does God use the songs of praise that *we* sing to Him as a holy covering separating us from anyone or anything that tries to separate us from Him? Only God knows the answers to those questions. But wonderful and powerful things happen to us when we sing praises to Him. Among them are breakthrough, deliverance, and transformation.

Just as music in the physical realm may strike a wavelength that shatters glass, so songful worship in the spiritual realm can shake Satan's dominion, toppling principalities of hell and extending the kingdom of God through Jesus Christ.

— Jack Hayford

When you struggle with difficult things and can't seem to break through to the other side of them, when you are unable to get beyond your circumstances, sing praise to God often every day. Praise will lift you into a realm where none of the normal limitations of this life exist.

When we sing our praises to God for who He is and what He has done, our worship becomes the very instrument He uses to set us free. That is the hidden power of praise.

What to Do When You Are Set Free

When you have been set free and are trying to rebuild your life in the Lord, the enemy will come and tell you, "You weren't really set free." "You're still the same old messed-up person you always were." "You haven't been transformed. You'll never be any different." "It didn't happen." "Nothing ever breaks through for you." When you start hearing those kinds of messages, recognize where they are coming from and remember who it is who set you free.

Say, "Lord, I lift up praise to You. I thank You for Your promises to me. I praise You as my Deliverer. Thank You that You have set me free and will *continue* to set me free. I know that all good things in my life come from You, and You are faithful to do all that You have promised."

Remember where the voice of discouragement comes from and determine to stay close to the Lord in praise and worship. Praise silences the voice of the enemy so you can better hear the voice of God.

When the Lord delivered David from the hand of his enemies, he gave God great praise for his deliverance saying, "The LORD is my rock and my fortress and my deliverer; the God of my strength, in whom I will trust; my shield and the horn of my salvation, my stronghold and my refuge; my Savior, You save me from violence. I will call upon the LORD, who is worthy to be praised; so shall I be saved from my enemies" (2 Samuel 22:2-4).

We must do that too. We must praise God before, during, and after any deliverance, breakthrough, or transformation in our lives. We can never forget that it is the *Lord* who gives "freedom to the prisoners" (Psalm 146:7). We must remember that "many are the afflictions of the righteous, but the LORD delivers him out of them all" (Psalm 34:19).

Praise God that He is your Deliverer, and thank Him for delivering you from everything that separates you from Him. Thank Him that He is all-powerful and is daily transforming you and your circumstances. Thank Him that He is able to break through any barrier in your life. We must never underestimate the power of praise when it comes to getting free of whatever keeps us from moving into all God has for us. We can be delivered from anything that seeks to imprison our souls or break down our spirit.

God delivers and transforms us because He loves us. He doesn't have to. He *chooses* to.

> ... the way we sustain a relationship with God. As we humble ourselves before Him as our Lord and King, we open up the channel through which He communicates to us and we respond to Him.

I Give God My Praise

I worship You, Lord. You are my rock, my fortress, my deliverer, my strength in whom I trust, my shield, my stronghold, and my salvation (Psalm 18:2). You looked down from above and "drew me out of many waters" (Psalm 18:16). You have brought me into a broad place and You have delivered me because You delighted in me (Psalm 18:19). You are my God and I will praise You (Exodus 15:2).

Lord, I praise You as my Almighty Deliverer. You have the power to set me free and transform my life. Thank You that You will break down every stronghold that the enemy of my soul has erected in and around me. You will break down every wall that separates me from all You have for me. Thank You that You have delivered me out of the enemy's hand, and You will continue to deliver me until the day I go to be with You. I call upon Your name, Lord. "I implore You, deliver my soul" (Psalm 116:4). I know that You, Lord, have begun a good work in me and You will complete it (Philippians 1:6). I know that in whatever state I am, I can be content because You will not leave me there forever (Philippians 4:11). I will praise You in the midst of any need I have for breakthrough, deliverance, and transformation, knowing that You see my need and *will* meet it in Your way and in Your time.

God Gave Me His Word

We had the sentence of death in ourselves, that we should not trust in ourselves but in God who raises the dead, who delivered us from so great a death, and does deliver us; in whom we trust that He will still deliver us.

2 Corinthians 1:9-10

Do not remember the former things, nor consider the things of old. Behold, I will do a new thing, now it shall spring forth; shall you not know it? I will even make a road in the wilderness and rivers in the desert.

Isaiah 43:18-19

The Lord will deliver me from every evil work and preserve me for His heavenly kingdom. To Him be glory forever and ever.

2 Timothy 4:18

And do not be conformed to this world, but be transformed by the renewing of your mind, that you may prove what is that good and acceptable and perfect will of God.

Romans 12:2

But we all, with unveiled face, beholding as in a mirror the glory of the Lord, are being transformed into the same image from glory to glory, just as by the Spirit of the Lord.

2 Corinthians 3:18

Giving It Some Further Thought

1. Read Psalm 106:8 in your Bible. Why does God deliver or rescue us?

2. Read John 16:33 in your Bible. How does this verse encourage you in your need for breakthrough and deliverance?

3. Read Luke 4:18-19 in your Bible. What has God promised to do for you, and how does this encourage you in believing you can break through all barriers in your life and find freedom and deliverance?

4. Read Isaiah 58:6 in your Bible. What does the fast that God has chosen accomplish?

5. Read Psalm 91:15-16 in the Bible. What are the promises of God to you in these verses with regard to seeing breakthrough and deliverance in your life?

26

When I Need God's Provision and Protection

I grew up poor. There were far too many nights when I went to bed hungry because there was literally no food in the house. Many people think having no food in the house means that the one thing they want right at that moment isn't there, even though there is plenty of other perfectly good food waiting to be eaten. They have never experienced the horror of going to bed hungry and not knowing when there would be any food to eat again.

Not long ago a very sweet wealthy lady asked me, "Where do you summer?"

The same place I winter, spring, and fall, I thought.

She waited patiently for an answer.

"If I'm blessed enough to get a week's vacation, I usually go to Florida because it has the closest beach," I replied.

"Oh, yes," she said. "It's only 45 minutes in your Lear."

"I never thought of it that way," I responded. "Eight hours by car is the way I look at it."

"You drive?" she asked incredulously.

"Yes, since I was quite young, actually. I find it clears my mind. And I can take my printer with me as well as my laptop."

"Hmm," she nodded unknowingly.

The conversation made me chuckle inside. I knew she had never known poverty. And I don't fault her for that. She was a very nice lady. But it made me think about how many people do not know the pain of real poverty.

In case you are one of those people, let me tell you that having financial problems is frightening. I'm not talking about being unable to make the payments on your yacht, private plane, or summer home in the Hamptons. I'm not referring to having to sell your shares of stock for a smaller profit than you had hoped. I'm talking about not being able to pay the rent on your little apartment or the mortgage on your humble home. I'm talking about not having enough food for you and your family or enough gas in your car to get to work. I'm talking about not having enough quarters for the Laundromat.

Been there. Done exactly that.

This isn't about never being satisfied with what you have or being greedy for more. I'm talking about simply having your basic needs met. When I was young, having these basic needs supplied was considered a luxury. Anything beyond that was only a distant dream.

When I received the Lord, I came to know Him as my Provider. Since then He has provided for me in ways I never dreamed possible. I have not worried about what I would eat or where I would sleep or if I had enough gas in my car or enough quarters to get my clothes washed. I could go to Him and ask for provision, and He always provided. I'm not saying there weren't lean times. There were. But they were not the frightening times I experienced before I knew Him. Now I always have the confidence that God will provide for me, and that's a tremendous difference.

From the time my children were little, I watched over them. I always knew where they were and what they needed. Most of the time, they didn't see me watching. They weren't even thinking about it because their needs were met and they felt safe. I was *al-*

ways thinking about it. I thought *ahead* about what they would need, even when they weren't thinking that far ahead for themselves. And I kept them from danger far more than they ever knew. I did all that because I loved them.

God's protection and provision are signs of *His* great love for us too. He loves us so much that He provides for us and protects us far more than we realize or give Him credit for. His provision and protection is happening in our lives every day more than we know, because He *loves* us more than we know.

God, however, will often use our need for finances to get our attention. He wants to keep us dependent on Him and teach us how to trust Him to provide for us. He wants us to know that He is Lord of the dry desert as well as of the fertile valley. And He has a purpose for both. He wants us to praise Him in the midst of our need, knowing that He will always provide for His children. He wants us to be thankful for what we have. He wants our treasure and trust to be in *Him* and nothing else, so we will love *Him* above all things (Matthew 6:21).

The Importance of Being Thankful

When Jesus saw the need to feed 5000 people, He took five loaves of bread and two small fish and *gave thanks to God for it* (John 6:11-13). If Jesus gave thanks to God before seeing what He had be multiplied, how much more should we do the same? Giving thanks and praise to God for what we have increases it to become something greater than it is.

There is a principle here that is worth repeating. Jesus gave thanks for what He had and God multiplied it to what He needed.

This is not about buttering up God in order to get something from Him. It's about being grateful to Him for what we have because we know all we have comes from Him and He will supply all our needs.

I know how hard that is when you are struggling. It's a step of faith to thank God for being your Provider and providing for you when you don't see the provision at the moment. But God has *promised* to provide for us. And it gives Him *pleasure* to provide good things for us. He provides for us because He loves us.

When we praise God as our Provider and thank Him for all that He has provided for us, we open the path by which He continues to pro-

vide for us and meet our needs. This is the hidden power of praising God.

When we *don't* praise God as our Provider or give thanks for all He has provided, we indicate we have taken what we have been given for granted.

If I ever found my children being ungrateful for what they had, I figured it was because they were getting too much. They always had plenty of necessities and more than what they needed in the way of luxuries. I was confident they were well provided for, so if they were not thankful, it meant they were spoiled and I needed to start withholding some things and help them focus on the needs of *others*. They needed to see that even what they thought of as necessities — food for example — didn't have to be as fancy and abundant as they had known it. My children are grown now, and even though they've been given a lot over the years, I know that they are genuinely thankful for everything they have.

When someone is grateful for what you have given them, it causes you to want to give them more. When they are not, you don't feel like giving them anything beyond the basics.

When we seek God and are thankful for all He has given us, we will not lack anything we need. And when we give to those less fortunate than ourselves, He will bless us (Psalm 41:1-2). But if we close our eyes to the needs of those around us, God will do the same with our needs. When we put all that we have — especially our finances — in His hands and do with it what He is telling us to do, He promises to bless us. When we give to God and to others, it shows that we trust God to provide for us. When we praise God as our Provider, and recognize where our provision comes from, we more easily open our hearts to share what we have been given with others.

By all means, we must pray that God will increase our finances and bless our possessions. We must pray that the enemy will not be able to rob and steal from us. We also must ask God to help us understand His will for our finances, His principles of giving, and how to be good stewards of all He gives us. But most of all, we must thank Him often for all of His blessings. We must praise Him every day that He is our Provider and thank Him that everything we have comes from Him. God promises that "the blessing of the LORD makes one rich, and He adds no sorrow with it" (Proverbs 10:22). What God gives us is pure blessing, and we should praise Him for that.

God loves that we appreciate all that He does, so be specific about what you praise Him for. Deliberately take your focus off your needs and focus on Him. Take time to stop looking for the provision and focus solely on the Provider. On who He is. On all the ways you appreciate Him. On the things He has done for you. Thank Him for all He has already provided. Thank Him that as your Provider He will always supply your every need.

Don't worry, this is not some means of getting God to give you what you want. There is this built-in control with regard to manipulating God — *it can't be done!* That's because God knows your heart. If you say words of praise that do not come from your heart, He knows it. It wouldn't be true worship. So you don't have to worry about whether you are praising in order to get God to provide. He has already set Himself to provide for you. He is just asking you to be thankful for what you have. To give some of what you have to Him. Some of what you have to others. And to trust Him for what you need.

God Provides Protection

I know what it's like to have lived in the "bad part of town" where people are murdered, mugged, raped, and robbed. Where it wasn't safe to go out of the house. Fearing for my safety became a way of life there. In fact, many times I wondered if I would ever make it out of that place alive. No one stays in the bad part of town if they can possibly afford to live anywhere else.

After I came to know the Lord, I found the greatest comfort in being able to trust God as my Protector. " 'For the oppression of the poor, for the sighing of the needy, now I will arise,' " says the LORD; " 'I will set him in the safety for which he yearns' " (Psalm 12:5). God did that for me. I intensely *yearned* for safety for years. He not only protected me in the dangerous place I lived, but He led me to a place of safety.

We should never take for granted the protection of the Lord in our lives. We should not enter a plane, train, or automobile without praising Him as our Protector. We should not enter a day without *asking* Him for His protection and then thanking Him for it in advance. How many times have we been protected and spared from harm or disaster that we are not even aware of?

448

> Over the years, I've become convinced that praise sets up a mantle of protection around the people of God. Praise is an atmosphere through which the Adversary cannot move.
>
> — Jack Hayford

There were so many times when I had to be in an unsafe environment, and as I lifted up praise to God I could sense His protecting presence. I have sung praise to God out loud in dark parking lots when I had to go to my car alone. Countless times when I felt afraid at home by myself at night, I would put on worship music and sing along to it. Each time I did that, my fear would dissipate and the peace of God would take its place.

One time I had to go to the drugstore late at night for medicine for my baby. When I left the store it was closing and my car was the only one left in the dimly lit parking lot. As I walked to the car, out of the corner of my eye I could see a young man coming toward me and I was afraid. I whispered praise to God as I walked and made sure my key was ready so I could quickly open the door and get in the driver's seat. When I was almost to the door of the car, the man reached out and put his hand on my back as if to pull me toward him. I turned on him so suddenly and spoke words to him with such force that he immediately released me. He looked as if I had frightened *him* more than he had frightened me.

I said, "Don't touch me! There is someone watching us, and He will destroy you if you do!"

I didn't explain that I was referring to God.

I'm quite certain that the words which came out of me and the force with which they were spoken were far beyond what I could have delivered on my own. The power of them shocked even me. It was definitely a supernatural power that I know was the Holy Spirit. The man stood frozen as I got in my car, locked the door, started the engine, and raced off, all in what seemed like one instant of time. That was the night I saw the power of God come to my defense as I praised Him in the midst of danger. There is no doubt in my mind that He protected me and enabled me to do what I did.

God always protects us from far more than we know and provides a covering of safety beyond what we realize. If God wasn't our Protector, we wouldn't be here. That's why we should praise God every day not only for being our Provider, but also our Protector. Never underestimate the power of praise regarding both.

WORSHIP IS

> . . . an outpouring of our hearts to God, not only in gratitude for all He has provided for our lives, but for who He is. As we offer up all that we have to Him in praise, He offers all that He has to us in love.

I Give God My Praise

Lord, I worship You as my Almighty God. You are my King and Lord over all my life. I surrender everything I have to You because I recognize that every good thing I have has been given to me by You as a sign of Your goodness, mercy, and love (James 1:17). Thank You that You are my Provider and You provide everything I need.

Lord, I praise You as my Protector. Thank You for hiding me under "the shadow of Your wings, from the wicked who oppress me, from my deadly enemies who surround me" (Psalm 17:8-9). "I will render praises to You, for You have delivered my soul from death. Have You not kept my feet from falling, that I may walk before God in the light of the living?" (Psalm 56:12-13).

I love You, Lord. I know that Your provision and protection are evidence of Your great love for me. I will call upon You, for You are worthy to be praised and I will be saved from my enemies (Psalm 18:3). My hope is in You. My heart rejoices in You. I trust in Your holy name (Psalm 33:21). I rejoice in You, I trust in You, I shout for joy because You defend me. Thank You that You bless and surround me like a shield (Psalm 5:11-12).

I bow down before You in worship, my Lord and my Creator. You are my God, and I am one of Your sheep for whom You extend Your hand of protection (Psalm 95:6-7). You are my refuge and my strength in the day of trouble, and I will sing Your praises forever (Psalm 59:16-17).

God Gave Me His Word

Because you have made the LORD, who is my refuge, even the Most High, your dwelling place, no evil shall befall you, nor shall any plague come near your dwelling; for He shall give His angels charge over you, to keep you in all your ways. In their hands they shall bear you up, lest you dash your foot against a stone.

Psalm 91:9-12

Those who seek the LORD shall not lack any good thing.

Psalm 34:10

He shall cover you with His feathers, and under His wings you shall take refuge; His truth shall be your shield and buckler. You shall not be afraid of the terror by night, nor of the arrow that flies by day, nor of the pestilence that walks in darkness, nor of the destruction that lays waste at noonday. A thousand may fall at your side, and ten thousand at your right hand; but it shall not come near you.

Psalm 91:4-7

I will both lie down in peace, and sleep; for You alone, O LORD, make me dwell in safety.

Psalm 4:8

The LORD is my strength and my shield;
my heart trusted in Him, and I am
helped; therefore my heart greatly rejoices, and with my song I will praise
Him.

Psalm 28:7

Giving It Some Further Thought

1. Read James 1:17 in your Bible. Write
    out a prayer of praise to God as Lord
    over your life, thanking Him that He is
    your Provider and Protector. Thank
    Him for all He has provided for you in
    the past, is providing for you now, and
    will provide for you in the future. Ask
    Him to show you if you have been a
    good steward of all He has given you.

2. Read Luke 6:38 in your Bible. What
    are we supposed to do? What will
    happen when we do that? Write out a
    prayer of praise to God, thanking Him
    for this promise.

3. Read Malachi 3:10 in your Bible. What is required of us? What will God do for us when we do that?

4. Read Proverbs 21:13 and Psalm 41:1-2 in your Bible. According to these verses, what are we to do? What happens if we don't? What happens if we do?

5. Read Psalm 34:9 and Matthew 6:21 in your Bible. Write out a prayer of worship and praise to God telling Him how much you reverence Him. Proclaim Him as your most valuable treasure.

27

When I Fight Temptation to Walk in the Flesh

Last New Year's Eve, as I was seeking a word from God about the coming year, He spoke two things very clearly to my heart. One was, *"Seek first the kingdom of God"* (*Matthew 6:33*). The other was *"Walk in the Spirit, and you shall not fulfill the lust of the flesh"* (*Galatians 5:16*).

It's not that I didn't know these two Scriptures before. I had read them countless times. I had memorized them. But I knew that this year in particular I was to hold them especially tight. Since then, I *have* held fast to these two words, and they have guided my decisions daily.

It wasn't that I was struggling with anything specific at that time, but I believe that God was wanting to do something special in my life, and it wouldn't have happened had I not heeded those words. So many times during the year, when I had a choice about what to do with my time, I chose to *seek God's kingdom first* and to *walk in the Spirit and not the flesh.* And each time I did, I received fresh revelation from God. I found something I needed for that day that I would not have found otherwise. I was saved from a number of mistakes. I was helped when I didn't even know I needed help until that moment. When I saw myself starting to cater to the flesh, I would praise God until I knew the Spirit in me was strong and the cry of the flesh was weak. In making decisions or reacting to something, I asked myself, "Am I moving in the flesh or the Spirit on this? Have I sought God first?"

Isn't it amazing how much more God knows than we do? We have a tendency to wing it in life. "Oh, I can handle this. I'll trust God for the tough stuff." And yet when we seek God first in *everything,* He shows us what we wouldn't have otherwise seen. There are countless things we will not pick up on unless we are moving in the Spirit.

The only way we can always be sure we are moving in the Spirit and not in the flesh is to worship God as a way of life.

Worship, however, is not something our

flesh wants to do. Praise is a sacrifice in that respect. It is only as we clearly see who it is we are really worshiping and why, and what the results can be in our lives when we worship Him, that our spirit and soul look forward to worshiping God.

Worship keeps us from being controlled by our flesh.

Moving in the Spirit

God wants us to live in stark contrast to the world. The world is absorbed totally in the flesh. One of the most common areas of moving in the flesh is in the area of sexual sin. Sexual temptation of one sort or another is everywhere. The attitude toward casual sex and immorality in our society has gone far beyond what most people imagined it ever could. Anyone who has any sense of their own purpose and who God created them to be knows that they cannot compromise in this area. The price is way too high. The consequences are far too great.

God says we are to "abstain from fleshly lusts which war against the soul" (1 Peter 2:11). The things we lust after, whether it be sex, material goods, prestige, money, or power, create havoc in our souls. They cause peace to elude us. It's not that God doesn't want us to ever have any of these things; it's that we are to look to *Him* for them. We are to submit to His way and His timing.

But there is a way to resist the temptation of the flesh — especially sexually. And that is to worship God. But it must be our *first* reaction, and not after the fact.

King David *should* have remembered this.

King David was the great worshiper of the Bible. A good man. A man after God's own heart. But one night he wasn't where he was supposed to be, and he wasn't doing what he was supposed to be doing. He was supposed to be out in the battlefield with his army. Instead, he was up on his roof watching the lady next door take a bath. The *married* lady next door, I might add!

If, instead of feasting his eyes on that naked woman, he had turned his eyes away, admitted his temptation to God *immediately*, gone right into the privacy of his own room, fallen on his face before God, and then worshiped the Lord until the temptation was gone, things would have turned out much differently. If he would have *continued* to stay there before the Lord in worship until the grip of temptation had *entirely released* him, the horrible tragedy that subsequently transpired would never have happened.

But he didn't. He kept on looking. He kept on thinking. He kept on lusting until his flesh had to act on it. He commanded that the woman, Bathsheba, be brought to his room and, while her husband was out fighting the battle that David should also have been fighting, he had sex with her. When Bathsheba soon after discovered she was pregnant, David tried to cover up the adultery by arranging to have her husband killed in battle.

This all began as one sinful thought.

No one ends up in adultery without thinking about it first. It's at the *first thought* that praise should arise.

David was later confronted by the prophet Nathan on what he had done, and to his credit David confessed everything and was deeply repentant. Even so, there were stiff consequences for his actions, not the least of which was the death of David and Bathsheba's baby boy. And from that time on murder, death, and treachery became a part of his family and his reign.

After the death of his baby, David went to the Tabernacle and worshiped God. Later he cried to the Lord, "Restore to me the joy of Your salvation, and uphold me by Your generous Spirit" (Psalm 51:12). He had lost his joy.

461

We will always sacrifice our joy and the full-ness of all God has for us when we move in the flesh.

Sex sins are the greatest example of walking in the flesh. And they are the most damaging to our lives because they short-circuit the great things God wants to do in us. Whenever we move in the flesh, and not in the Spirit, there are consequences. People are hurt by it. If all men and women knew the future God had for them, they wouldn't squander it living outside God's will in any area of their lives.

Temptation Can Be Controlled

You can hardly look at a magazine, the TV, or a film without having your spirit assaulted in some way. The question is, how do you walk in the midst of temptation without falling prey to it? The only way to fight temptation and walk in the Spirit and not in the flesh is through praise.

I am tempted like everyone else. Maybe more than most people. I seem to be one of the devil's favorite targets, probably because of the kind of books I write. But I have learned that the moment I am aware of an evil thought to confess it before the

Lord and begin to praise Him. This brings the greatness and holiness of Almighty God to bear upon the situation. I praise Him that He is all-powerful and thank Him that His ways and laws and commandments are good. I thank Him that life works when I live *His* way. I praise Him for His Holy Spirit, who guides and enables me to live the way I am supposed to. I thank Him for His grace.

I know that God has called me to a high standard of obedience, and I can't live that out if I am battling anything that minimizes God's truth in my life. I am allowed no excuses for sin. I may struggle with it, I may think of it, but I can overcome it because Jesus overcame it, and because of the Holy Spirit in me.

All of the selfish gesticulations of the heart come to a screeching halt when we enter into true worship. The heart is no longer susceptible to temptation because it is lost in the glory of an all-consuming God, "caught up in the rapture of love." And when we are truly in love, we want only what our lover wants.
— Michelle McKinney Hammond

One of the best ways to tell if there is something in you — in your mind or your actions — that shouldn't be there and that should be confessed before God as sin is how you feel when you begin to worship God. When you come before Him you can always tell whether you have a clear conscience. If you feel a little guilty over something you've done, or haven't done, or are continuing to do, or are planning to do, then your heart and mind won't be clear and your conscience will be pricked. "Beloved, if our heart does not condemn us, we have confidence toward God" (1 John 3:21). But if our heart condemns us, we lose our confidence to come before Him.

The only way to clear the air between us and God is to completely open up to Him in all honesty and confess our mistakes. That's how we become free from the bondage of our flesh.

However, all that being said, do not allow your lack of obedience to keep you from coming before God in praise. Don't avoid Him because of things in your life that shouldn't be there. Praising Him will break through the sin barrier and enable you to live the way you are supposed to. When you are feeling guilty, it's harder to come before God in worship, but that's when you most *need* to do it. Your worship can break down the barrier between you and God that sin has erected.

I know this may seem to be in contradiction to what people say about coming before God in holiness, but it's not. The more holy and pure we are, the more of the Lord we can receive in our lives when we worship Him. But the quicker we enter into communion with God in worship, the more we cleanse ourselves from all sin.

It is only because of what Jesus did that we can be cloaked in His righteousness. I used to think that being cloaked in His righteousness meant that we were still dirty underneath. It would be like putting on a new outfit without taking a shower and putting on clean underwear. Everyone would see the new clothes, but underneath you were still unclean. However, it's not like that.

God's cleanness, righteousness, and holiness make us clean, righteous, and holy. He's not just covering up something so He won't see the truth about us. He is taking the truth about us (we are sinners) and putting a new truth over us (He is righteous) and placing the capacity to not sin within us (the power of the Holy Spirit). When you truly get this, it will make a difference in your worship. You will be able to come to

Him anytime with greater love and appreciation because you will *know* for sure you're not worthy to come before Him. It is *His* righteousness in you that makes you acceptable before Him.

Living God's way is impossible unless Christ in us does it in and through us. And that happens when we deny the flesh, give up our own agenda, and let the Spirit carry out His.

Jesus told His disciples, the men who walked with Him in person every day and witnessed firsthand all His teachings and miracles, "Pray that you may not enter into temptation" (Luke 22:40). If even *they* could be tempted to do something wrong, how much more should *we* pray the same thing about ourselves? How often do we wait *until* we *are* tempted, are in the *throes* of temptation, or even until we have *fallen* headlong into temptation, before we pray about it?

Everyone makes mistakes. Don't let guilt over them separate you from God or make you feel distant from Him. That is the enemy's plan to keep you from all God has for you. The way to have victory over temptation is to go immediately before the Lord when temptation first crosses your mind or your path. Don't wait the way David did. Don't entertain it for even a moment. Go to

God immediately and confess it. Then praise Him as the God who is more powerful than anything that tempts you. As we worship Him, we are in His presence where He changes our conduct and purifies us from everything that contaminates us.

Repentance says that we are willing to submit to God's rule in our lives. Worship establishes His rule in our lives.

True worship is born out of love for God. God first loved us and drew us to Himself. We respond to His love by loving Him. Worship flows easily when we are filled with love for Him. Jesus said, "He who has My commandments and keeps them, it is he who loves Me. And he who loves Me will be loved by My Father, and I will love him and manifest Myself to him" (John 14:21). There is a definite connection between love and obedience.

Worship is *telling* God we love Him. Obeying His laws is *proving* it.

God won't listen to our prayers if we live in sin, but when we worship God and do His will, He does. "We know that God does not hear sinners; but if anyone is a worshiper of God and does His will, He hears him" (John 9:31). When we worship God, our prayers are being answered even before we pray them.

Expect to Be Tempted

The enemy would like nothing better than to inject something into your life and in your face that would cause you to stumble off the path God has for you. Because sin always starts as a thought in the mind, the enemy will try to get you to entertain the thought before he can get you to take action on it.

When we walk close to God in praise and worship, He shines His light on us and we can see our own sin more clearly (1 John 1:7). God wants to teach us His ways, show us our purpose, provide for our needs, and deliver us from the enemy's plan for our lives. He wants us to acknowledge Him as God in all that we do, and serve Him according to His will and in whatever way He calls us to do that. Respond to the greatness of God by worshiping Him and living in obedience to His Word.

The way to resist temptation, stand strong in what we know is right, and walk in the Spirit and not the flesh is to confess all sin immediately, even if it is still only a thought in the mind. A dishonest person will always minimize little things. But when you have an honest heart, even the littlest violation will bother you. Then speak the

Word of God and praise Him until the grip of temptation passes.

The devil tempted Jesus to see if he could convince Him to worship him (Luke 4:5-7). But Jesus quoted the Word of God to the enemy every time He was tempted. If Jesus can be tempted by the enemy, so can you.

The amazing thing that happens when you lift up God in praise is that you are lifted out of the realm of the flesh and into the realm of the Spirit. Out of a condition of emptiness and into one of fulfillment. Out of an attitude of discontent and into one of peace. Out of the same old thing and into something new. Out of the limited and into the limitless. Out of what is worthless and into what is worthwhile. That is the hidden power of praising God.

WORSHIP IS

. . . reaching up to God and allowing Him to elevate us into the realm of His Spirit so that He can set us free from the rule of our flesh.

I Give God My Praise

Lord, I worship You as my Lord and Savior. I praise You, Holy Spirit, that You live in me and enable me to move in the Spirit and not the flesh. I confess all my sins before You and repent of them. Specifically I confess (tell God anything you feel you need to confess). I don't want any sin in my life. God, help me to trust Your ways and love Your laws enough to always obey them. Help me to have such faith in Your goodness that obeying Your commands and directives is never even a question for me. Enable me to live in obedience. "Make me walk in the path of Your commandments, for I delight in it" (Psalm 119:35).

Lord, reveal anything in my heart and life that separates me from You. Holy Spirit, show me any time I have grieved You, and I will confess it to You as sin. Point out to me any idols I have in my life so that I can destroy their hold on me. Reveal the high places in my heart so that I can exalt only You. More than anything I want to please You, Lord. I know You hear the prayers of the righteous (1 Peter 3:12). Thank You for hearing my prayers.

Lord, when I am tempted, show me what it is that is drawing me away from You. If there is lust in my heart, I ask You to take it from me. I praise You in the midst of any temptation I am facing, knowing You have the power to break its hold on me. Help me to "walk in the Spirit" so that I will "not fulfill the lust of the flesh" (Galatians 5:16). Lord, I know that "it is no longer I who live, but Christ lives in me; and the life which I now live in the flesh I live by faith" (Galatians 2:20). Create in me a clean heart and renew a right spirit within me (Psalm 51:10) so that I can worship You with a pure heart.

God Gave Me His Word

Therefore let him who thinks he stands take heed lest he fall. No temptation has overtaken you except such as is common to man; but God is faithful, who will not allow you to be tempted beyond what you are able, but with the temptation will also make the way of escape, that you may be able to bear it.

1 Corinthians 10:12-13

For if you live according to the flesh you will die; but if by the Spirit you put to death the deeds of the body, you will live.

Romans 8:13

471

For those who live according to the flesh set their minds on the things of the flesh, but those who live according to the Spirit, the things of the Spirit. For to be carnally minded is death, but to be spiritually minded is life and peace. Because the carnal mind is enmity against God; for it is not subject to the law of God, nor indeed can be. So then, those who are in the flesh cannot please God. But you are not in the flesh but in the Spirit, if indeed the Spirit of God dwells in you. Now if anyone does not have the Spirit of Christ, he is not His.

Romans 8:5-9

Each one is tempted when he is drawn away by his own desires and enticed.

James 1:14

For we do not have a High Priest who cannot sympathize with our weaknesses, but was in all points tempted as we are, yet without sin.

Hebrews 4:15

Giving It Some Further Thought

1. Read James 1:12-15 in your Bible. What happens when you endure temptation and don't give in to it? What has God promised? Does God tempt us? How are we tempted?

2. Read Psalm 103:8-9 in your Bible. What should we praise God for in these verses? Write it out as your own prayer of praise to God.

3. Read Luke 6:46-49 in your Bible. What does being obedient to God do for our lives? How does it protect us? If we don't obey, what does that do to our relationship with Him?

4. Read 1 Corinthians 10:13 in your Bible. How is God faithful when we are tempted to do wrong? Write your answer out as a prayer of praise to God, thanking Him for all that.

5. Read Romans 8:12-17 in your Bible. What happens when we live according to the flesh? What should we do in order to live? What do we become if we are led by the Spirit?

28

When I Am Attacked
by the Enemy

The most ridiculous deception I ever experienced in my life happened before I became a believer, when I was involved in that New Age religion that taught there was no evil force in the world. (I mentioned this earlier in chapter 7, but it's worth mentioning again here.) They taught that evil only existed in the mind, so if you could eliminate all evil from your mind there would be no evil in your life. All the evil things that happened to *good* people were explained away by saying these people must have had evil in their minds and so they attracted evil to themselves. The premise was ludicrous, but at the time I didn't know what to believe. And I was willing to believe anything that promised some kind of peace in my life, no matter how ludicrous it was.

When I received the Lord and learned I

had a real enemy, it was such an enormous relief. It was also a major revelation. Suddenly everything made sense. Looking back now, I see how the enemy had me right were he wanted me. I couldn't see him. I didn't recognize him. I didn't believe he even existed. So he was free to do whatever he wanted in my life because I couldn't identify him. I was one of those who couldn't "escape the snare of the devil, having been taken captive by him to do his will" (2 Timothy 2:26). In fact, he almost succeeded in killing me so many times that I have lost count. But before he could, I met Jesus and learned how real the enemy was. And I learned how Jesus had not only defeated him on the cross, but He also gave me the authority in His name to stand against him.

Since that time my life has changed. I know who my God is. And I know who is my enemy. I understand more about the weapons God has given us to fight, resist, and defeat him. The greatest weapons are God's Word, prayer, and praise and worship. The Word says to "submit to God. Resist the devil and he will flee from you" (James 4:7). One of the ways we submit to God is by worshiping Him. One of the ways we resist the enemy is by proclaiming the Lord's praises. God blesses us with His presence when we worship Him, and in His presence we are kept safe. "You shall hide them in the secret place of Your presence from the plots of man" (Psalms 31:20).

You have an enemy. And the sooner you realize it, the better off you will be. You may be thinking to yourself, *Oh, I know I have an enemy. He's my evil landlord. My angry spouse. My cruel boss. My mean coworker. My perverted uncle. My crazy neighbor. The drug dealer across the street. The gang members across town.*

Actually, it isn't any of those people. It isn't a person at all. It's the devil. He is real. Jesus spoke of him, contended with him, let him think he was winning, and then defeated him for us. If he wasn't real, why did Jesus go to all that trouble?

The enemy comes to devour our lives, attack us in our most vulnerable areas and make us feel overwhelmed by our circumstances. He wants us to be overpowered by his tactics and so beaten down by feelings of unworthiness and guilt that we won't go before God in worship. But God says to "be sober, be vigilant; because your adversary the devil walks about like a roaring lion, seeking whom he may devour. Resist him, steadfast in the faith, knowing that the same sufferings are experienced by your brotherhood in the world" (1 Peter 5:8-9). We resist him when we worship God.

The devil hates it when we worship the Lord. It repels him and makes him miserable. It confuses him and makes him weak. It reminds him that he used to be the worship leader in heaven and he blew it. That's why he will do anything to divert our attention away from worshiping and praising God.

One of the best examples of the power of praising God when the enemy comes against us was when King Jehoshaphat found that there was an enormous multitude of enemy soldiers gathered against him. He was afraid, but he sought God and called his people to a fast. He said to God, "In Your hand is there not power and might, so that no one is able to withstand You?" (2 Chronicles 20:6).

Jehoshaphat recognized his vulnerability and his dependence upon the Lord, saying, "We have no power against this great multitude that is coming against us; nor do we know what to do, but our eyes are upon You" (2 Chronicles 20:12).

Our eyes are on You, Lord!

And the Lord spoke to Jehoshaphat one of the greatest promises of the Bible: "Do not be afraid nor dismayed because of this great multitude, for the battle is not yours, but

God's . . . You will not need to fight in this battle. Position yourselves, stand still and see the salvation of the LORD, who is with you . . . Do not fear or be dismayed; tomorrow go out against them, for the Lord is with you." And they bowed before God and worshiped Him (2 Chronicles 20:15-18).

The battle is not ours, it is the Lord's!

What a wonderful and exciting story. So full of hope and promise. This could be the story of our lives — yours and mine. We can learn so much from this about how to face our battles.

Ten Things to Do When You're in a Battle

1. Stop everything and worship God.
2. Praise Him for already defeating your enemy.
3. Thank Him for fighting the battle for you.
4. Ask God if there is anything He wants you to do that you are not doing.
5. Fast and pray.
6. Declare your dependence upon Him.
7. Recognize that the battle is not yours, but the Lord's.
8. Position yourself in the right place before God.

9. Refuse to have fear.
10. Quiet your soul in worship and watch God save you.

The Lord instructs us to put on the whole armor of God and "having done all," to stand strong (Ephesians 6:13). We stand strong against the forces opposing us every time we worship God. We can say, "Lord, I worship You in the midst of this battle. You are all-powerful. You are the one who saves me and defeats my enemies. It is You who enables me by Your power to trample the enemy who rises up against me."

Fighting on the Frontlines

Worshipers have always been on the frontlines. That's because it is through worship that you position God as *first* in your life.

Jehoshaphat knew the importance of worship, so he strategically positioned the worshipers ahead of his army. "He appointed those who should sing to the LORD, and who should praise the beauty of holiness, as they went out before the army and were saying: 'Praise the LORD, for His mercy endures forever'" (2 Chronicles 20:21).

The worshipers were in *front* of the army!

He didn't do that so the singers could get

killed while the soldiers hid behind them. He didn't do that because he thought the worshipers were expendable and easily replaced. He didn't do it because he was trying to trick the enemy into thinking they were facing a bunch of unarmed musicians who were naïve enough to believe they could serenade their enemy to death.

The reason he put the worshipers in the front was because their worship exalted God above all else. And nothing could prevail against the living God. The result was that when they faced the enemy with praise and worship, this so confused them that they destroyed one another.

When we worship God, we open the channel through which God works most powerfully to defeat the enemy on our behalf. We confuse the enemy and weaken him to the point where he has to flee. That is the hidden power of praising God.

If you are in a place where you need the enemy to get his hands off of you or your life or the people and things you care about, then praise God right now. Confuse the enemy with your worship and destroy his hold on you. Enter into God's presence and tell Him you need Him to fight the battle for you. Praise Him as your Almighty Deliverer and Defender. Say as Jehoshaphat did, "My eyes are upon You, Lord." Then position yourself in a stance and attitude of worship, and know that God is with you and will put you on a firm foundation.

How many times have you been faced with frightening opposition in your life? How often have you felt the enemy of your soul waging a full attack against you? How many times have you been afraid over the prospect of what *might* happen? Or what might *not* happen? How often have you been overwhelmed at the enormity of what opposes you? And of how little strength and power you have in the face of it?

It's not wrong to be afraid of what you see *could* happen. That's realism. What *is* wrong is to not seek God's help immediately and humble yourself in worship before Him. Among other things, our praise reminds the enemy of who God is and how well we know Him.

To be in the will of God requires us to put on the armor of God and go to battle against the enemy. Worship is our greatest weapon in the B.A.T.T.L.E.™ Bringing Attention To The Lord's Excellence. That is worship.

— Roz Thompson

Always keep in mind that the enemy does not want you to worship God. So every time you attempt to build an altar to God in your life, the enemy will try to stop you.

When King Hezekiah faced a strong enemy, he told his people, "Be strong and courageous; do not be afraid nor dismayed . . . for there are more with us than with him. With him is an arm of flesh; but with us is the LORD our God, to help us and to fight our battles" (2 Chronicles 32:7-8).

Keep in mind when you praise God in the midst of enemy opposition, that there is far more power with you than there is with the enemy. That's because God is with you.

Fighting to Win the War

We are not just in a battle; we are in a war. A *spiritual* war. Every battle is one more step in the war. Too often when we win one victory, we think we have won the war, so we put away our weapons and stop preparing for battle. We take off our armor and relax. But the war ends only when Jesus returns. That's why we have to continually fortify ourselves with God's Word, prayer, and praise, and learn to be always on the offensive against our enemy.

God wants us to *destroy* evil, not just try to outrun it. He doesn't want us to only try to defend ourselves and stay alive, He wants us to push the enemy back. He wants us to say as Samuel did, "I have pursued my enemies and destroyed them; neither did I turn back again till they were destroyed. And I have destroyed them and wounded them, so that they could not rise; they have fallen under my feet. For You have armed me with strength for the battle; You have subdued under me those who rose against me" (2 Samuel 22:38-40).

Praise is one of our greatest weapons of warfare. "The weapons of our warfare are not carnal but mighty in God for pulling down strongholds" (2 Corinthians 10:4). Our enemies have to turn back from attacking when we praise God, because they cannot stand in His presence (Psalm 9:3). Every time you praise Jesus for His victory on the cross, it reminds the devil of his greatest defeat. And he hates that.

Worshiping God positions Him as first in your life. It exalts Him above all other things. It reminds you of who He is and who you are in relation to Him. It prepares you for the battle. It helps you focus on the invisible rather than what you see (2 Corinthians 4:18). It shows your love for God. It unleashes the power of His love toward us. It washes away all that opposes us. It makes us "more than conquerors" (Romans 8:37).

No matter what is happening to you or around you, no matter how vulnerable you may feel about your situation, you can become immovable in the face of an attack from the pit of hell because when you worship God there is a strength infused in you against which nothing can prevail.

It makes you armed and dangerous!

WORSHIP IS

. . . our greatest weapon of warfare. When we praise God in the midst of an enemy onslaught, his attack is weakened and he must flee.

I Give God My Praise

Lord, I worship You as Lord over everything. I praise You as my Almighty, all-powerful King. You are the ruler of my life and the rock upon which I stand. Because of You I cannot be shaken. Thank You that "by You I can run against a troop. By my God I can leap over a wall." As for You, Lord, You are "a shield to all who trust" in You (Psalm 18:28-30). You deliver me from the enemy who is too strong for me (Psalm 18:17). I will "not be afraid nor dismayed" because of the force of evil that comes against me for I know that the battle is not mine, but it is Yours. I know that I will not need to fight this battle alone. Instead, I will position my-self in a stance of praise and worship toward You, and I will stand still and see Your salvation, for You are with me (2 Chronicles 20:15-17). Thank You, Lord, that my enemies will fall and perish at Your presence (Psalm 9:3).

Lord, I praise You as my Deliverer and thank You that You will deliver me from my enemies. I know that "we do not wrestle against flesh and blood, but against principalities, against powers, against the rulers of the darkness of this age, against spiritual hosts of wickedness in the heavenly places" (Ephesians 6:12). You will lift me up above those who rise against me and deliver me from the violent forces that oppose me. "Lead me, O LORD, in Your righteousness because of my enemies; make Your way straight before my face" (Psalm 5:8). I give thanks to You, Lord, and sing praises to Your name (Psalm 18:49). Thank You that You always lead us in triumph in Christ (2 Corinthians 2:14). I will sing praise to Your name (Psalm 7:17). Day and night I will call upon You to save me. I know You will hear my voice and redeem my soul in peace from the battle that is against me (Psalm 55:16-18). You, Lord, have the "power to help and to overthrow" (2 Chronicles 25:8). I know that You are my defender and You will fight for me (Psalm 7:10). And when the battle is over, I will be able to say that this was the Lord's doing, and it is marvelous in my eyes (Psalm 118:23).

God Gave Me His Word

"No weapon formed against you shall prosper, and every tongue which rises against you in judgment You shall condemn. This is the heritage of the servants of the LORD, and their righteousness is from Me," says the LORD.

Isaiah 54:17

Be strong in the Lord and in the power of His might. Put on the whole armor of God, that you may be able to stand against the wiles of the devil.

Ephesians 6:10-11

For You have armed me with strength for the battle; You have subdued under me those who rose up against me. You have also given me the necks of my enemies, so that I destroyed those who hated me.

Psalm 18:39-40

When the storm has swept by, the wicked are gone, but the righteous stand firm forever.

Proverbs 10:25 NIV

He sent from above, He took me; He drew me out of many waters. He delivered me from my strong enemy, from those who hated me, for they were too strong for me. They confronted me in the day of my calamity, but the LORD was my support. He also brought me out into a broad place; He delivered me because He delighted in me.

Psalm 18:16-19

Giving It Some Further Thought

1. Read Psalm 118:5-20 in your Bible. Which verses speak most powerfully to you about your life right now? Choose three verses that most inspire you to

praise God when the enemy attacks and you are in the midst of a battle.

2. Read 2 Chronicles 20:1-22 in your Bible. What do verses 3, 6, 9, 12, 15, 17, 18, and 21 speak to you about any difficult situation you might be going through in your life right now, or one you might face in the future? What do they inspire you to do?

3. Read Psalm 44:5-8 in your Bible. Who should you trust when the enemy of your soul rises up against you? What will God do? What are we not to trust in? What should we do for God?

4. Write out a prayer of praise to God thanking Him for all the things about Him that you are grateful for with regard to fighting the battles in your life.

5. Read 1 Peter 5:9 in your Bible. What are we supposed to do when the enemy attacks us? What should give us the strength and inspiration to do so?

29

When I Suffer Great Loss, Disappointment, or Failure

If you know someone who has never had a bad thing happen to them in their life, would you please tell me what planet they are from? I would like to vacation there next summer and get a glimpse of what that's like. On this planet, at least, each one of us will probably experience some degree of loss, disappointment, or personal failure in our lifetime. Even if bad things haven't happened to *us* personally, we probably know of someone to whom it *did* happen, and their loss affects us with grief too.

We all have a lot to lose in our lives. A loved one, a home, financial security, health, reputation, dreams, hopes, or a vision for the future. With some losses we can get over it, pick up the pieces, and move on. With other more tragic losses, it changes everything. Our lives suddenly have a big empty place in them that must be filled with something or we will collapse in on ourselves. That's the reason many people seek God more in a time of tragedy.

However, there are others who experience great loss, disappointment, or failure and feel that God didn't come through for them or this would never have happened. But the exact opposite is true. God has never been closer. God allows tough things to happen in our lives and only He knows why. But that doesn't mean it is something He willed or planned. Even if it were, indicting God for our circumstances is out of the question. That's because blaming God shuts off the very avenue through which His redemptive process flows into our life. If God is our Redeemer and He is the only one who can redeem our situation, then blaming Him for it happening is like shooting ourselves in the foot.

When our first reaction to loss, disappointment, or failure is to go to God in praise and worship, we open up a channel through which

His healing, restoration, and redemption flows.
That is the hidden power of praising God.

If some tragic crisis, loss, or failure has happened in your life, embrace God in it. That doesn't mean you have to be grateful for what happened. Embracing God in the situation doesn't make us delusional. We are not denying our circumstances, pretending that tragedy didn't happen, or believing that if we ignore it long enough it will go away. Rather, it's saying that no matter what has happened, God is still in control. He still loves me. He is still greater than what I am facing. He fully understands my suffering. And He is able to bring redemption to the situation.

One of the greatest signs of God's love is His comfort to us in times of loss, disappointment, and failure. He surrounds us with His comfort in a special act of mercy and grace to soothe our grief, despair, shock, and devastation. His love sustains us through to the other side. Otherwise we might never make it.

How to Overcome an Impossible Situation

I have suffered great loss in my life, but it is nowhere near the degree that others have experienced. What I am about to share may not be anything compared to what you have personally suffered, but I want you to know about the love and comfort of God I found because I was able to praise God *through* it.

To give you some background as to why my loss was so devastating to me, you need to know that the isolation I was raised in during my childhood affected me profoundly. When I started school, I was put on a bus and sent 20 miles away to a school where I knew no one. I was sickly, having nearly died from diphtheria the winter before, so I was fragile, shy, and terrified. I had no friends at all.

Shortly after I started second grade, my mother left my dad and went to live with various relatives. Whenever one of them encouraged her to go back home, she moved on to the next relative who would take her in. I went to three schools that year, and, of course, never made any friends.

When my mother finally returned home to my dad, I went to third grade back at the same school where I first started. But because I had been gone the previous year, I still knew no one. At the end of that year I met a girl who actually remembered my name and talked to me. Once she asked me to go home with her after school to spend the night, but I was too afraid. I don't even know what I was afraid of, it's just that I was afraid of everything. I'm not sure which I was more afraid of — being alone or being with other people. But on the rare occasion when I had to make a decision about that, I chose to be alone. At least that was familiar to me.

During that same year, my dad lost all his cattle in a terrible blizzard. They froze to death under enormous snow drifts that were higher than our house. That spring he planted crops to try to salvage our loss, but they were completely destroyed in a severe hail storm that came through. We lost everything and moved from the hard life and isolation of Wyoming to better weather and a not so easy life in Los Angeles.

In California we weren't isolated geographically anymore, but we were isolated by poverty. None of my classmates or neighbors were as poor as we were, and I acutely felt that distinct separation from other people around me because of it. Too often I went to bed hungry, and it was frightening. Rats ran across my bed at night, and that was beyond terrifying. There was nothing I could do about either of those things.

When you go to bed hungry at night, you can't wait for lunchtime in the cafeteria at school the next day. But when all the other children are making fun of how bad the food is and you think it tastes great because you haven't ever had anything so good, it isolates you. You don't fit in. When the house you live in is a dirty old shack behind a gas station and your mother is crazy, you don't make friends with too many people because they might want to come home with you and then they would find out the truth. The few friends I did have I valued, but I was never their equal. They had privileges and advantages I would never know.

It wasn't until I was a junior in high school that I finally met a girl who would become my best friend for years. Diane and I had been cast as the two leads in the school play, and with so much time together we soon became acquainted and discovered how much alike we were. Her mother was an alcoholic and inflicted the same amount of damage in terms of emotional pain and social embarrassment upon her as mine did upon me. Our mothers' conditions were a secret we shared but kept strictly hidden from others.

Diane became the only one in my entire life whom I ever told the truth about my situation at home. Having someone who understood was comforting. Of course, we never stayed at each other's houses overnight because it was just too risky. Neither of us ever knew what condition our mothers would be in. Would hers be passed out drunk on the floor? Would mine be in one of her delusional screaming fits, talking about the people who were trying to kill her by shooting laser beams at her through the television set or the bathroom mirror?

Both of them needed help, but back then help wasn't easy to find. Especially with the devastating social stigma attached to both alcoholism and mental illness. Doing something about it meant facing it, going semi-public, and, of course, there was the financial issue. You had to be able to afford it. Those options were not viable to our hard-working fathers, who found it easier to live with the problem. But *they* could handle it better than *we* could. They never understood the damage it was doing to us.

We stayed the best of friends through high school, and after college we shared an apartment in Hollywood until Diane was married. A few years later I received Jesus, married my husband, Michael, and led Diane to the Lord. She became my prayer partner, and we prayed each other through every struggle and challenge that came our way over the next few years.

When I had my two children and she had

her son, John, we got together frequently as families, and *always* for *every* holiday. When Diane's son, John, was six, she developed breast cancer, and two years later she lost her agonizing battle with it and died. I was extremely grief stricken. I grieved for her son and husband, but I also deeply grieved the loss of my best friend, the only person on earth with whom I had shared so much for so long. I know it was selfish to feel this way, but I thought, *No one will ever again know me the way she did.* Of course, my husband knew about my past, but she knew it in a way that only someone who had been there and lived through it could understand.

I took care of her son, John, for the six months before she died and for months afterward while her husband, Jack, did his best to pull their lives together. The only way I got through the grief of her death was to go before God many times a day and worship Him for who He was and what He had done in my life. I praised Him for Diane's friendship and thanked Him for the privilege of caring for her son. My family continued to spend more and more time with Jack and John, and they became an even greater part of our lives.

A few years later, I received a call from the

police saying that John's dad had been killed in a car accident that morning. The devastating news that John had lost both parents meant that I had to process my grief right away because I needed to be there to help him process his. In their will, Jack and Diane had given guardianship of John to me. It was one of those things we had agreed to when he was born, never dreaming it would one day come to pass.

John was a wonderful gift to our whole family, but the grief and the loss was again so great that the only way I was able to get through it and pull things together for everyone was by praising God through every step. Each time I felt the incapacitating pangs of grief, I would get before God immediately and worship Him. I didn't ask God why; I just drew close to Him and sought His comfort. And I found healing in His presence.

What Has Been Your Greatest Loss?

If you have ever gone through a tremendous loss, you may have thought, *Why did God let this happen?* But only He knows the answer to that. All I know is that when these things happen, if we draw near to Him in praise and worship, He will get us through. And He will somehow bring good out of it.

This doesn't mean we praise God *for* the tragedy; it means we are acknowledging His greatness and worth *in* it and *through* it. This does not mean we are joyful *about* the tragedy; it means we recognize that the joy of the Lord is *still to be found* and we will find it again. It means understanding that no matter what happens, even in the midst of the most devastating loss, the Lord has comfort for you.

The compassion and mercy of the Lord are best seen in the story of Job. He was a godly, worshiping man who suffered tremendous loss, not the least of which was his family and his health. He had done nothing wrong. He didn't deserve it. Even his friends tried to convince him that these things had happened because he had sinned. But Job knew better. The Lord called him "a blameless and upright man, one who fears God and shuns evil" (Job 1:8).

He could have blamed God, but he didn't. He trusted Him instead. His reaction to the tremendous loss was to humble himself and worship God. Job endured that terrible time without wavering in his worship of God, and his life was eventually restored. The Bible says to "count them blessed who endure. You have heard of the perseverance of Job and seen the end intended by the Lord — that the Lord is very compassionate and merciful" (James 5:11). No matter what difficult time we go through, there will be a time when life is good again.

Job lost seven sons and three daughters, and in the end God gave him seven new sons and three new daughters. "The LORD blessed the latter days of Job more than his beginning" (Job 42:12). You may be thinking as I did, *Yes, that's nice, but Job still had to lose the first seven sons and three daughters. You can't just replace a child the way you can a house or a herd of sheep.* It's true, he still had to endure the loss. But because of his attitude, God brought good out of it.

Job did not blame the Lord and say, "Why did You let this happen, God?" Instead, he said that our lives contain good *and* bad situations, and we should accept each with the same amount of reverence for God (Job 1:21).

What a powerful illustration of what we should do in response to tragedy in our own lives. God gives us what we have, and He takes it away as He sees fit. We are to praise Him for all of it. We won't always know the reason for our suffering, but we can know that God allows things to happen to us for His purpose. This doesn't make our suffering any easier, but it does give us hope for a future.

Don't give up in the midst of great loss, disappointment, or failure, or you will miss the greatest miracle in your life. If you praise God through it, you will see the birth of something new and good that would never have happened if this tragic thing had not occurred. I know it's impossible to imagine this when you are going through something terrible, but God will always bring good out of it.

People die. God allows it. Only He knows why. Why did Jesus raise up Lazarus, but not John the Baptist? Why were Jesus' disciples killed while evil men lived? Why one and not the other? This is something we can never know on earth. Jesus said that we will have troubles, but He has overcome them and will give us peace in the midst of them (John 16:33 NIV). Knowing the answers will not give us the peace we want. Knowing the Lord is what will give us peace. Whether we celebrate or we mourn, God's presence is there with us.

Remember, when you go through tough and tragic times, cling to God, refuse to let your sorrow silence your praise, and you will see how He sustains you. He will work something great in you and your circumstances if you keep close to Him. After Job's disaster had passed, he said to God, "I have heard of You by the hearing of the ear, but now my eye sees You" (Job 42:5). He had now seen God up close.

In the darkness we learn to stop worshiping our experiences of God and come to God Himself. We cease to be devoted to what we think He wants, and instead we become devoted to Him.

— Jim May

In your darkest time, God will give you a song in the night (Job 35:10). It will be a song of worship and praise, and your heart will sing once more. It doesn't matter how terrible or difficult your situation is. Every time you praise God, He will move into the situation to redeem and transform it in some way.

In Times of Disappointment and Failure

Can you think of a situation in your life

when things didn't turn out the way you thought they would, and it was such a source of painful disappointment that you were devastated? A time when you had big dreams or expectations about something, someone, or some situation, and then you were painfully disappointed when it didn't happen?

This can occur in any area of our lives. Perhaps it's happened to you in a relationship, or a marriage, where the person turns out to be nothing like you expected. Or you become involved in a business partnership that you think is going to be a great and profitable venture, and after you start the business rolling that person takes your money or your business. Or you make an important decision about something that you believe to be right, and it turns out to be so wrong you wonder if you ever had any discernment about it in the first place. Or a situation will come up in your life, over which you have absolutely no control, and you wonder, "How did this happen to me?"

We've all been there!

Everyone who has ever had a child has dreams about how that child will turn out and what they will do with their life. But if the child turns out heartbreakingly off track, the disappointment can be unbearable. That's why some parents end up disowning their children. The pain of the disappointment can be so great that the only way they can cope with it is to not see the child and be reminded.

Have you ever taken one job over another because you had high hopes that it would be a great opportunity and offer you a good future? But then once you got into the job, you found that it was not what you expected at all and it was too late to go back. It turned out to be a dead-end street, bringing only frustration, misery, and nothing in the way of fulfillment or reward. And to make matters worse, the job you turned down now seems to be the one full of promise, opportunity, and fulfillment.

People fail us, parents fail us, the system fails us, banks fail us, our judgment fails us, and, worst of all, we sometimes fail ourselves. We fail to make the right choice. We take a chance and our business fails, our marriage fails, our immune system fails, or our investments fail. When those kinds of things happen, we have to lay down our expectations and put them in the Lord. He is the only one who will never fail us.

The only way to survive these times of great loss, disappointment, or failure, and see a reversal in what is happening, is to surrender them to God, lift your heart and hands to Him, and praise Him in the midst of it all. Thank Him that He is all-powerful, all-loving, all-knowing, all-seeing, all-caring, and all-encompassing. Thank Him that He is sovereign and knows the end from the beginning. What we see as going wrong is often God's opportunity to do something great in our life. Our disappointments, losses, and failures don't have to destroy our future. When we worship Him, we invite Him to rule instead. When we praise Him in our failure, He uses His transforming power to work redemption and restoration in our life. He is a Redeemer and can redeem our greatest disappointments. We will never be disappointed in Him.

When you worship God for who He is, and thank Him for His great plan of redemption in your situation, you will see His glory revealed as He brings good out of it.

Even though loss, disappointment, or failure can be crippling, don't allow your faith in the goodness of God and His love for you to waver. His promise to you is that "all things work together for good" (Romans 8:28). That means that something good will come out of even your greatest tragedy. God's love, grace, and mercy assures us that even though we endure deep sorrow, "joy comes in the morning" (Psalm 30:5).

That's good news!

WORSHIP IS

. . . connecting with God in a deep and intimate manner to express your love and adoration to Him, no matter what is happening in your life, and letting Him wrap you in His love, compassion, and mercy.

I Give God My Praise

Lord, I worship You this day. You are Lord over heaven and on earth and Lord over my life. I praise You, my precious Redeemer and King. I thank You that You are a God of redemption and restoration. I surrender to You all my grief or sadness over any loss, disappointment, or failure I have experienced and praise You in the midst of it. I thank You, Holy Spirit, that You are my Comforter. Lord, I thank You that You allow no suffering that is without purpose. I know that You are a good God and what You allow will be used for good. I surrender to You the pain, disappointment, and sense of failure I feel with regard to (name specific situation). I draw close to You in praise and worship and look to You and not my circumstances. You know the deepest recesses of my soul. I put my hope in You, for with You there is mercy and redemption (Psalm 130:7).

I praise You and worship You, Lord. I love You and recognize that all I have is from You. Everything I have is Yours, and I surrender it all to You for Your glory. Therefore, whatever I have lost I release into Your hands. I praise You and thank You that this is the day that You have made, and I will rejoice and be glad in it. Thank You for Your grace and mercy. Thank You that You love me the way You do. Thank You that You will bring good out of my situation. No matter what has happened or will happen in my life, as long as I am alive I will sing praises to You (Psalm 146:1-2).

God Gave Me His Word

These things I have spoken to you, that in Me you may have peace. In the world you will have tribulation; but be of good cheer, I have overcome the world.

John 16:33

In everything give thanks; for this is the will of God in Christ Jesus for you.

1 Thessalonians 5:18

You number my wanderings; put my tears into Your bottle; are they not in Your book? When I cry out to You, then my enemies will turn back; this I know, because God is for me.

Psalm 56:8-9

Blessed are those who mourn, for they shall be comforted.

Matthew 5:4

Be merciful to me, O God, be merciful to me! For my soul trusts in You; and in the shadow of Your wings I will make my refuge, until these calamities have passed by. I will cry out to God Most High, to God who performs all things for me. He shall send from heaven and save me; He reproaches the one who would swallow me up. God shall send forth His mercy and His truth.

Psalm 57:1-3

Giving It Some Further Thought

1. Read 2 Samuel 12:20 in your Bible. After David's tragedy, what did he do?

2. What is the greatest loss you have experienced in your life? Were you able to praise God through it or in the midst of it? Why or why not?

3. Read Psalm 146:8 in your Bible. What is the greatest disappointment you have experienced in your life? How did you survive it? How do you feel about it now? What is the promise for you in this Scripture?

4. Read Romans 8:28 in your Bible. In light of this verse, what good do you see coming out of any difficult situation you find yourself in? If you can't think of anything, write out a prayer asking God to show you the good in your situation and then lift up praise to Him for that.

5. Write out a prayer of praise to God thanking Him for all His specific attributes for which you are especially grateful with regard to your loss, disappointment, or failure. (For example, "Lord, I thank You that You are a God of grace and mercy and redemption . . .")

30

When I Sense that All Is Well

I used to go mountain climbing. Small mountains, nothing dangerous. And it always took such a long time to get to the top. The trip up was hot, muggy, and tiring, and I couldn't see very far ahead because of all the trees and brush. But once I was on the mountaintop, there was a cool, refreshing breeze and I could see forever. The view was magnificent. Exhilarating. I remember thinking while I was up there that the mountaintop experience is always so short. Most of the time is spent getting there. And once you're there, the only way to go is down.

That's kind of like life, isn't it? At least for most of us.

We go through many things on the journey God has for us. Some of it pleasant. Some of it not. Some of it rough. Some of it a little more smooth. Most of the time is spent in one kind of struggle or another. We face a wide variety of obstacles, but we focus our efforts on trying to rise above them. And every so often things come together and life is good, and there is rest from the battle and peace from the storm. And there is no pain and the tears are not so frequent. And there is good news and the bills are paid and nobody is mad and things are going well. And there is peace in your heart. And you dare to let yourself think you are on the mountaintop. You climbed and climbed and you see the view and you say, "I think I finally made it."

You bask in it for a while, and you start getting used to the fresh air and the peace and the rest, and you think, "This is the life I was created for." Until one day when you wake up and find that your feet are pointing downward. You're still walking, but now you are headed back toward the valley. Only this is the *other* side of the mountain, and so it is a *different* valley. And once you get to the bottom of *this* valley, you're going to be climbing a *new* mountain. And then you realize that the mountaintop is just a reprieve from the ongoing journey.

The way to enjoy the mountaintop to its

fullest is to continue to worship God to *your* fullest while you're up there.

One of the biggest mistakes we make as believers happens *after* we start enjoying the blessings of a life of living God's way and walking close with Him. Things start going well, and we stop being as diligent to stay in the Word. We're not as careful to obey God in all His ways. We aren't as devoted to being in His presence in praise and worship as we once were. We stop being as fervent in our prayer times. After all, we don't have as many urgent prayer requests as we did before.

We always turn to God more when pain and discomfort get our attention. If times are tough we pray more, seek God more, spend more time with Him, prostrate ourselves before Him more, read the Word more, and praise Him more. We wouldn't think we would ever again forget to do such things, but we do. It's in our nature to gravitate toward catering to the flesh and forgetting the things of God.

Every time I have read the Old Testament from beginning to end, the thing that strikes me most profoundly is that the Israelites would always pray and seek God and repent of their sins when things were going badly. And then once things were going well and

514

there was peace and prosperity in their land again, they would forget about God and what He had done for them and start living their own way. They remembered God in the bad times and forgot God in the good times. This happened to them over and over again, so often that you'd think they would learn from their own history. But they didn't.

I used to wonder, *What is the matter with these people?* That is, until I realized that we all do this to some extent. We all pray and praise more fervently when things are going wrong. But maybe if we prayed and praised just as fervently when everything is going right we wouldn't have to slip back into the difficult times so quickly. Maybe we could spend a little more time on the mountaintop.

I have found that when everything is going well in my life, that is when I need to be *especially* careful to be in the Word and prayer and worship. That's because I know that the testing, the preparation, the stretching, the breaking, and the attack may be just around the corner. God is preparing me for the next thing He is going to do in my life, and I need to use this time to fortify myself in Him and get ready. In fact, if I ever hear myself say, "Things are going great," I stop and worship God right then because I know I am in dangerous territory.

The Bible warns us, "Let him who thinks he stands take heed lest he fall" (1 Corinthians 10:12). That's because Satan never takes a day off. He never has a time when he is feeling kindly toward us. That's why we have to stand strong against the enemy in the good times as well as the bad. If we are unprepared because we have not been watchful, the attacks that come upon us will have a stronger impact.

God wants us to draw close to Him in the wilderness of our pain, trouble, despair, and loss, but He doesn't want us to forget Him in the midst of the beauty of our blessings. Yet we tend to forget. That's the very reason He wants us to frequently take communion — the Lord's supper — so we won't forget what Jesus did on the cross. You would think we couldn't ever forget something as monumental and life-transforming as that, but we do. And God knows that. He wants us to walk close to Him and have our faith established in Him at *all* times (Colossians 2:6-7).

God wants to bless us and lead us into the future He has for us, but He doesn't ever want us to get to the point where we think we got there on our own. He wants us to depend totally on Him. That's because He wants to take us to places we can't get to *without* Him. In order to get to these places, we have to acknowledge Him in every part of our life. *All the time.*

How do we do all that?

By praising God often.

When we live a lifestyle of praise and worship, we keep our heart fresh and open to the working of the Holy Spirit in us. We keep ourselves in the right place to hear from God and be guided by Him. We rightly position Him as first priority in our lives. We keep ourselves always dependent upon Him, whether things are going well or not. This keeps us close to Him.

When the Spirit of God came upon Azariah, he told King Asa, "The LORD is with you while you are with Him. If you seek Him, He will be found by you; but if you forsake Him, He will forsake you" (2 Chronicles 15:2).

It can't get any clearer than that. If God is with *us* as long as we're with *Him,* that increases our motivation to be *with* Him, doesn't it?

The best advice when you are in a season of peace and rest is to use that time to build and fortify yourself in the Lord. Study His Word. Communicate with Him in prayer. Spend time in His presence in worship and praise.

Use that time to fall in love with Jesus all over again.

King Asa didn't always do everything right, but in the end "the heart of King Asa was perfect before God throughout his lifetime" (2 Chronicles 15:17 TLB). Even when we don't act perfect, we can show God that our hearts are perfectly in love with Him by the praise we give Him every day.

To worship is to act as an inferior before a superior. When I worship God, I am saying by my actions, "God, You are better than I am. You are bigger than I am. You are more than I am."
— Joseph Garlington

Part of standing strong in the bad times is recognizing that there will be good times ahead that will come as a reprieve from them. A time of rest from the ongoing battle. A hiatus from hell's onslaught. A needed pause before continuing on the narrow path. No one is immune to trouble, so in the times when you don't have any, praise God just as loudly on the good day as you do on the difficult one.

You may be thinking, *I don't remember the last time I thought everything was going well.* And I hear you on that. Often the good times are measured in smaller increments than a season. I once heard a woman measure the good times in her life as being when every family member was out of jail at the same time. It's all relative! And it's all attitude. If we praise God often and don't sweat the small stuff, we may find our good times extended beyond what we even thought they could be.

Every time we worship God, no matter what is going on in our lives, we take a giant step into the future He has for us. That is the hidden power of praising God.

One day we will be on the ultimate mountaintop with God, and we will see Him face-to-face and bask in the warmth of His love. We will be like lovers who share each other in a oneness that is complete and whole. We won't have to remind ourselves to worship Him, for we will not be able to do otherwise.

We will worship Him forever, without pause, because worshiping the Love of our Life is what we were created to do. Our minds won't wander. We won't be distracted. We won't be too tired, too sick, too depressed, too anxious, too tormented, or too tempted by other things. We will finally get over ourselves because we will know *Him* as He knows *us*. "For now we see in a mirror, dimly, but then face to face. Now I know in part, but then I shall know just as I also am known" (1 Corinthians 13:12).

Until that time, however, we're on a journey. And there will be situations coming our way that will try to steal our joy, and rob us of our peace, and cause our minds to focus on the source of our *misery* instead of the source of our good. There will be forces that want to make us forget how much God loves us. They will attempt to divert our attention away from the most important reason we are here — to love, serve, and worship God. Don't let that happen. When you go through difficult times, remember who sustains you. When you move into a season when all is well, remember who led you there. He is the Lord of the mountaintop as well as of the valley. So no matter where you find yourself, praise Him for all He's worth. Praising God will change your life.

> ... something we do for God, but in the process He gives far more of Himself to *us* than we can ever give of ourselves to Him.

I Give God My Praise

Lord, I worship You for all that You are. You are my Lord in the good times as well as the difficult. On the mountaintop as well as in the valley. You are King of Kings on the throne of my life in the calm as well as in the storm. I praise You in times of great blessing as well as in times of great challenge. You are Almighty and all-powerful, and I find my strength in You. It is because of You that I can stand strong, even when I feel weak. For I know that when I am weakest, You show Yourself strong. I am grateful for Your salvation, deliverance, protection, goodness, and blessings in my life every day. I know that everything I have comes from You. Because of Your great strength I go from glory to glory and "strength to strength" no matter what is happening in my life (Psalm 84:7).

I want to show my love for You every day by embracing You with my worship and touching You with my praise. Teach me all I need to know about how to worship You in ways that are pleasing in Your sight. Fill my heart with such great knowledge of You that praising You becomes a way of life. Teach me to make it my first reaction to every situation, no matter what the situation is. All honor, glory, and majesty belong to You, Lord, for You are worthy to be praised.

You are holy and righteous, and I have no greater joy in life than entering into Your presence to exalt You with worship and praise every day. I know that in Your presence I will find everything I need forever.

God Gave Me His Word

You must continue in the things which you have learned and been assured of, knowing from whom you have learned them.

2 Timothy 3:14

As you have therefore received Christ Jesus the Lord, so walk in Him, rooted and built up in Him and established in the faith, as you have been taught, abounding in it with thanksgiving.

Colossians 2:6-7

While we do not look at the things which are seen, but at the things which are not seen. For the things which are seen are temporary, but the things which are not seen are eternal.

2 Corinthians 4:18

There is surely a future hope for you, and your hope will not be cut off.

Proverbs 23:18 NIV

Do not be deceived, God is not mocked; for whatever a man sows, that he will also reap. For he who sows to his flesh will of the flesh reap corruption, but he who sows to the Spirit will of the Spirit reap everlasting life. And let us not grow weary while doing good, for in due season we shall reap if we do not lose heart.

Galatians 6:7-9

Giving It Some Further Thought

1. Read 1 Corinthians 15:58 in your Bible. What are we to always do, no matter what is happening? How can you apply this to your life in the good times as well as the difficult and challenging times?

2. Write out a prayer asking God to help you stand strong in all you know of Him all the time. Ask Him to help you not forget to do that when things are going well.

3. Read 1 Thessalonians 5:16-18 in your Bible. What are we to do all the time, no matter what is happening? Write out a prayer asking God to help you do those things every day.

4. Write out a prayer of praise and thanksgiving for all the good things God has brought into your life. Commit to praising Him for these things in the good times as well as the difficult.

5. Read 1 Corinthians 16:13 in your Bible. What are you to do at all times? How will this help you later on if you do this in the good times?

Dear Reader,

One of the greatest things you can do for yourself and others is to put on a CD of worship music and let it play through your home, car, place of work, or wherever you spend your time. Worship music will not only change the atmosphere of where you are, but it will also change your attitude and thoughts, and give you peace of mind and joy. That's why my husband, Michael, and I put 11 of our favorite praise and worship songs together and matched them up with our favorite singers and made a CD for you to not only listen to, but to use as the perfect companion to this book.

The songs correspond to the book chapters in their content and will inspire you to a powerful time of personal praise and worship of our awesome God. Michael's beautiful arrangements and production of these songs, and the anointed voices who sing them (each singer a worship leader with a heart for worship), will stir your heart to respond. In fact, I believe they will touch you so deeply that you will find yourself singing them throughout the day, long after the CD has been played.

The name of this CD is the same as the book, *The Prayer That Changes Everything* (Integrity Music). You should be able to find it wherever the book is sold.

> With many blessings,
> *Stormie Omartian*